THE JOY OF BEING

by

MARK KUMARA

Order this book online at www.trafford.com
or email orders@trafford.com

Most Trafford titles are also available at major online book retailers.

Print information available on the last page.

ISBN: 978-1-4120-4991-7 (sc)
ISBN: 978-1-4122-3245-6 (e)

Trafford rev. 12/18/2020

www.trafford.com
North America & international
toll-free: 844-688-6899 (USA & Canada)
fax: 812 355 4082

MY DEEPEST GRATITUDE TO

All of my friends who have played with me, cried with me, sung with me, loved with me, danced with me, and helped me, and who continue to help me.

And to the One that I love, who is yourself, who is my Self, and to all the birds that do sing, and all the dolphins that do leap, and all the animals that do revel in the purity and innocence of their being, in this beautiful world of ours - and to all the trees that do abide with such strength, and all the flowers that do give of their perfume, colour, and essence - to all the angels, and to all that just is - for nought else other than the joy of being.

Joy is the outer expression of peace
Peace is the inner origin of joy
Love is everything in between

Mark Kumara

Contents

We are the angels of a bright morning star,
We are the angels of a great loving heart.
When you want me I'm near,
When you see me I'm here.
Play and sing,
Let heaven ring,
And know that joy is here today,
Because we've come to stay.
And we will bless the way to a golden day.

Mark Kumara.

Joy is the most infallible sign of the presence of God.

Teilhard de Chardin.

AUTHOR'S NOTE

Let me explain how this book came to be written.

It was in my mind to write a book about my own personal search for truth and enlightenment being my path of service to the world, and, about the longing in my heart for union with the Oneness - that completion of the I AM - in that great and glorious adjustment which we term Self-realisation. I wanted to put down on paper the questions I had asked - and the answers I had arrived at during my search.

As I began to write, the words and sentences began to take on an emphasis and direction that I hadn't anticipated. It seemed I was often writing from a more authoritative Self, or from a more impersonal perspective.

I came to recognise it as my higher-Self, my whole Self, of whom Mark Kumara, my human self, is merely an aspect in human form.

My whole Self is the entity known as Sanat Kumara. Sanat Kumara had made Himself/Herself known to me some years previously. You would be correct in saying that Sanat Kumara with His (my very own) twin flame is my very own personal loving Father, loving Mother, and loving Self.

Just before publishing this book I was awakened one morning to a startling vision. Around my bed were standing about six or seven, marvellous, very tall, gently smiling beings in shining white light. I was surrounded by waves of love and a wonderful peace. One of them said to me, "We are members of the Earth Council and you are one of us. Your name is Sanat Kumara. You should assume it."

Years before I had been given this very same message by a clairvoyant. It was too much for me to assimilate at the time. I remember somewhat plaintively asking: "Why me!" The reply was a rather disconcerting, "Why not you. It has to be someone!"

As directed, I have now assumed the name Kumara, making my name into Mark Kumara, so honouring both my human self and my whole Self. Indeed, we are one entity. But what is a name? It is just a name. So, don't get caught up in names. I am still my Self whatever name I go by!

On occasions, Sanat Kumara impressed, as it were, the words of this book you are about to read into my mind with such power they seemed to pound through the typewriter, literally springing on to the paper in front of me with a power and emphasis which was not to be denied.

It was soon obvious that Sanat Kumara spoke in a much more precise and classical way than I do. As this was already happening, I allowed it to happen and tried to keep my editorial mind from interfering with it as much as possible.

Some of these passages I have put in *italics*; others, I have left in the text unmarked, for it soon became apparent to me that it was often too difficult to distinguish between the times I, Mark Kumara, was writing and the times Sanat Kumara was writing. I decided to surrender and leave it all to arrive on the page just as it did. So, as you can see, this book is a joint creation. Yet, this also a peculiar thing to say for, of course, we are one united entity!

Rather than edit out the occasional archaic language, I decided to leave it as it was, and, if I do say so myself, I rather like it.

In esoteric and some new age literature it is said that Sanat Kumara is that entity who is known as the *planetary logos* or *planetary sovereign* of Earth. Every evolutionary world has a planetary sovereign who, together with a council of other Kumaras and a family of Self-realised Masters, all with their twin flames, oversees the spiritual advancement of that planet.

For many ages, Sanat Kumara has been over-lighting and overseeing the awakening consciousness of this planet into a planet of light, as well as training another to take over that role. A planetary sovereign informs a world with His/Her life and energy. His etheric body encompasses the world. Sanat Kumara holds this world in love and has done so for many earth cycles, putting down many aspects of Him/Herself into incarnation at different times, as different personalities, all with his or her own loving mission to perform, of which I am just one. And yet, having said this, I am also, just as you are, the Oneness or Source manifesting as I AM.

Within this environment of love and joy, within His/Her aura of peace, and wise guidance, and despite the temporary terrors the world may undergo from time to time, all is moving forward in perfection and safety. I am assured of this.

Mark Kumara.

CHAPTER ONE

INTRODUCING LIFE

I am born to be love, to be joy, to be spontaneity, to be at peace. I am born alive, to be life and express life. This is my destiny. I am also God. Not the big, all wise, God in the sky lording it over everyone. That is a ridiculous idea. It is impossible. It is impossible for any entity, however grand, or however wise, or all-powerful or all-loving he or she might be.

There is no such *over-lording* God, either in the sky or upon earth, and never will be (you can breathe a sigh of relief at that!) But still, I am God. You are God. God is within me as myself. God is within you as yourself. You and I are God at the same time as being merely an aspect of God. It's no big deal. We all are. Everything is. It is also my choice to affirm that this is what and who I am, and to remind you that this, also, is who you are - and that you, too, have this choice whether to affirm it or not.

This is who you are!

This is not arrogance. From the viewpoint of the remainder of the enlightened universe and the seemingly vast non-physical realms that do exist, this is merely common sense. It is so obvious no one even mentions it!

Rather than using the term *God* (though, in this book I do use the term often), I prefer the term *The Oneness* or *Source* or *All-That-Is*, or *I AM.*

It is just as truthful, without being burdened by religious beliefs or other confusing stories.

Indeed, confusing though it might be to some, I should like to de-glamorize the whole idea of God. The whole is the whole. It is not served by having nebulous ideas about any special, or grand, or loving entity that we believe we are beholden to for our life. We are all life equally. We are all God equally. To a greater, or a lesser degree, everyone will one day realise this. Everyone on earth will be enlightened to this. This will be the first step. Then, Self-realisation, union with God for each individual in his or her own time, will follow.

The differences between us are often significant; but none of these differences are as significant as the fact that WE ARE ALL ONE, and that in the Oneness there are many billions upon billions of life forms, also Gods (if you like) just like you and me.

All these life forms, wherever they may be in this vast and wonderful universe, are embraced by the Oneness; indeed, *we are all the Oneness manifested in form*, and we are all linked, therefore, by the fact that we *are all equally of the same essence, being spirit.*

Only in awareness, in consciousness, and in the creative ability of each individual entity, is there a degree of difference. This is a difference of awareness and ability, not a difference of substance. The amount of light you hold differs, yet that same light is within All-That-Is, simply as itself.

Being born to express life does not mean that you can hope, or aim, to embody every attribute or every quality of life that life can possibly offer. This *idea of perfection* cannot be expressed in any one life form, however grand or galactic they might be, and certainly not in any one human being.

Being awake to the expression of your life does mean, rather, that you recognise and accept that every attribute of life, including that of so called *death*, and every quality of life, including that of so called *evil*, lies latent within you. It does mean that in your essence (spirit) you have found that you contain and have accepted that all possibilities exist.

It also means that in your human form - with your human talents - you can surrender to your humanity and your individuality, and choose, through your own (never to be repeated) unique combination of qualities, to express a natural and, above all, a joyful, expression of your own aliveness.

You are fire. You are electricity. You are energy. You are a spark of the greater fire, the One Fire.

In quality, in essence (spirit), there is no difference between a spark of the fire and the fire itself. Only in size and power is there a difference.

So it is with you and that in which you live. All is of this same quality and essence.

You and I, with all the creatures in the universe, together with all that is non-sentient, have this quality in common. Its name is LIFE. Its spirit is JOY. *It is the joy in all being.*

I will repeat this, in this book, many times, in many different ways. If you find it repetitive, forgive me. But, believe me, it is worth the saying.

Life has no favourites. Life is not exclusive. Life is merely the nature of all that is. There is no up or down, no great or small, no good or evil within life. Just as water has dissolved within it all the minerals of the seas, so does life have within it all the possibilities of creative mind.

There are creative minds (you may call them souls if you wish) that are awake to their essence (their spirit), and there are those that remain asleep. Those who remain asleep dream along. They live in a fantasy existence in which their conditioned mind has taken control and which this mind - and ultimately their own Self - is responsible for.

This dream-like ability of mind to be able to deceive itself and create for itself an identity which assumes it is not able to express joy, and that love and freedom is dependent upon the fulfilment of certain conditions, is the conditioned ego. In these pages I shall talk much of the ego and its conditioning.

There is a simple formula which applies. Being awake, and validating your essence in action, equals the happiness we term joy. Being asleep, and ignoring essence (your spirit), for whatever reason, equals stress.

Mere thoughts of joy don't go far. They don't go deep enough. *Thoughts must be translated into action on the physical plane for joy to reveal itself.*

Indeed, when the personality (the ego) loses its conditioning joy automatically reveals itself. It is always there, underneath, waiting. It is why the physical body, on the physical plane, is seen and known as the body of demonstration.

In these pages I shall use the term *entity* as meaning your true personality, which is none other than your whole Self (or higher-Self). They mean the same. I will not often use the word *soul*, for soul has resonance to do with religion, and religion upon this planet has a great deal to answer for in keeping up the illusion of separateness and ignorance which has been swallowed hook line and sinker by the conditioned ego of the masses. Further more, an entity is sexless. Spirit is without sex. Any entity, in harmony with its spirit, can change its polarity at will, to be male or female, *yin* or *yang*, any time it wishes.

There is always joy in union. There is always joy in essence (spirit) validation between entities, but I assure you that no entity, essentially, is in a fixed, or static, or irreversible, male or female role.

An entity that has allowed itself to dissolve into the essence of its *being* and has found that it still remains as an individual, yet is no longer apart from the Oneness, becomes an intensely creative entity. But, he or she, or he/she (if you are androgynous), now creates only in harmony with that life which is, non-exclusively, both the substance and the cause of all that is.

You are to do this. You are to be supremely confident, both in surrender to that life which is your very own essence (your spirit) and in surrender to your whole Self, being your own Father and Mother in heaven.

When you have done this you will have a perspective, not merely of your human self, but of LIFE, of all life, feeling your inclusiveness and empathy with everything around you.

How, then, you may ask, do you communicate to those entities who are asleep to the Oneness? How do you get through to someone who is operating through a mind construct of a conditioned ego which firmly believes - that sink or swim - it's on its own? This is an abiding challenge.

Basically, you have three choices. 1. You may approach them from spirit, from the I AM part of yourself. 2. You can try speaking to them from your whole Self, from the perspective of your higher-Self. 3. Or, of course, you can speak to them from your human self, from your human perspective.

In the case of your first choice, you immediately have a dilemma. The I AM never speaks, for there is nothing from spirit's point of view to speak about. All IS, as it is. All is going well. It always has been and always will be. There is just nothing to say. Anything said seems thoroughly irrelevant. The I AM exists within you as a state of permanent bliss and grace. It IS. It always just IS. The I AM never deals with specifics, in any event. Its role is just to be there within you and within everything, permeating the whole of existence with love and awareness of Itself.

With regard to choice number two, many men and women throughout the ages, by identifying themselves with their higher-Self, have, on occasions, used the pronoun *I* whilst indicating that they were speaking from the perspective of inclusive life, their whole Self and not from the exclusive human intellect. It has often confused those they most wished to reach. It has appeared arrogant, especially to those with a fear of authority who, perhaps unconsciously, still blame their parents or their teachers or society for their own lack of freedom or lack of feeling loved or powerful.

Of course, those who carry this fear find it difficult, in turn, to identify with the totally uncompromising nature of their own essence. Some spiritual seekers find it impossible to even imagine talking from their grand higher-Self. They remain at a distance from their higher-self, using many devices - trance medium-ship being one of them.

Few enlightened men and women have chosen to be spiritual teachers; and fewer women than men on this earth, though by universal law the feminine principle is more able to reach and nourish tender awakening consciousness.

In this age to come you will see women come into their own as the great teachers of life. Men will be there in shining support, embodying, and *being* the love and the joy and the power of the Father principle in bodily manifestation. Men will use their power as force, when - and only when - motivated by spirit, rather than being stirred by emotionally driven impulses. The feminine principle, the Mother, will bring meaning to a planet awakening into joy, whilst her male polarity, the Father, will bring joy to a planet awakening into meaning and purpose - lest meaning become the heavy tyrant unleavened by the lightness of spirit.

In these pages I will speak to you at times from my whole self and at times from my human personality which is Mark. The three of us, the essence that I AM, my higher-Self (which is my whole Self) and Mark, we are one. My higher-Self is likened unto a circle, for it is aware at all times of all my personalities wherever in the universe they may be. I am at all times aware of their every thought and feeling. In this manner I am in constant communication with them. Mark, Sanat Kumara, and the I AM. We are a threesome but we are one. We are a grand trinity. This does not diminish Mark, nor uplift Mark to a pedestal. It does not impose a set of values on to Mark or make Mark into a person without a will of his own. On the contrary, Mark is fulfilled by me and I am fulfilled by him. Fundamentally, the words "him" and "me" are illusory. From my view point they have little meaning. They are words I am using for your benefit. And, you may ask, who, then, does ultimately benefit? Well, is it not obvious. When one benefits, all benefit.

You also belong to such a trinity. Everyone does. Is not this a thrilling thought?

We are enriched in our togetherness, totally and wholly. There is no separation in me which knows where Mark begins or ends. There will be times when I shall speak with clear emphasis from the universal view point of all inclusive life and times when I shall express opinions from the human personality of Mark.

Sometimes, I shall denote clearly from which place I speak. Most times, I shall leave it to your intuition. In this way, there is a splendid freedom whereby you can see and understand that which you have made your own and no more.

Already, you can see the dilemma. In the previous two paragraphs I have implied that separation exists by using the words "from which place I speak" and "from my view point". I have apparently admitted that my being is apportioned into sides and places. Yet this is not so. I do not see any such sides, or parts, or opposites. There are none. Not from the reality of spirit. And this is the most real reality. Yes, joy is the most real reality. There are no words to express it, nor will there ever be.

Yet, in order to speak to you within the framework of this magnificent physical environment which we do presently inhabit together, where there is a clear idea of duality and where there are no invented words to express that which cannot be invented, I need to use words.

The very nature of words is that they are open to interpretation. They can mean *this* or *that*, as interpreted through the unique mind of each reader. They are splendid duality fixers! They lead to the taking of sides and the forming of opinions.

It could be said that for me to use words to explain the purpose of life is - at the best - optimistic, for life has no opinions. It is not limited by ideas about itself. Yet, you and I are life. We do have opinions about many things. And why not?

This, in itself, is a paradox, being open to much distortion by analysts who, by taking a position on words or on ideas, whether they are mine or someone else's, or, indeed, by taking a position on any person or any concept, have immediately lost the essence of what life is.

Try to avoid taking a position on anything material - and certainly, ideas, are, material. When you accept a position from truth, from your I AM, all is seen from a perspective of joy. Then, the decisions you take and the acts you do will be in harmony with the whole for the benefit of the whole. They will be wholly (or holy) loving acts.

In other words you will now be creating from resonance - being harmonic resonance - instead of from contrast which is no less than the making of decisions from a limited dual perspective of good or bad.

Separation, exclusiveness, rigid concepts, inflexible ideology: these are the great sins - one might say, the only true sins, for all fear stems from them.

Choice and analysis are, of course, legitimate functions in life; and in their place essential functions, too. You would be limited if you were not able to choose what to do next. But choice, being a product of thought, is not a causal impulse. Therefore it cannot decide what truth is. It cannot analyse or explain something which is of a prior impulse than the desire to choose or analyse.

Only in experiencing that prior impulse, only after identifying yourself with it, *knowing it is within your self, as your self,* can you then go on to use the creative powers of choice and analysis without distortion. You will be using power with love, love being another word for truth. You will be harmless, which does not mean being passive, for you will not be responsible for the feelings of those for whom you act in truth, and from truth. Later, I shall talk more fully about choice. It is a subject of vital importance.

I have said I am born to be joy and peace, spontaneity and love. I am that.

Now, how can we, together, realise what we are and delight in what we are? How can we awaken to joy and love and spontaneity, and be at peace with ourselves and each other?

There are seemingly so many problems; so many clouds obscure us from ourselves. Truly it was said, the Christ shall come in the clouds. Our own clouds, being emotional and mental contamination, obscure our Christ nature.

What are these clouds? These clouds are our very own thoughts, opinions, ideas, justifications, expectations, projections and rationalisations, and concepts and philosophies, in other words all that is unreal around us which suppresses - or, rather, hides the sun within us which is our Christ, this Christ being none other than our higher-Self. Every one of us has our own Christ or Buddha or Allah or Krishna, or Kumara, waiting there within us.

It is of supreme indifference what race or religion you belong to, or whether you are in perfect physical form, or crippled, in good health or poor, or even mentally incapacitated. No matter, your higher-Self is there. It awaits your realisation.

If you were as skilful at dispersing these clouds as you are at hiding behind them, this would soon be a shining planet filled with enlightened minds. The masses would soon have, as their only desire, the desire to be Self-realised as well.

On the non-physical levels where you come from and will return to all too soon, spiritual advancement is the major desire which all entities who live above the lower astral levels entertain. The question for the incarnated entity on the physical plane is always, can he or she make it their major desire there as well?

You fail to recognise who you are. And by this I don't mean in terms of your human family, or in terms of your role in society, or in any spiritual role, or in any role you may fancy you are to have in the new age; I am talking here about your real spirit self (your higher-Self, your whole self).

You have woven around yourself a misty cloud of miasmic form. Yes, on occasion, it has been somewhat protective. You have felt secure at times, even happy. But, it has been at cost; at the cost of joy. For, you have not known your *being*. And, to know the *joy of your being* is to know your birthright. It is to know who you are. I assure you this time of cloudy forgetfulness is now coming to an end. It has served its purpose. Now, it is time for the butterfly to emerge and try its wings.

Scary? Well, perhaps a little. Yes, it takes courage. There will be fear there. But that is *what you have your will for*: to confront the fear and see it fall away like the mist that it is. The choice is really simple: do you want permanent happiness in your life or a dreary on-going state of pseudo happiness underpinned by chronic stress? Stress slips its knife into you so fast, does it not, upon the movement of the mind and the uncomfortable reaction of the emotional body?

The question is: do you relate to the world, to your friends, to your partners, at home, at work, from your conditioned ego or from your essence?

I can hear so many of you saying: "Oh, that's not practical!"

You are not being asked to be practical. You are being asked to be permanently happy. Is this not really being practical? You will be so happy, that your love and healing energy will flow out all around you, with you actually having to do very little about it except to remain in the awareness of your joy and your I AM presence, and be present. You will have to do very little to heal the dreadful afflictions of the world, for around you they will begin to heal themselves. In the last analysis, is not everyone responsible for healing themselves anyway - or, rather, regaining the awareness that they are already whole.

Be a lover to your self. Be a joy to your self. Be such a joy, that it is, indeed, a joy for you and your whole self to be together. And be this uncompromisingly. This is the simple key to the great gate of universal freedom.

There is no other gate, though many are the twisting paths that humans tread to attempt to reach it.

Be a friend to your self. Be your very best friend to your self. In these pages I am communicating to you, not as a teacher to a disciple but as a friend to a friend. I am your friend who needs not your love but who would enjoy your friendship. I would like you to give yourself permission to celebrate with me the joy of being alive in a loving, joyful, universe on a stunningly beautiful planet. This earth.

When, within you, joy is happening - when you are feeling joy - love is there automatically. I have to tell you that love - for which you all crave so much - is the automatic result of living in joy. When joy is your all, love is both known and experienced to be your all, also. This is a realised fact. Joy is forever *prior*. It is a *causal* frequency. This is a new teaching to take you into a new age. It is the key to the future of this planet. Joy first, then love. Not the other way round: because in the attempt to love first, in the trying to love, there is effort, yet joy is effortless. This does not diminish love.

Jesus was absolutely correct. The Oneness (God) is love and love is all. But joy is also the Oneness, and joy is also all. In fact, this knowledge elevates love to its rightful and truly glorious frequency.

When joy is put first there is aliveness, there is energy and there is, in that very moment, no desire other than the grand feeling that you are at one with a creator and a glorious plan of thrilling life. Life is there in its essence, independent of the need to love, independent of the need to feel secure, or of the need to hide fears, or of the need to explore guilty feelings of not being loving enough. Or, of the need *to do your duty* as ordained by some temporal authority. Love is freed of all these distortions.

Love becomes crowned on the wings of joy. Other ideas of love, such as dutiful love, are not love, merely ideas. They are a shabby imitation and lead not to freedom and peace. I understand how well meaning these ideas are and the goodwill inherent behind them, but it is time to take a quantum leap into freedom and not be afraid. Look through the dark clouds of your feelings and look at the heavy thoughts you have of your responsibility for others which tie you to the murky clouds of guilt and resentment; and find out what ideas you are holding on to that stop you from living in joy.

I am uncompromising. I ask for the best in you. Would you have it any other way? Would you prefer it if I asked you to hedge your bets, keep a foot in both camps, live a life of mediocre satisfaction pitted with frustration?

I know who you are. I see the best in you. It is only a matter of time.

The crown you shall wear is indeed one of love, lifted up by your very own personal discovery that life is joy.

I do not wish to impose my views, my longings, or even my joy, upon you. That way leads to illusion. Any uninvited influence is an imposition. If my words do not touch inner chords, do not be the slightest troubled. Pass by confidently and know that, for the time being, your destiny is not upon this path.

My way is ever the way of freedom and the way of easiness and well being. It is not one of mental wrestling.

If my words bring you feelings other than resonance and expansion, do not increase your own inner resistance by continuing to give them thought. Allow your thoughts of this book, and of me, to drop entirely. Continue on your way, live your life and be at peace, wishing me well as you go. At least you will have discovered where not to look!

You may also have discovered a secret: which is, that what is written in these pages is not truth! As I have already said words are not truth. And neither are concepts. *It is only in the reality of your being that you can taste truth.* Maybe, therefore, it shall be our destiny to disagree in ideas but merge in our hearts which is where union can only truly occur anyway. And if you are open to that, you will find I am also. It matters not that you understand. It matters that you feel. Love is not a grand concept. Love is a feeling! It is personal to you. It is you who are to feel it. You may have lost sight of that!

And here is some advice: whenever a negative feeling arises, rather than blaming someone or resenting the outer situation, try looking immediately within your self. You will find resistance there. Follow it to its source. What is it? How has it arisen? What has happened to love or acceptance in this particular instance? You will almost certainly find you are carrying a belief that makes you believe that you are powerless to be a joyful person, maybe because of some complicated outer circumstance which you have a vested interest in perpetuating.

This vested interest keeps you tied to a frustrating self sacrificing path of mood-swinging pseudo happiness. It is a murky cloud put there by your manipulative ego to protect its scared vulnerable self.

Following resistance within you to its source, instead of blaming or resenting an apparent outer cause, is the beginning of wisdom. To live by the creed of loving yourself enough to love yourself into life, is wisdom matured. And what is life? Well, life is none other than joy in being, and being in joy. This experience alone brings everything into harmony.

It is your feeling of powerlessness that is, in fact, the cause of frustration. When faced with a difficult situation, you basically have five possible courses of action.

1. Do nothing, and hope the problem will go away. When it doesn't (and they usually don't) you are going to feel even worse.

2. Attack the problem, try to denigrate it, "kill" it, smash it into oblivion, or will it away. This solves nothing, usually making it worse in the long run.

3. Explain to the other party how you feel and try to resolve the situation. This is loving and helpful and certainly positive action and, between people of goodwill, usually restores peace to the situation and to those involved.

4. When all is said and done, when you still remain disturbed in mind, feelings or body, find a quiet place to sit and be undisturbed, let silence enfold your mind, let all thoughts drop away. Let feelings be acknowledged but not indulged in. Allow them to surface at first if they wish to be expressed, but then see them pass, dissolve and float away. And, now, look deep within yourself to re-acquaint yourself with who you truly are. From this perspective everything outside of you will seem rather small and irrelevant. Indeed, any identification with the outside, any entanglement with anything outside, is now seen to be what it is: misidentification.

Seeing this and after having done your best to resolve the problem, it is easy to let go of it, to walk away from it, knowing you have done all you can to try and resolve it, knowing that, in the ultimate reality, it was never really a problem in the first place. You wish yourself well - and if anyone else happens to be involved in the matter you bless them and thank them for showing you an illusion. It is an illusion, hopefully, you will never have to get entangled with again. It no longer holds any allure for you. You have seen through it! The vibrational frequency embodied in that emotional(astral) reality is no longer your reality. You go upon your way and get along with your life.

5. If, after all this, you are still holding pain and simply cannot find peace, this is the time to get some help in the form of emotional release, for you will probably find that the problem which you are now taking responsibility for stems not from the immediate situation but has its emotional roots in a core cellular memory going way back into your childhood, or even into a past incarnation. This

is important work which everyone, bar none, has to do at one time or another when entering physical incarnation. For more on this great work, see my Chapter on *Healing*.

When it comes to loving (or resenting) other people, we must understand that no one has to walk hand in hand with another unless they truly want to. But, taking responsibility, realistically, for our own pain and hurt, all eventually learn that this last option, our own emotional healing, is the only course of action we ever truly have that brings real peace and lasting light to a situation. It is the most positive, definitive, and effective course of action. It has finality to it. There is a closure to it where everyone is a winner - though, at the time they may not know it! From this ultimate perspective, from this point of correct identification, *from truth*, we accept another person's right to have a different view point or to have a different emotional frequency to us. We go upon our way, knowing that they have, for the time being, a different path to tread. We wish them well and from afar hold them in love. Indeed, to give someone their freedom in this way is a loving act. We may feel sad, we may feel lonely and we may feel disappointed that someone who we thought could be open to us is closed to us, but, nonetheless, we have done a positive thing. There will be spiritual growth in it for us and for them. Time and space allows healing to happen. This is a loving universe. Even in space - especially in space - there is love.

The origin of resistance always lies within you. The outer event, the apparent cause, has merely brought to your attention the fact that you are not accepting the right of others to hold a vision other than your own.

Indeed, you may be so enamoured by your own opinions and concepts, and your own vision, that you may have lost sight of your own sense of joy and aliveness. If you are following another person's philosophy, or vision of some outer magnificence, you are probably not being true to your own joy. This is not living; this is safe sterility where the waters of life quickly turn stagnant, and where hide the lurking monsters of fear.

Both the kingdom of heaven that Jesus spoke about and the nirvana that Buddha in his wisdom refused to talk (because he didn't want his disciples getting lost in blissful daydreams) are here now, in this eternal NOW, in your present body on the physical plane, NOW.

The possibility of experiencing the NOW in all its vibrant immediacy is a possibility that is open to every entity right NOW. Heaven is going to come to earth, not as a result of a perfected political or visionary system of state craft which promotes happiness for everyone, but is going to come in the ones and twos and threes and fours, and small groups, of individual entities. It will arise from within each individual, each in his or her own moment, each in his or her own NOW. And this is the only way it can possibly happen.

Your NOW contains infinite possibilities. It is infinitely flexible. It is the heart of your being. Both Jesus and Buddha were right. It is here within you. It cannot be explained, so Buddha refused to discuss it. It cannot be said to be this or that. It is a unique happening, that is happening NOW, to every entity in the vastness of the universe. It is the sum total of the Oneness (God) being present always as a part of the One, in the One, as One. It is salvation.

Yes, I am communicating to you with words, NOW, in this age of mass communication, but shall I fare any better than those who have preceded me? Shall some people place me on a pedestal and make me into a guru? Shall some do just the opposite and attack me with fierce mental righteousness as being an agent for some evil power? Both these views miss me. I am neither of the opposites. I am life. I am all possibilities. I embrace all and I choose that which I choose. It so happens that I choose to stand firm for that which leads to life and life abundantly.

The future always remains the future. If enlightenment lies in your future, it will always remain there. It will never happen. "Happiness one day will be mine but not just now!"

In fact, enlightenment is now and also ever changing. So enlightenment is changing, too. Change is the very nature of enlightened mind. The NOW is ever open to change. It is the paradox of life to be ever changing within the non-changing joy of self-realised life.

Having said that, there is also that which is beyond enlightened mind, which is beyond the whole enlightened Self, even. This is the ultimate Self, the All-That-Is, the Oneness, the I AM. It is supreme BEING, both everything and nothing, permeating everything as everything. It says nothing. It does nothing. It is nothing. Yet, it is aware and gives rise to everything, both the inner and the outer. It is both your origin and destination and everything in between, including light and enlightenment. It is your ultimate identity. You can find this Self which is your very Self, quite effortlessly, by relaxing and stilling your mind with all its thoughts and daydreams, and even your longings to find it.

You cannot find it with any part of mind because it is not of mind, not of the ordinary mind nor of higher mind. You don't need to go searching for it with your mind for it is beyond the mental search process. It can only reveal itself to you when your mind is still. Be effortless. Be Still, and then it cannot but help make its presence known to you, for it is *you,* the *you* which is underpinning and permeating all of you.

There is no fixed thing in life, no label, no absolute law, nothing to hang on to, to satisfy your ego, nothing to ultimately understand so that you can exclaim to the satisfaction of your ego: "Ah! Now I have got it! Now I understand."

The giving up of the idea of enlightenment is the enlightenment. The giving up of your concepts about life, or light, and the letting go of your *longing* for union with the Oneness, is the realisation that you are already in union with the Oneness which is your very I AM presence.

I ask you not to seek enlightenment but to look to your own joy and your resistance to expressing joy. The goal is not so much enlightenment but *en-joyment.* And, in this state of *being,* you will be as much *en-joyed* by life as you will enjoy the living of it. There lies unity. There lies the Oneness expressing itself so beautifully as your self, your whole Self. There lies the father principle. There lies your own Christ nature. I beg you, do not deny it.

Living in the NOW without any awareness of individuality is how animals live. Animals do live totally in the moment but without awareness of a self through which the unlimited nature of their higher self (their group soul) can be realised. They live largely by instinct which is an ability whereby they can tap directly into the consciousness of their group soul memory.

You are to live in the NOW with your individuality intact. This is a step up from the animal kingdom in terms spiritual evolution which is the evolution of consciousness in this galaxy.

Group consciousness (as animals understand it), or society consciousness with its archetypal underpinnings or racial memories, has nothing more to offer an individualised human entity on his or her path of transformation into self realisation.

The group can indeed offer protection, support, comfort and mirror fears and wonderful feelings, and press emotional buttons, but it cannot, in the final analysis, uncover for you the joy of your essence so that it remains a realised, *crystallised,* permanent experience for you in any situation, whether it be in a group or out of a group, whether you are in a relationship or alone, whether you are in a garden of flowers and butterflies, or in a prison of concrete walls.

You are being asked to live in the present, in the moment, in the NOW, with self awareness and self integrity. You are not to pander to any group, however sparkling, or comfortable - or wondrously therapeutic - neither are you to believe that the dictates of your family, or society, or nation, or a religion, new or traditional, should be in any way so special and important that you should give them your loyalty ahead of your own truth.

Be you in your own sparkling pristine, unique, Self. Be beholden to none for your joy, but your self.

Living in the moment without self awareness is somewhat like returning to being an animal, but you won't have the animal's natural innocence and purity of being. This is a return to living by impulses. These will be based on instinct, racial memory, ancient conditioning, and simple reaction to outside causes. The cellular body is beautiful and has its own intelligence, being very responsive to the Oneness, but it is very limited in its realisation of your higher self, being limited to pleasure and pain and subject to unremitting deterioration under the natural laws of its form life.

You are much more than this. To begin with, you are not an animal. You have been given the gift of individuality for a reason - for a hope - that you will find out who you are whilst in the physical body, embracing and holding to your personality all the wealth of experience that you have had during your journey in the realms of physicality. The Oneness gives you the gift of personality with which to make choices at whichever level you find yourself, whether it be physical or in the vast levels of the non-physical worlds.

Wherever you find yourself, *you will always be Three-In- One. 1. You are the Oneness. 2. You are your whole Self. 3. You are human.* The Oneness is your spirit or I AM presence, your God self. Your higher self is that which Jesus called "my father in heaven". It is your fully conscious whole self, a grand entity of light, containing the sum total of all your knowledge and wisdom from all your many life-times. It can equally be called "your mother in heaven". Or, "your beloved friend or lover in heaven!" Your human self you know all about! It is of course only of use to you on the physical level - and only on the physical level. It will, if you are not self realised, have a conditioned ego.

This is the eternal paradox. You are the One, you are your whole Self and you are the human personality. You are the One, yet you are the three. So, here we have it. At any one time you are the Oneness. At any one time you are your glorious higher self and at any one time you are your human self. Within you, you cannot separate any of these three and try to be, at any one time solely, or exclusively, just one of them, else you fall into illusion - be it spiritual illusion or materialistic illusion.

So, let us be specific. Who are you exactly: 1. You are spirit life, the Oneness, the I AM. 2. You are your whole Self, your soul, a creative mindful entity of light aware of all your many lifetimes. 3. You are a human personality in a physical body on a physical planet. 4. Until you regain the awareness of your whole Self in your human personality, you are operating out of a conditioned personality (the conditioned ego), which you are carrying along with you like a cloud of other ideas around your head.

Look at it this way: if I was to proclaim that I was the Oneness, God on earth, able to snuff out the planet in the blink of an eye, people would say I was unhinged. They would be correct. If I were to say I was a grand angelic entity (my whole kumara Self) and not really human, at all, they would shake their heads sadly. Again, they would be correct. For, I am not only this. If I were to say I am only human and that is all I am and all I ever will be, some would, perhaps, agree, but I tell you they would be the deluded ones. For, I am all three. Always, I am all three, wherever I go, wherever I am. And so are you.

Now, although I am all three it does not mean I cannot slip, in consciousness, from one to the other any time I wish. Indeed, I can. I can move my consciousness from one state of being(or one level) to another state of being anytime I wish.

In contemplation of the Oneness, I am refreshed by my perspective from this aspect of myself. Here, at this level of awareness. I know all is well. Nothing needs to be done. All is perfect. I am at peace. All is peace.

At the level of my whole Self, I am conscious of my compassion for all life. I am aware of the loving light that links us all. I am aware of the joy of my being, and I am aware that I have the ability to respond to outside stimulus and that I can be intensely and magnificently creative. It is from this level that I can teach and heal, and inspire, and be consciously aware that I am a grand entity of living, loving, light and colour.

I can also put myself down into human form, if I wish. I can learn about the challenges to be met on the physical plane of existence, and I can create that which I wish to create through my human form. At this level, I can never lose sight of who I truly am, but I am still learning and evolving, in consciousness, into ever greater awareness and light.

Now, when I am cleaning my teeth, doing the washing up, cleaning the house, putting out the dustbins, doing the gardening, driving my car, my awareness is very human - and I do delight in being very human.

At this level, the human level, I can forget, if I do not keep very awake, who I am. I can forget the other two parts of my self. It is easy to do. I admit it. I have often forgotten. Yes! And this is when you do things that you later regret, just because you lost sight, momentarily, of who you truly are - the grand Three-In-One! Haven't we all done this. Oh, yes! It is certainly being human. But, it is not very fruitful; for, as you can see being solely human is not who we truly are. Our distortion of truth creates the distortion in our behaviour, and the disease in our bodies.

This is how it all works. Like three fingers on a hand, all three of us - Oneness, whole Self, human self - our joined together but at anyone time we can choose which finger to point with!

The un-awakened masses look mainly to the human personality. They look only to form and its instinctual needs for security and sex, and consequently live in suffering.

Symbolically speaking, you could say that the addiction to form, the belief in materialism at the expense of the spiritual, is *satanic*. Spiritual seekers, however - seekers after truth - fall into the trap of wanting *to be* the Oneness, of wanting to be supreme being, having no actual idea of what that might be, but wanting to be only that! This is a more subtle addiction. You might call it the *luciferic* illusion of wanting to be spiritually perfect, or perhaps of wanting to *white-out* into the permanent bliss of the Oneness and never have to think again. It is an understandable desire considering the suffering there is in this world, but it is an illusion. It can never be attained as a sustained living reality. What is forgotten, is the higher self, your whole Self, being your Christ self, your Buddha self, your Allah self, which stands between the two opposites. This Self stands in the middle. It is the integrating principle of harmony between the two opposites of form and spirit. You will never be without it. It now needs to be accepted and realised within you on earth. You will recognise it when you find it, because it is the *joy of your being.*

A fine illusion amongst human beings concerns both the truth of your sameness and the truth of your differences. One day you are demanding you should be the same as others, wanting what they have got. The next day you are at war with the same people so as to retain your individual identity. Can you not see that you are both. You will always be different from one another. Enjoy this. Relax around it. Do not strive to be the same. However, from the perspective of your Oneness, you are the same. You are from the One. You are the One. This is a profound truth, so do not believe you are better than another because of your race or religion or the colour of your skin, or because you believe you are more evolved in your higher self, or because you believe in the new age!

The truth to be aware of, when dealing with anyone, is not whether he or she is the same or different from us, but what is the quality of consciousness (which is the light) being manifested in and through that person. Always look beneath the form and serve its needs - the needs of consciousness. See that, when dealing with everybody. When you do this, you are looking at truth and you will act out of truth. And truth always serves truth - however hard it may seem and however long it takes!

Remember that consciousness and light are the same thing. They are words for the same thing. The advancement of spirituality is nothing other than the expansion of consciousness and, thus, the shining strength of your own light.

It is now time to bring the kingdom of heaven to earth, and to dismantle the belief that materialism has the power to reduce or suffocate your spirit on the physical plane of existence.

The important spiritual growth is to be found on the physical plane. When you die there is a re-assessment as to what you have achieved and a re-absorption into your higher self. This assessment process is ongoing for many lives until you can stand on your own two feet on earth in awareness, at least, of your whole Self. Then, WHO YOU TRULY ARE is walking upon the earth. At this point, you have earned the freedom to enter a new life, at new levels of creation.

You cannot attain liberation unless you have learned that, the physical level - the most challenging of all - is no barrier to joy. Until you have truly pierced this illusion, you remain asleep to your self, and open to fantasies and fear.

You cannot be a master (one who has mastered the art of remaining awake to his or her higher self, in realisation of the Oneness) until you have achieved this realisation upon the physical plane. The physical plane is a part of the whole. You cannot be whole, be at peace with the whole, or be liberated into greater service in the service of the Oneness, until you have realised that joy exists throughout the whole of creation right through to the physical plane.

If you do not meet and confront fear on the physical plane, which means confronting it right down to the cellular memories in your physical body, memories which have been frozen there, long forgotten or long denied, you will be travelling the universe - the non-physical levels (which you do after death) - only in a state of partial realisation. You will only be able to as far as you can go, and no further. There will be levels of consciousness you will be unable to access, for you will still be, in your consciousness, in a reality of limitation. You are not yet experiencing the whole as the whole.

But, the physical plane is not apart from the Oneness. IT, the Oneness, is merely the whole experiencing itself in physicality. It is the Oneness manifesting in physicality, and its nature is joy. It is for you to make this your reality. For most of you, it is why you keep coming back. It is the only reason you keep coming back!

It is not so difficult. It needs a little courage. It needs the will to look inside oneself and confront one's fears, admit to them, accept them with a loving heart, release the emotions tied up with them, if any, and see them disappear, then use the will to act again in a new way without the fear. The pain, if it comes, is resistance to change, the fear of which may have been dammed up inside you as a wall of fear for some time. The greater the time the fear has been there, the greater the fear of confronting the fear, and more than likely the greater the release of emotion required..

Fear, if not confronted immediately, cements itself into the ego until it becomes the very fabric of the ego (moving into a clever unconscious state) so that, as in the difficulty of seeing the wood for the trees, it is difficult to find, or to pin point. It may appear not to be there or to have vanished. However, you can always tell by the symptoms of stress, or disease, or sadness, that fear is there, lurking. And, oh my, does fear love to lurk!

Religion cannot make the fear go away. Religion cannot make anything go away. If you put your dependency upon church, or upon an annual pilgrimage to a shrine, or upon a master, to relieve you of your fear, to give you sufficient respite to get through the week, or the next year, you are buying into the ego's subtle scheme of camouflage (avoidance) and just delaying the moment when you are alone with your self and your fears, and have to accept them and face them.

Fear, not confronted, cements itself into the ego and attracts more fear, then attracts guilt, then looks for an outer saviour. Moreover, this kind of illusion - that an outer saviour - either can, or will, cure all ills, is endemic upon earth. It is hard to find the courage to face this illusion when it is defended by so called spiritual fervour and the fanaticism of religious zeal. It seems hard to be powerful and joyful when faced with such savage reprisals, even - or especially - when they are only mental reprisals. But, then, are we not often held in thrall by this fear - the fear of being in our own true power - whatever the reason.

The kingdom of heaven is an *in the present*, in the moment, experience.

It is an inner reality with an outer significance. Few in the world live knowing its reality or trust in its outer possibility for them personally.

The clouds that obscure your self from your self need to be gently blown away. It is the work that confronts every entity on earth. It is the need that must be now recognised as the first great need. Government at all levels, family, town, state, should now recognise this need as the great need and direct their energies and resources towards it.

"Oh, now you are really in the clouds?" I hear some of you say. No, not at all, I am here, with you, with my feet right on the ground and I hold out the only hope for the human race. Look to this need. It is the great need of the indwelling life of the human race which longs to express itself with joy upon this bountiful green and blue planet, which can be, I assure you, the most magical of homes and a perfectly exquisite place to experience the God of your being.

My message to you is simple. You are free. You are free to do as you wish. Give your self permission to be free and do as you wish. Look at the guilt which stops you from doing this. Love yourself for having got stuck, then un-stick yourself, advance, and be stuck no more. Live in your reality, create your reality and take responsibility for it; then you will be *co-creating* with God. Yes, God and you, with God within you. A joint effort! Make it one of joy and you shall be here, manifested as a god. Not as a miracle worker, but as a god of joy, for this is how a god feels and only how a god feels. Miracles are low down the list of *doing*. Give them no thought. It is a miracle enough when you live in your joy: then watch what happens around you!

To those entities who reject the idea (and it is an idea until you *experience* the living truth of it) that they are God in action, or who reject the immortality of their personality, I say to you, you are always free to do and believe whatever you wish, but as long as you continue doing as you wish without recognition of life's unity and without recognizing your personal responsibility for all your own uncomfortable feelings and situations, you are ever in peril of creating ever more disease and suffering for your self and those with whom you share these beliefs.

Those of you who do believe in life's unity and the survival of consciousness after so called *death*, and you probably do if you have read this far, (unless you are reading this book out of curiosity which, by the way, is also a legitimate reason), need have no fear of the so called "left hand path". You need have no fear of being led astray at this point in your evolution with all the support that is now readily available around you, under the in-pouring of fine energies now entering the planetary body from the hearts of vast entities who are actively, at this very moment, stimulating the awakening of hearts and minds of human beings.

It is shaking the very core of society, so that, in the shaking out of the mud, the gleam of gold will be seen at the bottom of the pan.

Believe it. Take my word for it. You are now sensitised too firmly toward your goal for you to become *lost*.

The time of the great awakening is upon the world and for you who have sensed it and work toward it there is no possibility of you being separated from the fruits of this awakening upon this very planet.

In this sense, and only in this very limited sense, you are one of the "chosen ones".

So have great courage. Be free. Create your own joyful reality. Take responsibility for it.

Don't be paralysed by fear of what is happening and fear of "doing the wrong thing". Trust your feelings and act. Don't talk so much, or think so much, about the problems. Your feelings of the moment will be your guide; it is your higher self speaking to you minute by minute about your direction and choice of behaviour; for there is always a choice between the joyful and the not so joyful. The choice is yours. Have courage. There is no "wrong thing" to do. There is only experiencing. And that still small voice within shall lead you by the hand to the final place you seek.

Feelings of being stuck or "lost" will only be temporary; fear them not when they come. Welcome them (without wallowing in self pity which is a waste of energy). They are valuable lessons. They are not to be looked upon as going wrong!

The idea that something is wrong leads to great illusion and unnecessary pain and mental anguish...it gives you a hard time. Be gentle with your self. Never give yourself a hard time and you will never give anyone else a hard time. Such a simple formula! One of the key qualities of a manifested God is gentleness. See to it in your self.

Fear of "going wrong" is a very painful reality to be trapped in: it sucks you into a depressive state of being.

Many spiritual seekers are at present benumbed into inaction by this fear. They live in a state of limbo, fearing to examine their feelings as to where their own joy lies, not knowing what to do about it.

The answer is to bring oneself right back to the present moment, this very moment, NOW, and start to express the feeling that is emerging right now. Do not "think grand". Do small things, work with your hands, maybe, and feel, vividly, the movement of your own joy and life energy within you, then do whatever it is that allows you to keep the feeling of that joy present.

Entities who live in a paralysis of fear, fearing that by their actions they shall harm "the plan", or hinder "God's work", are living out of touch with God within them which never judges anything as wrong. Yet, it is this very inaction, this very fear of taking responsibility for their own feelings which is harming the plan.

The fear, behind the fear, in this limbo state is the basic fear of death and annihilation. This then expresses itself as anti-life and anti-action.

For fear of being "lost", which is really a fear of dying, these entities either do nothing, or live by ego impulses, being a moment to moment reaction to outer stimuli, which they call being spontaneous. It is a false spontaneity.

They actually feel lost and helpless. And so they are. They have drawn to themselves the very thing they fear.

The recipe, if I may call it that, is to give yourself permission to do what you want to do, and to do naturally that which is deeply satisfying to you, to do that which gives you the greatest feeling of aliveness and expansion of your being. *It is not to do what you think the plan requires of you.*

If you are given guidance by any entity as to the direction of your path, listen, but then put it to the test of your own intuition and your own truth. If there is an immediate and abnormal reaction of fear to the advice, it might well be worth looking into, if nothing more than to find out the cause of the fear - a most valuable undertaking, because when fear is present there is blocked life energy.

On the other hand, if there is no emotional reaction, or a feeling of boredom, or a feeling of "I have been there and done that", on no account waste your time with it. Do not waste your life being bored, even if you are trying to do the right thing.

Resist the subtle control of members of your family, and of society, who want to run your life for you so that it fits in comfortably with theirs.

You are life the creator. *You* are free to do as you wish. Take responsibility, not for others, but for your self, and know that what you wish for is O.K. Yes, O.K!

There is no point in waiting. Waiting looks for something to happen, someone to come, someone to take responsibility for you, for the world.

Life is now. Enlightenment is now. Creativity is self-responsibility NOW. If you wait, you wait for ever. The human race will wait for ever.

Humanity is a collection of individuals. Self-realisation is the awakening of each individual in turn to their individual joy nature. It can only be attained by each individual, each in their own way, one by one. When individuals realise the nature of the Oneness, humanity as a whole will be at peace.

It will not be a static dreamy boring peace but a peace of vibrant life, passion, colour, excitement and sensitivity. The individual will live at the peak of his or her self expression, at the same time being given the opportunity to move into other areas of self expression by looking for new values or by freshly interpreting existing values.

In this book I am going to talk to you about concepts which are often, from my view point, stood upon their head and woefully misunderstood.

What better topic to begin with, in my next chapter, than that which attempts to explain the unexplainable. I shall once again, paradoxically, attempt to do this very thing.

It is a theme which, for many, is the ultimate mystery. And they would be quite correct: it is the ultimate mystery. Whole libraries of works will never solve it. Yet, there is a solution.

What, then, is this eternal mystery to which there is ever a momentary solution?

Yes, you have got it. It is life!

In the meantime, here is a song. Make up your own music to it.

SURF RIDER

CHORUS: Hear the wonder and the thunder
Of the rolling roaring surf.
It's the singing and the dancing
Of everything on earth.

1. Riding on the breaking sea, going along so easily
I'm alive and my soul is free!
Skipping and diving, swooping and soaring,
I ride on the sea.

2. Misty spray with curling foam, the mighty waves I do roam,
In green tunnels I'm at home.
Skipping and diving, swooping and soaring,
I ride on the sea.

3. Sparkling whiteness and the roar of explosions on the shore,
I am thrilled to my core!
Skipping and diving, swooping and soaring,
I ride on the sea.

4. King of the waves I am, all I ever wish to be,
Rider of the waves, that's me!
Skipping and diving, swooping and soaring,
I ride on the sea!

CHAPTER TWO

LOVE AND PURPOSE

The question of life's purpose has occupied the world's thinkers throughout the ages, and rightly so. It is worth giving thought to.

Religions imply it's all too difficult for us mere mortals to understand but that there has to be a motive behind "God's mysterious purpose". Well, is there?

Let me tell you this immediately. Then we can discuss it. There is no mystery to love. There is no mystery to joy. There is no mystery to peace. And they need no motive. They already exist. Indeed, they are the existence.

Now look to the title of this book: THE JOY OF BEING. Ha! So, now the mystery is solved.

Yes, this whole existence of ours is nothing but love manifested. This is the reality. Love holds everything together. It is truly like the cosmic glue. I have said: joy is the outer expression of peace, peace is the inner origin of joy, and love is everything in between. It is so. This is the reality we exist *as*. And we exist *in*.

Perversely, though, on the physical plane the conditioned ego would have it otherwise.

You see, in striving to be loving, in seeing love as a motive in life, while remaining frustrated (either consciously or unconsciously) you are failing to BE life. Yet, in the *joy of your being* lies the key to the whole mystery.

Philosophers, who spend many happy hours - and many not so happy life-times - delving into the meaning of life, generally look for meaning with such focused intent that they miss out in living the life they are looking at.

Religions (and in this category I also place the many esoteric groups and new age philosophies) generally place emphasis on the working out of a plan with revelation as an end result, with final bliss for those who have done what the religion or cult has asked of them.

This hoped for revelation may be nirvana, or atonement with Jesus, becoming a master, or becoming a member of a "white brotherhood." Or, it may be to enter a heavenly world in paradise where all emotional and carnal desires are taken care of eternally.

What I wish to say is that life can be - indeed maybe - all or any of these, or none of these, as you wish it to be. However, life is not, finally, as a permanent reality, any one of these or any other end-product event.

Life is what you wish to create of it. If a group of like minded entities wish to form themselves into a brotherhood to undertake a creative task this is what they wish to create. If you wish to extinguish your consciousness and "go to sleep" for a long time, waiting for a trumpet call to wake you up, you can create the conditions for it to happen. If you wish to live at one with Jesus, you can create for your self an image of Jesus which will reflect accurately your every whim and desire, except that, being merely a mirror of your desires, it will have no independent life of its own and will remain attached to you for ever.

After a while you may find that being at one with Jesus - or your *idea* of Jesus - to be rather on the boring side. Yet, if this is your will, so will it be. Jesus himself may have other ideas! He is, indeed a lovely being, sovereign unto himself, able to exist very happily and gratefully without having disciples hanging around, or in needing, himself, to surrender his own will to a master! Are you able to be as such?

Life is never any one thing. It has within itself all possibilities at every moment. Therefore, how can there be any ultimate purpose other than harmony?

Joy and love and peace, however, do exist as the very nature of the Oneness, and humanity does have a very real purpose to wake up and find this out.

And what exactly is it, what is this sleep, this altered state of dreaming, this altered consciousness, you may ask, which humanity has to awaken from?

Well, it is nothing more than the conditioned ego. The conditioned ego is the cause of all the disharmony in the world today. Each individual in his or her own unique way has enveloped themselves in conditioned ego. And, it is the responsibility of each individual in his or her own unique way to remove it. Teachers can help, healers can help, governments can help by creating an environment in support (once they understand the necessity of doing so) but they cannot do it for you. No one can ever do it for you. It is up to each individual to first take responsibility for this great work, and then to go about sincerely and systematically dissolving all the elements of their own conditioned personality as they go about their daily lives.

The outcome of dissolving the conditioned ego is Self-realisation. This is the great union, the fusion of your higher-Self with your personality minus your conditioning. It is the final adjustment made between spirit and form which ends the false dreaming, bringing clarity and blissful union to the Self where, finally, all is seen and known and felt to be God. It is the goal which lies at the heart of all longing and yearning in every human breast, and it is achievable, and will be achieved by every entity in his or her own way, in his or her own time.

I do make a distinction between Self-realisation and *enlightenment.*

Enlightenment is yours as soon as you wake up to the fact, and truly believe, you are a being of light, and that light is within All-That-Is. Many are enlightened in the world today and the number is growing at a quite astonishing rate. There are families and groups of enlightened people now forming and living everywhere. This light is very attractive and attracts to itself an ever growing light, spreading like wild fire, until its momentum will overflow into enlightenment for all on earth. This is a great first step. It will put you, and all on earth, well on the way to Self-realisation.

I talk more about enlightenment and Self-realisation in the Chapter on *Meditation.*

However, I might add that when you are awake to the nature of God both within you and outside of you, purpose becomes rather meaningless, for you realise that love and purpose are one, and that in being joyful you are being purposeful; and in being purposeful, and being aligned to your whole Self, you are being joyful, and thus quite naturally loving; with peace (harmony) being the constant factor behind everything.

At the same time you cannot help but be aware that love, also, is the constant factor that always *is*.

This is why I have placed love and purpose together as the heading to this chapter. They are, in truth, together.

We have already touched on who you are. Let us go deeper. Yes, you are here on earth in a human body, but in essence you are life. Life has no titles and no particular identity. It has no sex. It has no particular form. It has no age. It has no purpose other than to BE. This is where you and me and all others are equal within the Oneness.

We do, however, by individualising out of the Oneness, take upon ourselves various roles in order to experience that role for the sake of that experience, and, of course, even more importantly, to experience ourselves as *the other*. This mirroring effect allows us to see ourselves through others, by bouncing off others, by loving, playing with, confronting others, and just being with others - and finally by fully accepting the other. In this way we experience our Oneness-self in a way that we could not otherwise do if we were to remain in that ineffable state of harmony (the peace) that is pure Oneness alone. It is inevitable, of course, that we help each other, as, in so doing, we are obviously helping ourselves. In this there is spiritual growth, better called spiritual advancement, or, even better - expansion of consciousness. And, remember, consciousness is light.

This on-going experiencing is as true for our whole self (our higher-Self) at its own level of light frequency as it is for our own individual personality in our more dense reality on earth.

From the outside looking in, our role seems to define who we are, except that each viewer will see us differently. For instance, to those who see me as an artist, I am that. To those who see me as a writer of songs, I am that. To those who see me as a spiritual teacher, I am that. To those who see me as rather strange, I am that. To those who see me as loving, I am that. To those who see me as irreverent, I am that. To those who see me as arrogant, I am that. To those who see me as wise, I am that. These are roles that most people feel comfortable with. But unless they are as flexible as life is, their ego takes a knock when I say I have long ago accepted as a reality (indeed, it is but just another role to play) that I am the human personality (a human aspect no less) of a planetary sovereign or loving Father of this world of ours, this earth. And those who look to me as a spiritual teacher, healer, guru, or father figure are not altogether delighted when I take no interest in teaching, or in any of their opinions, but take to my hammock and watch the birds.

So, are you and I to be defined by what we do, or are expected to do, or are we free to live our life according to the joy of our being, which is to be in moment to moment aliveness, in splendid innocence and in truth with our spirit.

What do you think? How would you like to live? And, if you vote to live according to the joy of your being, are you prepared to give that same right to others?

Those who look to me to demonstrate a particular mode of behaviour are gratified when I do so when it fulfils their expectations, yet, when I do just the opposite, the ideas they have built around me become insupportable. And then, of course, it is not their ideas that get the blame, it is me!

I am not special in this; see how it happens around you all the time, and see how you let yourself fall into this pattern with others when your own expectations are not being met.

On a personal note, my choice is to live according to the joy of my being, and my wish is that every human beings on earth come to know this way of living, too. You have nothing to lose in trying it out. It is wondrously loving and thrilling in its vistas. My experience tells me you will like it. And, you know, experience does count for something.

Many organizations on earth, many brotherhoods, past and present, have been created to meet the need of entities seeking to awaken to the joy of their being. Many more such groups will be created to serve this need for many ages to come.

Though a self-realised entity does not need to belong to such groups, he or she is always free to do so. He or she might join such a group out of simple joy - the joy to serve and the joy to participate - but not from need. Please, do remember, that, the God of your being, the spiritual you, together with your higher self, is your own sufficiency. You already *belong*. You are not going anywhere in order to belong. You are not joining anything, or anybody, in order to belong.

Joy is to be your experience. Joy is to be your purpose and joy is to be your fellowship.

Without need there is no need to plan.

Now, and this may seem to be a paradox: having no need to plan does not preclude being able to plan.

In other words, if the moment calls for planning, you make plans.

If you were unable to plan this would severely limit you. Yet, are you not life which is unlimited?

When there is no need (and I am using *need* to denote the ego's demand that the outcome of its plan should be entirely favourable to it) plans can be made for their own sake, for the sake of the joy inherent within them which is the joy within the doing. Then we have such beautiful living, understanding that: *being is in the doing and doing is in the being.*

Without the ego's demands of a satisfactory eventuality, without the ego's insistence upon a vision that is in accordance with its pet philosophy of how the world should be healed, there is no stress, no strain, no urgency about the planning, and no blockage in the creative doing.

To *need* to get somewhere, implies failure if you don't get there. An element of strain and frustration enters in. Fear of lack, fear of failure, gives rise to even more fear. There is an endless cycle of irritation, resentment, guilt and anger which is a fertile breeding ground for all sorts of disharmony, and diseases in the body.

The opposite of disharmony is harmony. When you sit in meditation, don't try to get anywhere or go anywhere, solve anything, or make anything happen - either inside yourself or on the outside. It is enough to imagine yourself as harmony incarnate, in the flesh, in your body, harmony inside and harmony outside. All accepted. All is well. Past, present and future, all has always been well and always will be well. Drop into this harmony. Harmony, you could say is the ultimate purpose behind everything. You can jump right there in a moment! And remember, what you can imagine may become your reality. Here the mind is helpful. Here it gives you a key. Here the mind comes into its own. After all, it loves to create new realities. So, get the mind onside, be a friend to it, and ask it to imagine for you what harmony might be like. Then, as you continue to sit in wondrous peace, allow even your mind's thoughts of harmony to drop away, and experience it.

The very words we use: *planning, doing, creating, undertaking, manifesting,* all mean much the same thing. They are absolutely interchangeable in the context that I am speaking about here. When you look into your self, stop for a moment before you do any creating, doing or planning, and say to your self: "Am I doing this out of joy or am I over riding my feelings because I think (*it is the ego doing the thinking*) that what I am doing is very important and has to be done?"

Ask your self this many times a day and decide which master you are going to serve: the conditioned ego, for which no goal or plan is ever quite perfect, or your whole Self which is aligned with your spirit, out of which you can begin to do things in a small and simple way, but only those things which give you an inner lift and a feeling of excitement and joy, and deep satisfaction. It is possible. When you live in harmony with yourself, it is possible.

In creating the belief that it is possible, and in acting upon it, you are jumping, so to speak, into the fire of ego destruction, and once upon this path there is no turning back. Once started you have to see it through. So, courage is required. Have faith in your self and the will to act, and the will to see it through.

Before I continue, I must say this: don't ever go and do something just for the sake of doing it. This will actually reinforce the ego. If there is nothing to do which comes out of a feeling of joy, do nothing. Sit and feel your body and just continue to sit with it and watch and feel, and experience harmony. This, just this, by itself, is the most creative thing you will ever do for yourself - and for the planet. Please believe it.

And, as I have mentioned, when sitting on these occasions, do not fall into the trap of *doing* a meditation in which you are expecting something to happen (or have any results in mind). These meditations have their place but they are still *doing*, still controlling the situation.

I am asking you to sit still and know that nothing needs to be done. Achievement, or perfection, is not the issue. The issue is for you to be present, here and now, in your own joy, in your own peace, in your own harmony, and make that a permanent reality. All else will follow from this. What it might be, who knows. Give it no thought. It is not of the NOW. Not of your present reality.

You are being asked to refuse to give away your power (your joy) to any outside person, to any situation, or to any *ideas* you may have of what to do which may be trying to seduce or manipulate you away from your truth.

In a sense, your joy is the dragon within you. Let it come forth and confront the fear and guilt that you and others have about living in joy. It is your very own dragon of wisdom. In Tibet and ancient China the self-realised ones were called The Dragons of Wisdom. Now you know why. All because of joy!

So, when you don't know what to do and you feel that nothing is particularly joyful about your life, make this a valuable time for your self, and sit, not in meditation, nor in day dreams, but just sit, fully awake and present, and be with your self and know that you are a living God at peace and know that in this state all the universe can fulfil you, and you in turn fulfil the universe.

This, let me assure you is the most useful thing you can ever do for those around you. The conditioned ego will resist this seemingly useless activity tooth and nail. It will feel far from happy at this inactivity when so much (as it sees it) needs to be done! Resist the ego with your *will*. It is the best use of *will*. You will notice that your will remains the detached observer.

Allow the joy and love of your life to manifest around you, then come out of your aloneness and stillness, and start *doing* again, carrying the new insights and the possibly unusual feeling of harmony with you. And do *what is yours to do, being none other that what you want to do!*

Just sitting *and being* is absolutely essential for you: it is essential because it allows essence (spirit) to make its presence felt. And the longer you have denied your spiritual vibration (the frequency of light of your higher self) as being a part of your life, the longer you may need to sit, allowing the different feelings inside you to sift themselves out so that you can sort out what is what.

Life is not divided into two camps, rest and activity. There is more to it. In rest, you will discover activity. In activity, there is rest.

In sitting, in just *being* and doing absolutely nothing - except to be present in the presence of the Oneness - you are doing something profound - and rare to be seen on this earth. But not rare in other worlds, on other levels of existence. It is common place. The norm. It is as vital a part of existence as the breath that moves within all existence. Without the inner, the outer goes not out.

This state of being is called contemplation. See to it that contemplation becomes a part of your daily experience. It is the most loving and joyful and peaceful thing you will ever do for your self, and at this time it is much needed in this planet to balance the frenetic and distorted energies of egos who are grimly hanging on to personal visions of ever diminishing satisfaction with ever more frenzied control.

When you have recognised and accepted your essence vibration, no longer do you create your reality out of lack, or from pressure by some authority, or from any feeling of being duty bound to do any particular thing.

You now choose. Using your sovereign will, out of your enthusiasm, from your own validation, you commit your mind to your plan, and nourishing it with your feelings (which bring it to life), you will your plan to manifest. You will it to be. You empower it with all your feelings. And then it happens.

This comes out of the moment. This comes out of the abundant expression of your own sense of joy and aliveness.

You are not here on earth "to do your duty". There is no duty other than that which you may like to create for your self. And if this is so, why call it a duty? Why feel it as a burden?

Duty is a heavy word. But does it need to be?

I repeat, there is no intrinsic need to achieve anything, no intrinsic need to get anywhere. Life has no motive. It is it's own motive. It is it's own movement. It is not *having to make* movement. It does not have to move to get somewhere because there is nowhere where it isn't!

Life has no obligation (or duty) to be either this way or that way. So, why should you? All your personality needs to realise is that if you wilfully hurt others, you end up hurting yourself. And, if you are in denial of the Oneness (either within or outside of yourself), you will be permanently lonely because you will feel permanently separate.

Plans which are undertaken with motive but without attachment to that motive, have a purity, a freedom of their own. They are in harmony with life which needs no motive and has no plan to experience itself. Do enjoy making plans such as these.

You are here to experience your self as joy and spontaneity. This is the nature of life. This is you. This is your nature. This is fundamental to your being. Do this, and nothing more than this, and all that is required of you is done.

Out of joy and spontaneity comes love. Joy is love expressing itself very much on the physical plane in the physical body. It is particularly a quality of the Oneness on the physical plane and I shall speak more of joy in a later chapter.

To talk of love and purpose is my present theme. And this purpose is definitely not mysterious. There is no mystery about joy and laughter and spontaneity. There is no mystery about a kind of happiness which floods your being with such intensity that a lasting peace (harmony)is the abiding companion of your laughter.

What is stopping you being awake to this? What is the pay off, and is it worth it?

Your synthesis point in the physical world is where you link up with, creating with, others in a natural way. It can be anything you want it to be but it is uniquely yours. It can be in music, in art, in administration, in science, in colour, in healing, or in nature - even in sex, or laughter. In fact, it can be in anything.

It is the place within you that resonates, without judgement, or desire, to all that is outside of you. *Love,* is the medium, as it were, in which all these faculties swim.

Your path is unique to your self and only you can feel the appropriateness of the time when to choose and change direction. There is nothing wrong in having a teacher and there is nothing wrong about being alone. In many lifetimes you will have experienced all facets of these experiences, so just allow your self to flow easily to which ever path seems, at the present, to be the most rewarding. Choose a path which calls you to excitement and challenge; it will probably be tinged with a little apprehension - or may be a great deal of apprehension - but no matter, choose it!

There are many teachers in the world now and more shall arise. Seek them out, live near them, they may have something to offer you. Love them, enjoy them and respect them but do not become attached to them or their methods, or copy their behaviour.

You are to have nothing to do with attachment, or method, and nothing to do with surrendering your self to a teacher lest you become like a clone with a whole lot of other clones of mesmerised disciples. Be, instead, self reliant and self- motivated and keep moving.

Your purpose is to realize that there is no longer any ego-mind goal-orientated purpose, that there is no point in waiting for anything to happen, and that there is no need to have a purpose. You are to realise that your will (when you are attuned to your own essence) is the will of God because you are God. In other words, you are the Oneness, and also an aspect of it.

Waiting for something to happen is the companion to duty.

Doing your duty for a later reward is to suffer *now*, hoping something better will come along later. Indeed, it is like a pat on the back for being a good girl. How degrading can this be. It reminds one of animal training. But the Oneness, or your higher self, is not your trainer and you are not animals to be put through your hoops to get a sugar lump as a reward, and then to go to heaven for getting it right.

This belief is a terrible burden to put upon yourself. And, if you have put it there, so must you remove it.

You do create your own pain or happiness, and karma is only a philosophy of burdens if you let it become so. The end of fear is the end of karma. And, the end of beliefs such as this, behind which fear is hiding, allows the fear to be unmasked and confronted.

The path I speak of is not burdensome unless you make it so. It is, in truth, a way of great ease and celebration. It is a way of joy, of dance and laughter, of gaiety and music and colour, of sensitivity and intimacy, of nurturing and caring, of richness, and freedom to feel your own spirit and use your will, using your mind to create in harmony with the whole of life.

It is a way, also, of occasional tears - often many tears - which will wash through you like a rushing waterfall, sweeping clean away all that has been held in as tension from the past - whether it be from yesterday, or from childhood, or from many lifetimes ago. There is no self realization without tears. Rainbows are seen through the rain. Use them frequently to wash away your pain: tears are the way to glory. Be not afraid to let them flow. They are a sign that consciousness is expanding and beginning to glow again with light and colour.

Remember, joy is of a higher vibration than the astral emotion that we call feeling, yet it resonates to feeling. It also, therefore, has a resonance with sadness.

If you can feel a feeling intensely (such as sadness), you will be able to feel all feelings intensely. Never try to squash your sadness, but neither indulge in it, or believe it has any special merit for spiritual growth. It is just sadness.

When you can feel to your greatest depths, you can feel to your greatest heights. The resonance to joy is then naturally obvious. It is easier to drop into harmony (and thus into wholeness) from a place of deep feeling resonance than from a state, say, of confusion and resentment. Reserve your compassion for those who are so self-conscious about their feelings that they live in a grey world of emotional and spiritual mediocrity. Their conditioned ego is holding them as in a vice. They are, for the moment, stuck.

Sometimes, maybe quite often, you will feel ecstatic with joy and seem to go crazy, not minding what others think of you. Marvellous! If you *mind* what others think of you, you will never live in tune with your spirit.

Think what this means, to you, in this life, here and now. How far have you got to go *before you cease to mind*? It is a good clue to where you are now. How often do you live in denial of your essence?

Denial of joy, denial of peace, denial of love, for the sake of a duty that you consider your family, or society, or your religion, or current partner, or your karma, requires of you, is a wonderful ego belief that weaves its spell around you to keep you stuck in loneliness and unresolved discontent. Sadly, this belief and the emotional charge it carries with it, remains with you when you pass from the physical plane, holding you in thrall in the astral levels for a while until you can be shown how to resolve and remove it. To have this belief linger for so long in your life here is a calamity. To still be holding it when you pass over is not exactly disastrous but you will come to see it as wasted time.

For, this is not to say that choosing duty, for a while, so as not to hurt others, or to help others (as maybe in the case of bringing up children), even if burdensome, is not right for you. For, there is no right or wrong in these choices you make. There is only experiencing. And, let me say, that hurting others, either consciously or unconsciously, to do your own thing is just such another experience. From it, wisdom grows. The day comes when you see that there is an easiness to everything. There is certainly an easiness to right timing. Making choices from clarity shows you that the timing of all things can be natural and easy and worth waiting for. It makes all burdens lights. In the meantime, you can find moments - precious moments - to sit and drop into harmony.

Placing duty upon a pedestal, under which you sigh with weariness, believing you have no choice but to endure, worshipping it, and perhaps hanging on to it like some sort of meaningful life-belt, is anti life. It is anti the NOW. It is like a big cloud, swirling endlessly. It will end up strangling you.

When caring for others comes out of essence, from a clear choice, this is not duty. This is an act of love. An utterly different feeling is there. There are no burdens. Only joy is there.

Clarity comes out of seeing things clearly - where there are no hidden agendas lurking about in your psyche being fed by the conditioned ego. With clarity comes real choice. This is a choice that empowers you rather than a choice that you feel is forced upon you - be it even by God (as your religiously conditioned ego might have it!) - which deep down you are in conflict with, thereby draining you of energy, and denying you the joy and love in your life that you crave.

So, we see that love and purpose are connected to joy, joy being the apex of this triangle. Love without purpose does not truly exist, nor does purpose without love, and neither of them can wholly exist without joy.

It is therefore essential that you find, recognise, accept, and crystallise, within your self, your essential joy frequency. This is the purpose before you as human beings. It needs to come first, else humanity will sink into a dismal and cloudy morass of well meaning but dutiful boredom, out of which will erupt much frustration and rage and aimless violence, and suicide, as, indeed, you are witnessing in your youth of today.

The kingdom of heaven on earth is not going to be here tomorrow. It is here now. It is your purpose to express it now. Is not living from your essence uncompromisingly, a splendid purpose? Is it not enough? If not, what other would you have?

Life knows nothing of duty because life is a feeling and duty is always an idea. Duty implies a task to be performed, usually for others. Yet, if you are the Oneness and Oneness is all there is, then who are these others? Are they not wishing to live in essence also?

Yes, of course they are, and here we have the solution to this matter of duty versus caring. Caring for, or the helping of others, is expressed by spirit when, and only when, the desire to be helpful is derived from the urgency of spirit to free itself and others from the ego's dominance. In other words, when spirit is calling to spirit, the helper may look to the indwelling life beneath the conditioned ego, and help to set this life free. A great task, this is, and it is a place where all will one day stand in service in *the joy of being*.

This, then, is the true meaning of sacrifice - the making sacred the helping, and the caring, which when done with joy has a natural outflow of love and purpose, going toward more joy. It is none other than serving from spirit for the benefit and freedom of spirit, and never for the desires or benefit of the conditioned ego.

Now, let me say, that if you are of a mind to serve and help others whilst you are in the process of awakening to and discovering your own essence, this is fine. You are awakening to yourself and helping others at the same time. This is an economy of energy. It is a grand road to awakening, very swift, very direct, as long as you don't get bogged down in the pride of ego satisfaction and the belief that you have no choice in your area of service and begin to wallow in self pity.

Whenever resentment or weariness begins to happen, let go, pull back from your helping for a while, and re-connect with your inner self in contemplation: it will soon show you another direction to take, or show you how to help in another way. Remember, when your helping has a lightness and a joy to it you are on track. When it hasn't, you are helping no one and reinforcing your ego. These are the clouds that karma is made of. This is all that karma is. It is your own ego entanglement in illusion, originated in past life times by fear.

When you help and serve from essence, no karma is generated because no clouds are precipitated. All is clear and all remains clear, despite the fact that you might be serving in the muddiest of arenas - of which this earth, at present, has quite a few.

To be true to your own sense of joy and aliveness is not a mystery. It is open and easy. Only your ideas and the ideas of others which you have made your own, make it into a mystery.

Life is not to be waited for. The kingdom of heaven is not to be waited for. If you wait you will wait for ever, and waiting will be cemented into your ego; waiting will become your habit. You will even remain waiting when you are residing in other levels of the universe.

The leaving of the physical body is no automatic passport to the kingdom of heaven. Paradise shall ever dance in front of you like a mirage.

When you put duty before living your truth, you remain sick to the soul; and you will stay like this just as long as you refuse to look to your essence, awaken to it, and allow it to be the life in your life.

There is nothing more ugly than placing duty, which arises solely from your conditioned ego's perceived purpose, before one's own sense of joy and aliveness. Indeed, it may ease the pain of others, but unless it arises out of your essence in spontaneity and joyful aliveness, it would be better abandoned before it further pollutes the world with well-intentioned but distorted ideas regarding the nature of spirit (which is another word for essence).

Service (true sacrifice), undertaken by men and women who are drawing upon their inner life, who are living from a centre of peace and joy despite outer hardships is rare. It is also what they choose or like to do. If you like to do something it can hardly be made out to be a sacrifice as in the appalling idea of some religions in which the idea is, that, if you put your self down sufficiently, out of that self abnegation must come merit.

This is a travesty of what humility truly is. Indeed, it is the arrogance of the ego appropriating to itself ego satisfaction in the belief that it is playing an important role in the expectations of spiritual fruits. True humility lies in being open and vulnerable enough to express your true feelings in any situation, and living your life according to your truth.

What would you like to do if you were free to do what you would like to do? Well, you are free, so why don't you up and do it!

I hear you saying, "That's all very well, but I've got children to look after, bills to pay, and a husband who wants his meals on time. How can I go and do what I want to do?" Well, you have dug your self, temporarily at least, into a hole in which you have decided that what you want to do in life is to deny your own feelings of joy, as a pay off, maybe, for the security of having a home, for the warmth and delights of sexual comforts, for the delight of having dependent trusting children around you which makes you feel loved or needed, or for going along with what society expects of you, or, perhaps, just for the love that you missed out on when you were a child.

Now, if this is really what you want to do, there is nothing wrong in this. To be a home maker and create around you a loving environment in which incoming entities can feel at ease, in which they can become acquainted with the intricacies of human existence, and be helped to awaken to their own true life and spirit within is a fine service. Very fine. It is not unlike being the guardian of a planet. Indeed, it is good training for this particular path of service. But, again, it is really only *permanently* helpful when undertaken with spiritual awareness, with non-attachment to the outcome, and with a light heart. Then, and only then, is it not so much a duty as an act of love. Underpinning it is joy.

So, what to do if you have dug your self into a hole?

Well, first you have to admit to your self that, at one time, it is what you wanted to do, but now you no longer want to do it. This is a simple truth. It is better faced as such. Do not have any guilt about the fact that life is always about doing what you want to do and measuring it against personal happiness and satisfaction; but, let me say (before you walk off and leave your family), this needs to be looked at from essence (from joy), not from the conditioned ego's attempt to merely avoid pain.

The next stage is to confront those you are living with and share your thoughts and feelings with them as openly and honestly as you can. To your surprise, you may find the hole disappearing, or circumstances may suddenly alter around you without any obvious volition of yours, which begins to make life for you fun again.

There is no right or wrong behaviour in anything you ever do; there is merely life for the adventure of it and the experience of joy or pain for yourself, for which you are totally responsible. And, if you cause pain and suffering to others, it will certainly cause pain and suffering for you because all is One. When you hurt another you are indeed, in truth, hurting your self. So why do this? It seems a rather pointless experience.

When you begin to share with those around you your deepest feelings, fears, and longings, and let them know that you would like to begin to live from your essence in the joy of your being, and invite them to do the same, at the same time letting them know that you will provide all the support that you can give them whilst they attempt to do the same, then life can become very exciting indeed! It burns away the karmic entanglements, and the glamour, and illusions, exceedingly swiftly - maybe in a few hours, or in a day, or even in minutes. Joy is seen to be the reality again. Love is there once more. And personal satisfaction is immense. Purpose has returned. Happiness reigns.

When you hurt yourself you hurt others and when you hurt others you hurt your self. So, any logical person will see that the trick to life (if I may use that expression) is neither to give your self, or others, a hard time. This has often been likened to a fine balancing act, and so it is, but like anything, practice makes perfect. In this case the practice is the practice of keeping awake and alert and being absolutely so present in the moment that you don't go chasing off into day dreams, get into the same habits, fall asleep and fall down the same familiar old holes.

To plan is to be creative. In the physical universe this universe is full of plans and diverse purposes. This earth, our solar system, and this galaxy, are carefully planned creations. We live as creative cells within the bodies of cosmic beings which have plan and purpose. But I say to you the purpose which is behind all purpose and which is sufficient unto itself and ever shall be so is *joy* and the awareness that all is love. And this is the great purpose before humanity: to awaken to this knowingness. All else shall follow.

The key is self reliance. Cosmic beings - your higher selves - are life-realised beings. You do not have to have solar or galactic awareness or knowledge of inter planetary affairs to be a cosmic being. You are aware, simply, that you are life, a God, living within God (the Oneness), self reliant and self responsible for all your own feelings which is, indeed, your own aura of loving radiance.

Many human men and women have become self realised having little knowledge, but they have all had lots of courage to live by their truth. It is the easiest of paths.

No one human being on earth knows, or will ever know, the details of the creative plan for the evolution of this galaxy and it is well that they do not ... not only would it boggle your mind, but too much dwelling upon plans and hierarchies leads to irresoluteness and confusion - or fear that the so called plan may not succeed! Please let go of all this. It may be fascinating, and a little knowledge may be useful at times to expand your horizons. But pay it scant attention.

The knowledge of humanity's galactic origins might seem to be useful for the people of earth at this time, but this is only in so far as it will help them awaken to their own joy and love nature, which they now need to know is the very same nature as that of the Oneness.

And yet, this kind of knowledge - any knowledge - for you at this time is relatively unimportant. It will come to you in its own good time. Awareness of your spirit and the knowledge of who you are (your higher self) is all important.

The present plan for earth entities is not, in fact, for you to be particularly creative. It is not for you to go searching after miracle powers. It will be a miracle enough, I assure you, when *each of you awakens to the joy of your being and trusts it.* Then will pain and suffering end. Is not this purpose enough?

All else shall follow from this awakening - with miracles a plenty, arising from this awareness. This holds good for the planet as it does for the individual.

So to sum up: what is your purpose? What is the purpose for the three-in-one that you are, human, whole Self and spirit?

Let's again be specific:

1. For spirit (your source), *harmony is the ultimate reality and already exists.*

2. For your whole Self, expansion of consciousness (being your light) is your purpose.

3. For your human self, the bringing of your personality self into alignment with your whole Self is your purpose.

Peace is the first corner of the eternal triangle. Love and purpose, together, make the second corner of the eternal triangle of life which forms the nature of the manifested Oneness. The third apex, which humanity now needs to become responsive to, is joy.

So, your purpose is to re-discover joy. In re-discovering one aspect of the triangle, you will naturally, without effort, re-discover the other two aspects - of peace and love. For they are truly not separate. Some entities will be more inclined to concentrate on peace, others on love, others on joy. It matters not. All have the same triangle with them. However you approach the Oneness, the Oneness responds. Finding One finds all. Harmony reigns. Your purpose here on earth is then achieved. Other vistas await you.

CHAPTER THREE

SPIRITUAL MESSENGERS

Running like a golden thread through all world religions is a belief in a coming saviour. For Christians, it is the return of the Christ. For others, it is the Maitreya, or the Bodhisattva, or the Imam Mahdi, or the Masters.

For some, the Avatar of the Age has already come and gone, recognised by only a few of the faithful.

For some, he or she is here now, and disciples flock around, convinced and readily proclaiming.

This longing, this general expectancy, surrounding some man or woman, or some hoped for super being, has become a habit.

It has nonetheless been a useful and, oft times, beautiful expression of life's urge to be free and humanity's longing to awaken to the One life. This urge has expressed itself sensitively in discipleship when the disciple has been sincere in his or her desire to do the inner work, and, importantly, has been loving and tolerant toward other faiths.

More often, the initial beauty and sensitivity of discipleship is dragged down into the mire of organised and mundane ritual; it becomes degraded when discipleship becomes crystallised into an organised religion or cult. This results in intolerance, self righteousness, zealotry and fanaticism, not the least of which is silly adulation of the recipient of this worship.

This expectation of a coming Avatar expresses the cyclic nature of life as it experiences itself within form and within the consciousness of human beings.

In other words, when present beliefs are no longer an adequate vehicle for the awakening consciousness and life is being suffocated, life asserts itself. Using the vehicle of one - or many - entities, life speaks through its vehicle, or vehicles, saying, " Wake up! Wake up! Remember who you are! Remember what you are looking for!"

A few entities do wake up. The impact of these can be world changing on a world. But, for those who have not yet gone beyond beliefs, there then begins again an immediate conflict between old beliefs and new beliefs.

Of course, after a while, for those still putting their faith in beliefs, the new ideas begin to take root in the consciousness of the aspiring disciples. They once again make them into beliefs. The disciples seize upon them hungrily and gratefully, and begin to proliferate around the life-wave carrier (which is what the master really is) like barnacles on a ship's bottom, dragging his (or her) teaching through the water ever more sluggishly until the day arrives when all is sunk in a welter of religion, theology, organization, administration, superstition and fantasy.

This is when a new Avatar arrives upon the scene.

To break through the cement of old beliefs is not an easy task. Some entities can be seduced into dissolving their beliefs, others need a sledgehammer.

Life-wave carriers - they are both the destroyers and the awakeners - come in many shapes and sizes with many tricks up their sleeves. And they come again and again in many different guises until spirit and the Oneness is finally revealed in all its glory, united with awakened personality and surrendered ego.

Upon the day that all beliefs cease, there is only life, a loving life, revealed as the joyful and profoundly peaceful existence of all that is and all that ever shall be.

Life has no idea of itself. It has no beliefs that must be believed in before it shows itself to you. Life is here. This is it.

If life could talk (as, indeed, it does through an awakened one) it would say, "Your *ideas* of what you *think* I am, do cloud you from what I am. Drop them all and find me. There, I AM."

Life continually affirms its nature, and with such obvious aliveness, that all beliefs concerning its nature do, eventually, fall away.

How often have you seen a child exasperated by its parent by their insisting upon a socially correct behaviour that the child should follow? It is usually obvious, as you observe this little domestic scene, that there is a blockage in the flow of the life energy of the undoubtedly well-meaning parent. The child, expressing life in an unconditioned state of being, unerringly homes in on this blockage and more often than not gets thoroughly squashed for his or her insight.

Here we have life trying to free life in its simplest, but probably most irritating, manner. How much can children teach you!

And, whilst giving this as an example. It does not mean I condone the total indiscipline of children. Of course, they have to learn to fit into the society they find themselves born into. Of course, they need to learn (with love) what is acceptable and what is not. This is not only to stop them from being brought up as selfish little monsters, but to alert them to the kind of society they have incarnated into, to which, as adults, they can give a measured response. The mind should also be well trained, being brought up to realize that it is ever the creative master, being the master of emotion - not, of course, existing at the expense of emotion, but living in awareness of it and with it.

A life awakener (an awakened master) feels the blocked life-flow just as a child does, but, being fully conscious, he or she can make conscious decisions as to the appropriateness of his or her reaction to the blockage, and make choices regarding his or her methods of assistance.

Hence, the Christ's admonishment to become like a little child.

Indeed, the child within you must take you by the hand and show you the way. Remember how it was to trust. Remember how spontaneous you used to be. Remember how you used to play so intensely in the moment, thinking of nothing but that which was embraced by it. It will lead you back to your self.

Look to your childlike impulses and see how often, when it comes to a choice, you betray your self, vacillating between openly doing what you want to do, and doing the right thing. And see how cleverly you conceal your frustration and justify your decisions !

It is so important for you to *feel* again - to feel the life flowing through your veins as you did when you were a child. Ideas and beliefs obscure the nature of life. This leads to such concretisation in your ego that your aliveness becomes the merest glimmer, suffocated by your nebulous ideas of what life is about and constricted by fears which lie in your deeply held unconscious beliefs.

Life is God. There is nothing more powerful. It will burst forth again and again to declare that it cannot be suffocated, conditioned by, or limited by, fixed ideas about itself. It is always a natural emergence, appropriate to the consciousness and the forms in which the concretisation has occurred. It also accounts for the outrageous behaviour of little boys who will constantly tease their mothers and test their fathers!

Names such as Master, Christ, Avatar, are names. And a name is no more than a name. A name gives rise to ideas about itself. A name says or implies something to happen or not to happen, to do or not to do, to be gained or not to be gained. And then there are the ideas: the implicit ideas, the unconscious ideas, and the vague nebulous half-formed ideas, the concepts and opinions.

Unquestioned religious beliefs carry a mystical aura about them which appear to be beyond analysis, beyond all argument. They are deep in the psyche, but they are still ideas. Life is none of these.

If you have the remotest idea about the Christ and his or her coming or the remotest idea about any other master or spiritual messenger, how they will behave, how they will put the world to rights or how they will differ one from another, you are missing the point of life within you which is you. You are indeed missing the whole point of life and you will always remain confused as to who is the real Coming One.

My dear friends, the real Coming One is you. Truly it is. The truth of your abundant self, your Father in Heaven, The Oneness, *the joy of your being,* is inside your self as your self. It can only be found in the *here and now* by your self. No one can find it for you, give it to you, or initiate you into it. If you think they can, that very thought becomes a strong barrier to you discovering and awakening to your own free and natural life expression.

Yes, it is helpful at times to be in contact with an entity who is self-realised. Their presence may act upon you like a catalyst and precipitate you into a turmoil of emotional crises which confront you with your mental duplicity and denied feelings. Their presence may act upon you subtly, as in osmosis, to give you a flavour, or a taste, of what you are looking for.

More often than not, their presence increases the dependency of the disciple upon the master. It increases the longings, the expectations and the idea that there is an emotional relationship between master and disciple. These are strong ideas. They lead to great difficulties.

To taste is fine. It is a good way to get encouragement and get a feeling for what you are looking for. But to *keep tasting and hoping*, making this into a way of life, is to live in splendid illusion which the ego will make every effort to prolong, because it gives it such a satisfying feeling of accomplishing something of a spiritual nature without ever having to make itself vulnerable to real change.

Each time you go back for more you strengthen the illusion of the relationship. You increasingly cement that idea and that habit into the conditioned part of your psyche, the ego.

You, yourself, however, are the very source of joy and energy which, when you are awake to your essence, you can dip into, in contemplation, at any moment, at any time of the day, be reconnected to your source and emerge refreshed. Self-realised entities are self-reliant entities, being *self-refreshing* entities.

This is the main reason why so few who become awakened proclaim themselves to be teachers: teaching disciples to be self reliant by gathering them around you, allowing them to become dependent upon you, inevitably leads to confusion. Entities at a certain level of awareness are just longing for someone to come along and tell them that everything is now going to be hunky dory, as long as they just fall in and worship the master.

When you rely on another for your feelings of worth or purpose, you are not being self reliant. Instead, you become addicted to a powerful idea in your head about what the master is going to do for you. You begin to copy. Or, try to surrender a little better! And then you begin to rely on a group of like minded individuals for emotional support. Then you wonder why life is not so hunky dory, after all. You wonder why you get tired, why you are caught up in the politicking and bureaucracy going on around you, and why you are moaning and complaining to the master about all kinds of trivial and tiresome problems in your life. You are trapped in a grand illusion.

Yes, you may have had a taste; but the truth is, the taste is not the real thing. A taste comes and goes. The real thing never comes or goes. It is coming from nowhere and going nowhere: it is always here. The real thing is *you being here, NOW,* always. Beware of becoming addicted to the taste or to the trappings through which the taste is dispensed. These trappings come in many colours and they can entrap you if you allow them to.

You can become temporarily lost in the trappings; and a sure sign of this is a feeling of being lost. There is bewilderment, resentment, nothing happening - the limbo syndrome. It is a sure sign of your dependency upon another.

Within your self you are all colours.

Well, then, you ask, what about surrender?

Surrender is great. Indeed, it is! But do surrender to your own life energy. Surrender to your own loving joyful energy. Surrender to your own self reliance upon your own energy. If any one outside of you reflects this to you, well and good, but, if not stay clear. Don't fall into a master. Fall into your self.

Not until you have fallen into your self, can you fall into another and remain as free as the wind without imposing your own fantasies upon the other.

You are LIFE in a capital way. You are a capital joyful spirit. You are joy. Call it what you like. You cannot put a name to it. I am it. You are it. It is beyond analysis. It is, exasperatingly, far beyond explanations such as these words of mine. And, yet, I do go on!

How to awaken is the knotty problem. Anything you think it might be - or think about doing - may add to the illusion, yet, if you refuse to open up your mind to the challenge, you will add to the illusion by default. The secret is in watching. By watching, and by using the will to keep this watching process going, the ego's clouds disperse and the sun begins to peep through.

It requires courage and confidence in your self. It requires trust, even to the point of death to the conscious mind. It requires, from time to time, a trust in living without any idea as to what living is or where it is going to lead you.

If you like to call this a trust in God, so be it: that is fine. You are God, and many gods of great loving consciousness trust alongside you, and yet you are so utterly unaware, most of you, of this fact. This fact alone is the cause of astonishing ignorance and great loneliness at this physical level of universal existence.

From the abyss of the death of the conditioned ego (being only an apparent abyss) a self reliant, life affirming, being emerges. This being is causal and original, unique, integrated and identified with life as life. This is harmony. This is for you to realise.

Upon attaining this realisation, you can say, if you wish, that you are the avatar of the age, and many in this century have said just this.

It was just their way of looking at it. Life is the avatar of the age. It is the avatar of every moment, too. All who awaken to it know it (and have the right to say it if they wish). A world full of avatars would know no strife - though, their disciples might end up killing each other!

Every one who awakens to the one life is an avatar of the one life, and, as life is the one life, each awakened one is absolutely no greater an avatar than another.

You might well say, why use names at all if they have all these connotations and possibilities for confusion? Why, indeed? Why, indeed? But, again, if it is going to be helpful, why not!

I am all for avoiding confusion. As I have said, names are just names and have no significant purpose anywhere in the universe, other than for the very reasonable and practical application of identity. This is especially so in the physical worlds, but loses its relevance at other levels.

Do remember, your identity at higher levels of frequency is more to do - in point of fact, is everything to do - with light and frequency, rather than with titles or status.

Any name that gives hopeful aspirants the idea that one master is in any way more special than another is a lot of nonsense. When you are self-realised you know once and for all that you are not in the slightest degree special. Any pandering to a belief in speciality is a fine sign that the "master" is still expressing a measure of conditioned ego.

Life is equally within all, as all. It is not exclusive and it is not special, and for those who identify themselves with life as the Oneness, it is not special. In fact, it is very ordinary and being ordinary is like coming home where everything is familiar, where all is accepted, where you feel free to be you and in each moment you feel absolutely safe and loved. How can joy and peace not be the abiding feelings in such a place?

Only to those who are still searching, does it seem special. Seekers love special names: it makes the search important, gives the ego status and makes it feel all worth while. The names and the beliefs associated with them are sticky like glue; they give rise to symbols and superstition which further cloud the simplicity of the search, and, before very long it has all become more mystical and confusing than ever.

Life - the Oneness - contains all possibilities. When you identify with life, and live from your essence, you contain all possibilities and these possibilities do not exclude anything that has gone before.

Life is not exclusive, but inclusive. Life has, at any time, at any emergence, within it, all the possibilities of past and future Christs, Avatars and Masters. Life contains all names, all concepts, all memories, all personalities, yet life itself is none of these.

Life is beyond personalities. It has not been this person before or that person before. Life cannot be before anything or after anything. It is *now* just as it is, always has been and always will be, unlimited in possibility.

Life has been, and is, and will be, all personalities reincarnated, past and present. One who is life knows that all past events are here NOW, and all future possibilities are here NOW.

Essentially - in essence (in spirit), that is - you have not been anyone before. You are life. All has arisen from you as your self and shall do so in infinite possibilities for ever.

This is a part of you that you need to honour. The Oneness. All else follows from it, and emerges from it. Your higher self which sends out many aspects of itself into incarnation is aware of the Oneness, even if you, in physical bodies here on earth, are not.

For many a Christian, the Christ represents the ultimate in perfection. He is the Son of God who embodies the qualities of love, wisdom and power. There is the belief that the Christ will know all about them, personally, and will be personally intervening to forgive and heal their weariness and uplift them into heaven to be at one with God the Father; or, maybe, He will absorb them into his own body (the Body of Christ) where they will be at one with Him in peace and glory for ever.

Now, this is a very healthy dream to have. There is nothing wrong with it whatever. As dreams go it is much healthier than most. It is embodying, through the power of imaginative thought, all that is the most loving and beautiful in life. It also expresses the desire to surrender to something greater than oneself, and the longing to be in unity with the Oneness.

These thoughts and feelings are fine as far as they go. They have served the world well: they have been the guiding inspiration for people of goodwill for thousands of years in the Christian world.

The time has come to explore these thoughts and these dreams a little more deeply and take a new look at what they might mean. For, indeed, they are but dreams.

Knowing they are but dreams in no way invalidates previous thoughts and feelings. It will expand them, enrich them and promote a new dream - one which will lead you, not into Christ's body but into your own. Then will the outer glory end, then will the dream end, and then will you be *awakened* to the glory of the Oneness which you yourself are; and, paradoxically, of which you are, also, truly a glorious aspect of.

You will, indeed, be surrendering to something greater than your self; you are to surrender to your essence, your spiritual nature, the Oneness, which is at one with the Christ principle in every meaningful way.

At every age, a new message, a new vision, is given to humanity that follows on from, expanding and enriching, all that was best in that of the age gone by.

But more importantly than that, a new vision reveals a new quality of divinity for aspiring humanity to attempt to embody in the age that follows.

Love was the quality of divinity introduced to the world by Jesus. What will this new quality be and what form will its revelation take?

As is always the case, the new quality to be revealed will be revealed by those who bring the vision - and they can only reveal it to the extent that they themselves can identify with it, embody it within themselves, and express it through their own natural living (or *being*).

What, then, is this new quality of divinity for this age to come? Can it be said in one word? Indeed, it can. JOY!

I shall be repeating it endlessly - and go on repeating it. JOY!

You are the joy of the world. Together, we are the joy of the universe. God is joy. The Oneness is joy. We are it!

Joy is particularly a quality associated with aliveness, and the vibrancy of being alive, and knowing you are part of a greater unfolding purpose. It is also the celebration of life for no other reason than for the sheer joy of being alive and revelling in it.

This is the new quality of divinity you are now to embody. You are now ready to embody it and express it in your life.

Like love, joy has always been here, but there has been little recognition of its power, or its beauty, or its rightness in being in the divine scheme of things, where solemnity has so often been the accepted norm in the world's religions.

Joy, though, has as its value the one sure indication that we are living in wholeness. If you are not feeling joy in your life, you are not living from essence (which is the experience of being directly connected to spirit), but out of the conditioned ego where joy remains an illogical dream; and happiness is, at best, but temporary.

Joy is all, just as love is all. They go hand in hand, and in no way does one ever make less the other. The Father is joy. The Mother is joy. Always has been and always will be.

Joy has the power to cut through to the heart of love. Joy has the ability to dissolve illusion with a sureness that nothing else can. Within your inner life, you can measure anything against joy and see if you stand the test of remaining joyful: if it does it is of God, of the Oneness; if not it is of illusion or glamour or hypocrisy.

The expression "cutting through to the heart of love" can be expressed thus: love arises out of joy, and only love that arises out of joy, is love.

The theme of this book is the importance of joy, how we measure it, how we recognise it, how we shut it out, and how we can affirm it and be open to it. At the end of this coming age, men and women shall speak of joy as having the spiritual value that love now commands. Think on this.

To return to spiritual messengers, it is a fact that you cannot recognise anything until you have first experienced it. It is impossible to recognise in another person, or in a spiritual messenger, let us say, qualities that you your self have not, at one time or another, observed in your self. It is impossible to imagine something that you cannot imagine.

Now, this image building process, which is your supreme creative ability, must start with images that arise from within you.

With joy this is easy because the very feeling of joy is already lying there within you, waiting for you to give your self permission to say hello to it.

When you imagine, as Christians do, the image of Christ, and when you endow this super being with magnificent qualities, you are, in fact, building and imagining a possible image of your self. This is great work.

That is not to say that Jesus and his great qualities do not exist with exactly the qualities you so much admire, but the manner in which Jesus expresses his qualities will almost certainly be different from the way that you would.

This is due to the unique, original and independent nature of personality with which every created life form is endowed and through which it expresses its independent and individual life.

Your personality is unique to you. Your expression of life through your personality will be unique and original in every moment. It is true, there will never be anyone quite like you. Get used to this idea.

You will always have personality. What you will lose is the distorted part of personality that has made for itself a very limited and conditioned ego, feeling that it is exclusive, special and separated from the all-that-is.

If you like thinking in pictures: the ego is rather like a grey balloon that you carry along with you on a string and then end up believing it's your real self.

It is impossible for your *imagined Christ* to have an independent reality of its own exactly as you have imagined him. Everyone's dream is different because everyone is different and, therefore, everyone's imagination is different.

Every Christian person's Christ is differently imagined. And this is exactly how it should be. See, how hopeless, it is, therefore, to get theologians to agree on the nature of Christ.

It is great work to use the imagination beautifully in this way and attempt to live by the precepts that the Christ embodied, but what if you were to step into this image you have so lovingly created and see that it is your self; that, what you have been mentally creating and desiring, so preciously, is nothing less than your own possibility; and that you are the Christ to come forth and be revealed in all your glory.

Do try to avoid the compulsion to seek outer validation for your imagination. The conditioned ego longs to get support from its peers for any beliefs which give it a feeling of worth.

When ever you want anyone to agree with you, watch carefully what is happening inside you and look at the fear at the back of this need, and then pin point what it is that you are afraid of. This is wonderful work.

Theologians spend their lives looking for common ground, or proof, or agreement for their beliefs and theories: it is such a waste of time. They should be looking inside themselves, uncovering all their fears, all their shame and guilt, and acknowledging their deepest fear of being unloved.

Why is there this great need to debate, to agree upon, the nature or validity of this or that saint? And why is there such a strong reaction against any person who proclaims himself to be self-realised and enlightened?

This is simply answered: it is a matter of desire. The conditioned ego generates both the desire to be dependent, and the desire to be independent. The very desire is the problem. The *need* is perceived as being for or against.

The stunning implication of the phrase "the Christ is within you" has been all but forgotten and ignored; or passed off as a religious turn of phrase. It is so much easier to devote one's attention to meaningful discussion than to admit you live a lovelorn frustrated life and to look to your denied feelings.

Every one has, latent within them, a fine and accurate "knowing" as to how their own Christ self will be. Every entity has within them their own complete blue print for finding their own place in the scheme of the universe in the fullest expression of their life. And this is the reason for the strong reactions when a so-called awakened master fails to live up to your expectations (which of course they never can). Herein lies the answer for the feeling that this master "is not my master". There is an understandable reluctance, which comes from deep within you, to surrender one's will to the will of another (which, however, the conditioned ego may desire to over rule.) You need to trust yourself in these situations.

Sometimes to surrender to a master is helpful (for a while!) Sometimes it is not. In the last analysis, surrender or not to surrender - to anything outside of yourself is not the issue. Surrender to your self, though, is very much the issue.

Indeed, you have your own enlightened master, your own Christ, waiting within you; it is your own blue print for you, and a part of you will always resist making another's blue print your own. And rightly so.

The only desire an awakened entity has is to lead you to your own awakening. It may be helpful, in the earlier stages of your spiritual quest, for you to try living in a group situation; yet, later on, entanglement within the group can lead to much illusion which must again be confronted.

Followers are never original; they need the master. But, above all, you are to become original. By all means be a disciple to a master if you wish to be but keep very awake in the process. Disciples who jump to do your every bidding, who fawn at your feet and kiss the ground you walk on, who hang on your every word and take every utterance as gospel, who gaze at you with adoring eyes, who mimic your life and every appearance, who expect you to deliver the "goods" if they stay around long enough, are well meaning but, quite frankly, very boring - and deluded.

If you still like to think in religious terms, know that *you* are a Christ - at least you can be - in your own right. Not Jesus The Christ or any Christ you may have read about or heard about, or any new age Christ, but Christ, nonetheless. Acknowledge it. Be it. Live it. And laugh and have fun and share with others how you would like life on this planet to be. There have been many gentle Christs upon this planet, but none who have volunteered to shoulder such a burden as Jesus. But the time for burdens is over. Do not fall in love with them all over again.

Truly, forget all about being a Christ - and just be your self. Forget about duty and burdens and sacrifice, and original sin, and religion, and all that nonsense. Be your innocent, unique and original self. Find again the original joy within you.

The Buddhists have a saying: "When you meet the Buddha on the path kill him". This is an excellent saying. It doesn't mean you have to go round annihilating teachers. It does mean that you would do well not to give away your power, compromise your spontaneity, or dilute your joy, for the sake of any entity or his or her followers, however glorious or enlightened they may appear to be.

However, to *believe* that you are the Christ or the Buddha or Allah would be as misleading as if you were to truly believe, in the last analysis, that you are a disciple of the Christ or the Buddha, or, indeed, that you are the particular or exclusive thing of anything. In the final analysis, from your truest truth, you are neither one thing or another, neither black or white, neither good or bad, neither master or disciple. All possibilities are yours. And, therefore, you are unique.

The use of the definitive article _the_ implies definition and limitation. Being defined means it has expectations woven around it. Yet, your nature is unlimited. It is not defined, certainly not by human expectations. And to be a Christ is not special. Do remember this. It has become special because of beliefs woven around the name and because of what has gone before. If you use the name of that which has gone before, will you be able to remain unique and untouched by these beliefs which, by their very nature, are limiting? This is always the question one must ask oneself when ones takes on a name around which lie so many beliefs and expectations.

Give your self a name by all means. Names can be fun and they are useful for identification as long as you don't actually believe they are your identity. Your identity is spirit. It is the living truth of your self which has no name.

If you choose a name that leads others to have expectations of your behaviour this is for you to take responsibility for; and if you allow a master to give you a name, you still need to take responsibility for choosing the name and the effect, if any, it will have upon you or others. If you do not, and if your name colours your life without you consciously acknowledging it, then you are living in a dream world. You are probably living according to a belief which has an unconscious hold over you. Your whole life will be coloured by this limitation and there will be unease and frustration. There will be a constant struggle with choices in your life.

There is a simple answer for this. Choose your own names, and alter them whenever you like. Don't be so serious about them. They are the least important thing about you. Take responsibility for what you call your self, and, if after a few days you don't like it, change it.

By all means, take names of beauty and joy which will remind you who you are but don't get attached to a name. Play with names in your life: it will show you much about your ego and how it longs to identify with a name and thereby run your life for you.

If you are going to live a joyful life don't get stuck in any idea at any time. A name which gives you ideas about your self is a great trap. Even the word "self-realisation" is a trap.

How can you be joyful if you are always thinking about this thing called self-realisation which is going to solve all your problems.

Your mind will get in the way of your joy absolutely. There is a great difference between watching and thinking. Do watch your life as you live it at all times. This is so useful. Thinking has its problems!

If you keep thinking about (judging and monitoring) your life as you live it, how can you be joyful ? How can you possibly be joyful ? Do be aware of this difference, between "thinking about" and watching. "Thinking about" is the origin of all limiting self-consciousness. Watching reveals to you, sooner or later, pure consciousness.

You don't have to keep putting your behaviour to the continual test as to whether it is in the best interests of your goal of self realisation. You know what you are at this moment. You are in constant change, yes. Change is the nature of life.

When you live in the moment, however, there is something always there within you that does not change. You are always there and you know who you are. It matters not that one moment you are sad and the next you are happy. Just be in the moment and be who you are in that moment. And watch.

The moments will continue to be moments and in the watching you will experience the moment. Only in the moment are you ever fulfilled and complete.

Do not dwell on self realisation; but do keep watching. Affirm joy always, knowing that you are in service to the Oneness and a part of that great purpose. Deny not fear and sadness when they arise, but don't go hunting for them either. This is the way to become self realised.

The first three sentences in this paragraph say it all. They are important sentences. Rejoice! Dance! Dance on the grass, be it in the sun or in the rain or in the moonlight, or in your living room. Be naked if you wish! Be a joy unto your self. And, only continue reading this book if it brings joy to your being. In fact, from now on put joy to the test of all you do. Rediscover joy as your God within you. JOY! Live in this truth. And have courage!

All spiritual messengers are on a mission of joy. Please do believe that. And don't waste time with those who say ought else. But understand that no teacher knows all that there is to know; none has unfathomable wisdom. So don't put that on to them and believe that they have. Teachers are learning, too.

Self realisation doesn't mean you stop learning; it just means you are awake. You now start learning what joy is all about faster than ever!

Beware of teachers who make you comfortable and pander to your personality needs. They may still be wanting to be liked. Teaching may be the way that their ego is keeping them comfortably protected from their own fears of being vulnerable and open to the joy of their own being. This is very common.

If the ego has tried everything in life and failed, it will eventually have a go at being a teacher, making the spiritual path its fabric for identity. Everyone of you will experience it. It is one of the last ploys, a final illusion, and a very difficult one to pierce. It is the final ploy of an ego with its back against the wall, so to speak.

The ego will either make itself into the great teacher or the great disciple; either of these will do as long as it is appropriating to itself the esteem and satisfaction of doing something really worth while.

Do not condemn teachers for this reason. To teach and to heal is a great path. It is a wondrous path of service. It matters not who is self realised, or, to what degree anyone you have heard about, or know, is enlightened. It only matters that you look to the joy of your own being without pointing the finger at anyone else.

If God is joy, you need a teacher of joy. This is the simple fact of the matter. Don't be with any teacher who doesn't make you feel the possibility of joy arising within you. This is a simple test. Put it to every teacher, and do not have the slightest qualms about showing the door to anyone.

Take responsibility for all you do, but especially for your own teachers. I tell you, your teachers will breathe a great sigh of relief. Teachers all over the world will be skipping for joy like spring lambs!

The crux of this chapter about teachers is, of course, that you, not they, are the most wonderful entity in the universe. They know that they are, and they know that it is only a matter of time before you know that you are, too.

No Christ or Avatar is the one that you are looking for. The dream that you may have projected on to an outer person is your own possibility to attain.

You are an aspect of the Oneness and you are also the Oneness. You cannot will it to be so. It is already so! But, if you keep watching and being open, *feeling deeply* in every possible way, and, above all, relaxing ever more deeply into your self, then you will begin to discover to your amazement that the Oneness is your very self.

No greater sanctity exists than the sanctity of the individual. Anything that prejudices or restricts the right of the individual to full knowledge of himself or herself is worse than even the deliberate taking of physical life: it is thrusting an entity into deep fog. So beware of teachers you don't feel comfortable with.

The reason humans get so aroused, so fiercely condemnatory, or so protective, about a teacher is that they are defending their own selfish interests. There is nothing so deeply interesting to an unawakened entity as his own desire to become awake.

If you are a committed Christian you cannot help but measure what you are looking for (or what you think you are looking for) by your own inner yard stick which is your own imagined Christ, or, if your a Buddhist or Hindu by your own imagined Buddha or Krishna. And, quite rightly, you will settle for nothing less. But, if it doesn't measure up, you condemn the master. Then again, if it happens to goes along with your projection, you defend him or her to the death!

Neither of these two reactions are helpful.

Unconsciously, you are placing your beliefs concerning an outer saviour alongside the blueprint of your own inner saviour and finding them irreconcilable. Once you are awake to this, your tendency to swing between guru worship and guru bashing ceases.

When you realise that your emotional reaction against anyone has, as its origin, your non acceptance of a part of your own nature, it will be a happier day for teachers and all independent thinkers who, presently, suffer a great deal of abuse in the world.

Symbolically, your nature is like that of a triangle. It can also be likened to a pyramid, but for the moment we will take the triangle. You are a three pointed star. First, there is your life, your essence, where you are united with all that is in the Oneness. It is sometimes called the Spirit within you. Secondly, there is your whole feeling-mind self which is your fully conscious self, a radiant and beautiful entity which always lives out of essence, never needing to deny it. This is your higher self, a multi-dimensional personality self (sometimes called your soul or cosmic self). And thirdly, there is your human personality which is your current lifetime personality.

Becoming a self realised person simply means that the human personality, the third star of the triangle, has awakened to the presence of the other two stars and has accepted their place and its role in the whole triangle. All these parts, when they acknowledge each other, can then function without stress as a whole.

As I have said in Chapter 1., your self is made up of: 1. You as spirit, the Oneness, God. 2. You as your higher self, your cosmic, multi-dimensional, whole Self. 3. You the human personality (which may be enmeshed in a conditioned ego).

In Christian terms this would equate to: 1. The Holy Ghost. 2. God the Father/Mother. 3. God the Son.

The only difference between you as your higher cosmic self and you the human personality is when, as a human personality conditioned by ego, you do not taste and feel the Oneness as a daily living reality. In not trusting life, in not believing in a joyful loving universe, you are out of touch with the only truly stabilising factor in the universe, which is the Oneness.

You will note that your fully conscious higher self does exist already on the physical plane. It is here! It has absolute awareness, from moment to moment, of all that you are doing and all your thoughts and feelings. It is utterly linked to you, at all times, for it is you.

However, the unawakened human personality, immersed in its conditioned ego, has the power upon the physical plane to block out the whole Self from expressing itself here.

Now, what can be blocked, can be unblocked, and this can be demonstrated. And, indeed, this is for you to demonstrate. Hence, this earth plane is often called the "plane of demonstration".

Thus, it can be seen that your fully conscious cosmic self, is your real master, your true teacher. It is not so much mastering that you require, but your surrender to the living *being-ness* of your own fully conscious self.

This self you can always be aware of because its presence within you is your very self.

Difficult disciplines are not required. A surrender to your own sense of aliveness and radiant *well being* is all that is required.

Surrender, my beloveds, to your own joy, without compromise to reason. Love is fun, is it not! Yes! And joy is ecstatic!

We are all expanding in consciousness together in this galaxy of ours. And, for consciousness, read joy and peace and harmony, and light - with love as an understood.

We are embraced by super friends who have a super vision in a super galaxy. They are our brothers and sisters, messengers from time to time, and loving parents, in this beautiful galaxy of ours. Yes, they do have super vision, but their one uniting characteristic which they have with us, with you and me, which is more important to them than the least of their grand visions and the least of their great powers, is down to earth love, a solid practicality, and - might I say it - more than a healthy dose of down to galactic JOY!

CHAPTER FOUR

RELATIONSHIPS

The understanding of relationship is the understanding of who you are and your place and purpose in the cosmic life of the universe.

Everything that vibrates within your personal sphere of observation and influence, whether for a long or short period of time, has a direct relationship with your self.

All that is outside your personal sphere of direct relationship has an indirect relationship with your self. To you, all is related. All is related to you.

Every living creature, every green plant, every drop of moisture and air, and all the seas and all therein, and every stick and stone upon this planet, and its great molten core, vibrates within your personal sphere of influence. This planet is your present realm of direct influence.

Outside of this planet you are, at every moment, relating to everything in the universe whether you are conscious of it or not. Here you have an indirect influence. This is a fact which many of you find hard to believe but which is a fact nonetheless.

In this chapter I am not going to discuss how to repair, patch-up, avoid, work at, or how go about finding the perfect relationship. There are a million books on the subject, recording well the machinations of egos, their devious desires and their problems in relating. And sometimes most helpful they are, too. I am more interesting in talking to you about fundamentals, and giving you a vision to work towards. When the basics are understood, all the tedious heartache over relationships will come to timely end.

I tell you this: the reality of your relationship with others is usually very different from that seen from your human viewpoint, which is the viewpoint of the conditioned human ego.

This, and this is a tragedy in the human world, means: that there is seldom a meeting between you and another entity. And, by this, I mean a meeting between entities, were clarity is present, where truth is validated - as it were, from spirit to spirit.

My previous analogy of the ego being like a grey balloon trailed along on a string holds good here: can you imagine all these grey balloons bumping into each other, believing they are having meaningful relationships. This is what human entities do. It is rather bizarre, is it not?

Whenever you relate to another person out of desire, or need, or duty, without spirit being present, you are relating out of the simulacrum of your self; you are relating from a grey balloon. Small wonder you spend so much time and energy protecting your self from them!

Whenever you relate to another entity out of joy and empathy, you are truly in relationship, and both the nature and beauty of a relationship such as this, is that it is entirely without expectations.

Can you not understand that should you be granted your every wish, should you be granted your heart's desire, whilst you still have expectations concerning your relationship with another, you would be reinforcing your conditioned ego and thus delaying the day of your self realisation.

Indeed, more than anything, it is your ideas concerning relationships that you need to dispense with.

The reason is this: when you dictate how a relationship should be or the boundaries it should take, you are placing limitation upon both your self and the other person.

Unlimitedness, however, is the truth of your being. And unlimitedness is also the truth of all others.

To live by, or be party, to any other reality, is to gather clouds of illusion around you and to live within them.

A meaningful relationship, my beloveds, is one that is entirely meaningless apart from the joy and empathy that arises out of it. All else is of the ego.

It is best to live your lives together as friends without the placing of any expectation upon the relationship. Even the least expectation, when unfulfilled, may leave you feeling hurt and blaming the other.

No person can fulfil all the needs of another, so don't expect it. Ever! Just as you, yourself, will never be perfect in all things, don't expect perfection in a relationship. It is an impossibility both for you to be perfect and your partner to be perfect. Be clear about this. Communicate your needs and desires to the other by all means but never demand or expect the other to fulfil them all.

Now, on the subject of morality, the nature of purity has nothing to do with morality or ideas concerning good or evil. Purity is a state of being which is unrestricted by any conditioning factor, unsullied by any thought of limitation.

When living in innocence - not an innocence as dictated by another person or religion, or as perceived by society, but in your own spontaneous NOW - you are living in purity, even if it be that you are enjoying intimate union with many entities at the same moment.

There is nothing intrinsically wrong in honest lust or in desiring sex and sex alone. There is nothing right about it, either. For, it is not essentially a matter of morality. It is a question of: are you relating to someone from your truth? Or, have you blocked off your spirit to satisfy urges of the conditioned ego?

If it was your spirit that was sending you out on the streets to hunt for sex, you would be living in your truth. It would be your truth for the moment and a perfect truth it would be.

Of course, prostitutes rarely relate to their customers from truth. They can usually only perform many sex acts a day when they close off spirit. The conditioned ego (the grey balloon) is doing the relating. The other essential part of you remains detached. This detachment, in fact, is seen as being necessary. It is considered an indispensable part of the job.

Detachment from spirit is also considered useful by many a housewife who keep the peace at home, as it were, by trading sex for security. But, I tell you, this is not considered by me to be useful, but harmful. Detachment for this purpose, hardens the ego. It increases the belief in separation from your cosmic self, from your spirit. And, if sin there is, this self-hardening of your ego is it.

When you live from truth the sex energy does not move so readily to the genital outlet, instead it nourishes the heart. It vivifies your creative centres (which are your solar plexus, throat and head centres) and is felt as flowing life energy by every cell in your body, thus bringing into balance and harmony the outer life with the inner.

When you live from truth you can do no harm to others. Perhaps, on occasions they may not like what you do or say if it goes contrary to their expectations, but it will never cause them any fundamental harm in the sense that you are reinforcing the clouds around their ego.

Your spirit-self, calling to the spirit of another, is the greatest calling card you will ever have. Call upon everyone with it, but don't get caught up in reactions - if any arise. The reactions of others to your energy is not to be your concern, unless, out of compassion, you make it your concern. Rest assured, you will never be hurting anyone by living from the truth of your own vibrant joy. You may rattle a few egos that could do with a good rattle. And one day, yes, they may thank you for it.

Purity and freedom are one and the same. Purity within a relationship means allowing and accepting the other person's right to be how he or she wishes to be.

Pander not to those who would wish you to be other than the reality of your own living truth, which is to live in joy.

Be true to your own reality; take responsibility for it; take responsibility for both your hurts and your joys. And lay not blame upon the other. EVER!

One of the hardest things, is to allow those that you care for to behave in a foolish manner; in other words, to make mistakes (as it would seem to you).

Remember, everyone comes to earth with their own unique vibrational energy. You cannot alter a person's vibration just to make you feel better or to make them *fit in*! You can only accept (which is another word for love) them for what they are and move on, finding for yourself a place where your own joy of being, your own energy, feels nourished and in turn accepted. Never stay anywhere where you feel you are being unappreciated and put down.

Of course, if it your children who are bugging you, or someone that you are caring for who you love very deeply, you can't just walk away. Indeed, this is what the working out of karma is! It is an unescapable (for the moment) obligation. But, you can hold in your heart the awareness that one day, when that obligation is completed, you will be able to follow - and should follow - the joy of your being and your heart's desire. This is an expression of wisdom in operation and a demonstration of compassion on the physical plane.

Doing all of this with awareness is what is called magnificent living!

Be wise and be compassionate, accept the right of the loved one so to behave. You don't have to like their behaviour. You don't have to agree with it, you don't have to go along with it, you don't have to stay around for it, but you do need to absolutely accept their right to behave in such a way.

When you live from the truth of your being you can make observations, but not critical judgements, because you are coming from a place where nothing will ever be split into rights and wrongs. You will see what is happening, the issues involved, the hurts developing, but you will not judge any of it. You see it for what it truly is: merely experience.

If you wish to be helpful, wait patiently, until the one you care for moves again toward you and then, without blaming, share what you honestly feel about your own hurt. And, if you should be so awake as to be living in your NOW where all hurts are illusory anyway, share your peace. This is the way of wisdom and a loving heart.

If they do not move towards you again, no matter, give them the freedom to move where they will. If you are destined to help each other in another place, at another time, or you are already in an affinity relationship in the universe with this person - and these do exits - you will be drawn together again and again, and you can be assured your joy will be validated together soon enough.

You can never lose a loved one, neither can they lose you. Not for long, anyway. There is no where for them to go where you cannot also be. Affinity rules! Vibrational frequency rules!

When you are living as your free, whole, and unlimited self, everything is open to both of you. It is all one universe. It is our home, which is all the more reason for us to heal our relationships with those who we believe are not lovable! In your home, there may be hiding places, like the cupboard under the stairs, but sooner or later, you are going to be discovered! As I say, there is no where to go.

Our home in this universe is a defined home only in the sense that it is the Oneness, and there is no where outside the Oneness to go. You cannot escape! You are going to be discovered!

Where the Oneness is known and honoured, it is not possible to hide behind a new name, and disappear like you can on earth. Names are good for nothing in a universe where love reigns supreme. The most truthful identity that an entity is known by, by which one entity recognizes another, is not by any name or title but by that entity's unique auric vibration which every personality wears around himself or herself like a kind of sensory finger print.

Every entity is known by and identified by the quality, the radiance and vibratory note of his or her aura. Names have very little relevance once you are out of the physical body. This is why I say play with them, have fun with them but don't take them seriously. They often get in the way of your relationships with each other because of the undue importance you place upon naming yourselves.

Having said that, just as the clothes you wear and the stars which shine in the heavens can bring their influence to bear on your personality in a positive or negative way, so can names. So, if you don't feel comfortable with a name, change it for one that you do!

The belief that a name has a power in it is ridiculous and the idea that if someone knows your secret name they will have a power over you is sheer superstition. If you give your power away to these stupid beliefs you'll give your power away to anything.

The moment you blame or criticise, or even think poorly of another, a link is created between you both which creates a difficulty. You are now tied to the other person by this creation of yours. It allows no freedom to move. A paradox arises: the link becomes a karmic bond, a tie; and yet, a rift - a gap - develops between you both.

Of course, it only becomes a rift where the Oneness is not being honoured. A rift is not the same as space. Where there is space, freedom to move exists. Where a rift exists, some fear is present, either within you or the other, or in both. This fear is blocking *acceptance* - which is another word for love.

When there is acceptance, the gap dissolves. The other feels free to approach you once more, or you to them, sharing once again both of your experiences without judgement. Acceptance, and this I cannot repeat enough, is the key.

Acceptance! Acceptance! Acceptance! Say the word a hundred times a day. Accept everything about your self. Accept every thing about others. And live in love and peace and joy.

By accepting your self first and foremost, and by never giving yourself a hard time, either mentally or physically, your mind-feeling aura will begin to grow and glow around you, radiating and releasing your healing energy into, first, your body and then into your environment around you. In loving your self you cannot but help to begin to love others.

Accept, always, the right of others to be how they wish to be. Don't give your self a hard time by getting entangled in mental analysis about other people. It makes your aura shrink!

If you spend too much of your life analysing others, you will get into such a state that you will probably persuade yourself that you need to go and see a psychologist, which will get you into even more analysis; then you'll both be shrinking together!

I am talking here about your mind. You cannot dissolve a rift with another person by just saying a few nice things to them when your mind remains in an attitude of resentment and non-acceptance.

Remember, your mind is your creative power. Any thought you have is yours to take responsibility for. On the physical plane you may not be able to see a thought in action but you can certainly feel them when they stir up the astral currents. Every thought has a direct and powerful impact. Do recognise this in your life.

You can see the power of thought in action in your daily life every time you resent someone's behaviour but try to put a good face on it. It never works does it: your body language gives you away, your inner feelings of restriction give you away.

And, remember, an unconscious thought is very much a thought. It is just as powerful in its action of constraining your life energy. How often have you noticed this, whilst trying to pretend that all is well?

Your own thoughts are absolutely responsible for how good you feel in the presence of other people: it does not depend on their thoughts, it depends only on *your* thoughts, conscious or otherwise. So if you want to live in joy and not give your self a hard time, see how important it is to penetrate your daily mind to determine what unconscious thoughts are sabotaging your life.

And they will be; more so, in fact, than conscious thoughts. It is your unconscious thoughts that give you a hard time. When you can make these unconscious thoughts conscious, when you can look at the fears and the feelings associated with these thoughts, and, by just observing them, throwing the light of your loving awareness around them, they will dissolve back into the light of Oneness and will no longer have a hold over you.

In other words, these thoughts will no longer give you a hard time when you see the fears behind the thoughts; when you observe, then acknowledge, the fears which you buried under the threshold of your consciousness at a time when they were too hard to look at, or too hard to understand, such as when you were a small child. When the fears have gone, the tendency of those thoughts to hang around you unconsciously, will also go.

So here is great work to be done: the making conscious of unconscious thoughts which habitually hang around you making your life a misery instead of a joy.

How is this to be achieved? Well, it so happens, you are alive on earth exactly at the right time; there are thousands of helpers ready to help you with a whole variety of different techniques and therapies to assist you in making conscious those unconscious thoughts which are hiding your fears from you.

They are here to help you. Use them and appreciate them. However, above all, keep watching and be sufficiently disciplined of will to resist re-thinking the habitual thought once you have seen through it and have become aware of it. In other words, don't self-indulge in the regurgitating of these old thoughts for any vicarious pleasure they might continue to give you, basically impotent though they might be.

Your helpers can help you and guide you but that is as far as they can go. They cannot live your life for you; they cannot be your own watcher. Your own awareness has to be alert enough not to allow further clouds to re-form around your ego, which, for a time at least, after you have confronted the fear, will be only too ready to take up its old habits.

You must not only want to change: *you must use your will to change*, so that the change becomes crystallised into fact, otherwise all the therapies in the world won't help you.

A combination of helpful guidance, wise therapy, meditation and watching, with the use of your will directing the change, is an excellent formula for a life's work.

And remember, you are your own guru. And gurus are very good at watching. You must become very good at watching, and then you must use your will to act upon what you have found. It is not a difficult thing to do once you get the knack of it and once you set your self upon the path of truly desiring to get to the bottom of your frustrations.

Nothing can get done without watching. And nothing can get done without you using your will to desire to change and making that change a fact upon the physical plane. These are perhaps the two most essential ingredients in your formula.

I shall talk a lot more about fear, the denial of feelings, and how to dissolve the conditioned ego, further on in this book.

Accepting the right of others to be how they wish to be does not mean condoning their actions; neither does it mean that you should help them if they ask for your assistance in actively doing something that you do not wish to do. A man of wisdom might say to his friend who, in his opinion, is undertaking an unwise course of action: "My friend, I have love for you in my heart, but this action of yours I cannot personally go along with, as it does not feel to be in harmony with my spirit, within the Oneness. I, none-theless, fully accept your right to go ahead with this project if it is what you really want to do. But, I must warn you, however, that I may act against you in this matter rather than compromise my spirit by inaction."

Be aware, that by inaction you can be helping and condoning the action of another. In these matters trust your spirit uncompromisingly. It is so easy to listen to when you get the knack of it. It will guide you when to stand back, when to act, how to act, when not to interfere. And, when you act, act from the truth of your spirit and have no fear of the consequences.

Everyone is growing in knowledge and wisdom. In a sense, everyone is a child on this planet. There is a difference between what a child is and what a child does.

A child grows up to be an adult. We all know this and make allowances for childish pranks. A child's acts are seen in this context. We are compas-sionate. We make allowances. We know that the child is an adult in the making. So, also, should you be aware that a human entity who does stupid things, is, both potentially, and in reality, a glorious entity of love and wis-dom. He, or she, is growing up, too.

Look not at the acts but at the awakening sun behind the acts. Forget about the popular saying: "You shall know a man by his deeds." It is an absurd jingle. Back to front. Deeds are important, of course they are. They reflect your maturity, they demonstrate, on this physical plane, your love and your wisdom, and the joy of your being. But to truly know a man or a woman, look beneath the human ego, look beneath the deeds and see the glory of the cosmic self; look even deeper and see the Oneness, the One Self, which is also your Self.

What you do is never as important as what you are. Only when you are at one with your whole Self can it be properly said that a man is known by his deeds. Until then, his deeds are but products of his conditioned ego. They are the product of illusion and are in themselves of partial useful-ness.

When you do something without being there in your whole truth whilst doing it, how can it even be said you have done it, for is not your whole self the most vital, indeed, the only, real and enduring part of your being?

This in no way abrogates you from the responsibility for your acts. It is up to each human personality to bring forth his or her will, to acknowledge the existence of spirit, and surrender the personal will to that inner life which lives for the joy of being. Spirit wants to be a living force on earth, through its much loved higher self and human agency. It is a co-operative venture.

When you regard the actions of entities, especially those close to you, from the viewpoint of their inner life and their progress into glory, you are seeing clearly. Now, at last, there is no judgement of the type that condemns.

Wise observation and clear sightedness are the creative tools of the compassionate entity who is available for help when asked.

This is not the same thing as judgement. Judgement, which condemns, is the mental attitude of someone still caught in the clouds of ego. It is based upon the desires and the expectations and projections of the one who judges.

Judgement which condemns sees only the outer scenarios. Compassionate observation observes the human ego and the latent inner glory, and is aware which is the most real. *I say to you, let all your outer glories pass away and the beauty within your inner light be revealed. Let no outer beauty veil you. Stand revealed as I AM.*

It is the old story: if distortion is your reality, then you will be distorted and all your relationships will be distorted. If you are happy, your relationships will be happy ones. And, the truth is, you will never have a totally happy relationship with anyone until you are first able to be totally happy on your own, alone, in relationship with your Self.

And, this is not to say, that just because you understand this fact in your mind, you should immediately rush off to be alone and try and force the issue.

Never force any issue with your self. Once you start forcing your self to go through enlightenment processes, force becomes the energy you also start sending out to others, and there is nothing so tedious as someone who is demanding that you should become enlightened. Further more, the very stress you are causing your self makes your goal of self realising the Oneness very difficult.

Be alone when it is easy to be alone. But do take responsibility for being alone. Most of you could be alone far more than you are. Only in aloneness can you feel who you truly are. Then come out of your aloneness, with joy, and be that which is yours to be.

All who live in joy are healers, for joy is of essence, which is of the whole, which is of God. There is nothing special about being a healer in joy. You don't have to set yourself up as a healer. Don't imagine you have to go around healing everybody. You just live in joy. You live simply. You have discovered Zen!

Now, everything begins to vibrate to a new frequency around you. That which can sustain the vibration stays, that which cannot, burns away through insight or emotional catharsis, and even, on occasion, through direct physical change.

Your relationship with everything outside your self is one of consciousness. Every single thing in existence is conscious. When you are fully awake to clear consciousness, instead of the clouded variety, you will be amazed how consciousness exists within you. You will be amazed how all is linked and unified by the very same essence that is your Self.

Other than loving you absolutely, spirit does not have any particular interest in you. Why should you be more special than anything else in creation? You do not have to be special. You do not have to be particularly good, or particularly spiritual, or be particular about anything. You need to know that all these fears about being particular fall away. You are not, essentially, a part of anything. You are the very total of life itself. It is only the ego that wants someone to take a particular interest in you.

When you say yes to everything, nothing is special. It is only when you say *no* that resistance arises. When you are saying, "No, I cannot accept that." You are setting yourself apart from that which you cannot accept. You are making it special. You are being particular.

Don't be partial about anything. Hold no opinions good or bad or mediocre. See everything, including your relationships, just as they are.

Whenever you make an opinion about anything, you are excluding other opinions; you are being dogmatic, and when you are being dogmatic you are digging your self into a fine hole - not to put too fine a point on it.

Pulling words to pieces is not the most elucidating of pastimes, but have you not realised that the word *dogmatic* is made up of *dog*, which is god spelt backwards, and *matic*, which comes from the word *matter*. Whenever you are holding forth with a cherished opinion, being dogmatic, you are giving support to the dogs of illusion.

Look to this tendency within your relationships. I tell you that the taking of a stand, the needing to be right, then stubbornly sticking to your opinion and patting your self on the back for being firm and not "giving way" is the modus operandi of the ego. It is the ticking time bomb in any relationship.

Saying *yes* to everything doesn't mean you have to surrender your power to live in your own joy, or surrender your will to another. It does mean you accept the right of the other to be unpleasant if they want to be. But you don't have to stay around to cop the blame or the bad vibes!

In extreme situations, you will leave your body (death), if your antagonist so disapproves of you, or is so violent towards you, that he forcibly releases you from it. This is an opportunity you can - believe it or not - take with your full consciousness being present. I am not speaking here of suicide, but of sustained or lethal violence to your human person by another human being. Always confront unpleasantness with the clarity of who you truly are. Dare I say it...with joy! Or, at the very least...with awareness. Well, why not? You have a choice, you know. You really do. Fear is the only thing that freezes you. Face everything with this awareness. Then, anything that happens to you is all for the best. It can only lead to more joy.

Never be afraid of the consequences if, and when, your physical body is taken away from you. To give away your physical body is a small thing; to give away your joy, surrendering it to fear, or to live in denial, is to deny your god within you. How can you enjoy the wondrous freedom of the non physical levels of the universe if you have given away your joy before you get there?

I might mention, here, that suicide is a different case altogether. It is an act of force, usually from desperation, by the human ego against its own ego. It comes out of ignorance as to the true nature of reality. It is not an act of joy. The human ego has decided it cannot, for whatever reason, confront the illusion which apparently holds it in thrall, so it decides to destroy itself instead. This is not a solution for the gaining of self realisation. Force never is. It is an act behind which hides overwhelming fear.

Now, it is a fact that you have no need of any outer experiences to feel fulfilled, or to be fulfilled. Yet, in your human reality you do need outer experiences against which to test your reality and to enjoy the adventure of physical reality, to experience the amazing feeling of living within that which you and I have created, namely the trees, the skies, the open plains, the oceans, the snowy mountains and the volcanoes, the wind, the rain, the sun, and the night, with loving friends with whom you can taste and share these delights and dance in the dew to the morning song of all the birds.

See how lyrical I can be at all this beauty, in this wonderful planet we live in together. To be lyrical is my reality. It is a joyful reality. Try it.

How many of you have enjoyed the exhilaration of doing this? Well, start right now. Loosen up. Take a dive into joy. Dance about with your hands in the air, and in your heart feel the joy that will come bursting forth from you in song, perhaps singing the greatest meaningless words you will ever sing.

Stop trying to work at your relationships. Allow the other to rant and rave, allow the other to work hard if they want to - but you, you just let go, and live in joy. Stop trying, and just be. Whatever is happening around you is whatever is happening around you. Don't put the mind to it.

What is more important: you, the eternal Oneness, or everything else which is swimming around in the great mirror of life around you?

The answer is neither. Neither you nor the mirror are more important than the other. There is no division. This is your illusion.

But, and this is a giant BUT - to live in *the joy of your being*, you need, first and foremost, to be true to the only place you can be sure of finding truth without any distortion.

And, where is this to be found? Why, inside your self of course!

Be accepting of all that is, so that, when relating, you can relate beautifully without becoming lost to your own beauty.

You are beautiful.

Here is a song:

KISSES AND CUDDLES AND CUPS OF TEA

CHORUS;   Kisses and cuddles, kisses and cuddles,
             Kisses and cuddles and cups of tea.
             Kisses and cuddles and cups of tea,
             Life is easy as can be!

1.   On top of the world on a sunny day,
       Every thing is going your way,
       All you have to do is go along,
       With the words I'm singing in my song.

2.   When all is grey and the world is dull,
       Remember this is just a lull.
       Watch when the storm clouds blow away,
       And soon you'll see another way.

3.   Don't listen to friends who put you down,

It'll only give you an awful frown.
But don't hit back, that makes it worse,
For violence is a dreadful curse.

4.   When those you love have foolish turns,
Resist the urge to make them learn.
In good time they will see,
When in love you set them free.

5.   When all is lost it's good to cry,
And in your depths ask, Who am I?
Do I have a purpose and what's my goal?
Where is my place and what's my role?

6.   How to change and what to choose?
Are you afraid that you may lose?
god is here and god is you,
And this, my friends, is what we do.

7.   If you're expecting this or that,
Life will dump you on the mat.
But if you allow it just to be,
Joy will grow like a mighty tree.

8.   Now, that's my song, it's all I know,
There's nothing more that I can show.
All is All and ever will Be,
And Joy is here like a mighty tree.

CHAPTER FIVE

SEX

Within all the spheres, within all levels of being, where light is known and seen to be the reality that it is, the coming together of entities, in union, produces greater light.

This is the energy released for the purpose of creativity, not as humans understand it solely for the making of bodies of flesh (for having babies), or for the gratification of sex desire, or to consummate companionship, *but for the bringing of light into your body and for the transforming of that which is in disharmony into harmony.*

The union of human entities provides energy which naturally recreates your bodies of light into the perfect replica (on a miniature scale) of the vast sun of light which shines in your physical heavens. You have your existence within the aura and etheric body of this great entity.

Without these grand entities, the suns, you would not exist. And without you, they have no existence. You are in relationship with your sun as you are within everything else in the universe.

At no time have you not existed. Neither, therefore, is there any time in which your sun has not existed - whether it be in its present (incarnated) body of form, as in its wondrous radiant nucleic energy and raging fire, or in its more subtle body of stupendous golden light. Know you not that the sun is an intelligent life ? Many of the ancients knew this and worshipped the sun. But the sun does not want to be worshipped. As I have already said to you, to worship anything outside yourself is to fall into illusion and distortion.

Now, there is nothing sinful in the creation of bodies. You are creator creatures and are able to create whatever you wish; yet, to create that which brings disharmony to the whole is to create disharmony and disease.

Sex union between mutually consenting humans for the gratification of desire or for the cementing of companionship is not, as many religions would have you believe, by itself any cause for *disharmony* (which is a better word for *sin*).

Much fear surrounds sex union in this world. There is a fear of the power, a fear of the pleasure, and a fear of the peace which the light brings to you at these moments. This has created such astounding guilt and shame complex within humans concerning this wondrous act that human beings have become alienated from their own natures.

The body of flesh which clothes you is also a body of light but for many it has become a thing of shame to be wrapped up, not merely for reasons of warmth and comfort, but from shame of its naked beauty and natural functions.

This shame for the body, for which your ego finds many ingenious rationalisations, is a blight upon the so called civilised human races.

Nakedness is my true form. Ever do I revel in openness and nakedness. Neither in me nor upon me is ought hid. The naked glory of all manifested form am I.

This shame, this guilt, has come about, not because of the nature of the body or its nakedness but because long ago the true and all important function of sexual union was forgotten and the lesser functions substituted.

When you and your partners understand the underlying principles of sexual union, desire is gratified and harmony naturally results, but if these basic principles are not consciously acknowledged, if they are forgotten or wilfully ignored, then disease and disharmony and its accompanying bed fellows of guilt, shame and fear, will take over.

These creative energies, being released within you, are for the revealing of your own glory. It puts you in touch with the Oneness. It reminds you who you are. It balances energy in your body. It is infinitely healing. *It affirms the joy of being.*

In the remembering of this, whilst uniting with another entity, all else will follow.

Why is this such a basic principle? Because spirit is the living truth of your being: it is the causal, the original self, within you. Uniting with another either affirms this with glory - or depreciates your existing ego.

Two grey balloons bumping against each other may produce, at best, a little friction. It is a pale substitute for the glorious light of spirit which is released, resulting from a union undertaken in joy.

When you join with another with an awareness of your whole self there is a release of light and creative harmony for both parties.

But if the union is a meeting of egos in denial of the Oneness, the energy that is released goes, not for the balancing of light within the body, but towards the strengthening of ego desire and domination.

Remember, my beloveds, when you live your life with the awareness that all is joy you do so with grace and sensitivity, even if it be in the midst of passion and irresistible sexual attraction. In moving toward one another in Oneness, honouring the joy of your being, you can be as peaceful as you wish, or as passionate, or as lusty as you like. Your nature is unlimited in its expression and its possibilities.

In a union between whole entities there is never strain or anxiety. There are no expectations. When there are no ideas as to how your body or the other body should perform, when there is just the moment, being there, being with the body of the other, who is also just being there, light will surround you both.

If thoughts start coming in to take you away from being present with another, then these thoughts are coming from the ego.

The ego wants the union to be something other than what it is. It has other ideas.

It is the ego that says it is not enough just to unite in joy and feeling. The ego says this must happen or that must happen. Maybe it wants to push for orgasm. Maybe it wants to feel more stimulated in the sex organs in a certain manner. Maybe it wants the activity to be as satisfying as it was the last time, and so on, and so on.

The ego's demands, the ego's expectations go on and on. When they are not met stress creeps in, inevitably giving rise to anger, or disappointment, or loss of self-esteem. These are the results of an ego dominated union.

Spirit is not the slightest interested in whether a penis is erect or quiescent, whether a vagina is lubricated or dry, whether you do, or do not, feel like genital gratification, or whether you do, or do not have orgasms.

Being present in the moment, being in the joy of your being, does not preclude enjoying any form of bodily pleasure, but it does mean that you allow your essence energy to move in your body rather than using your mind to demand that the desires and expectations of ego are met.

Your spirit energy, being at one with all, has a knowing of its own. Trust it and allow sex to happen when it feels like happening. Don't push it. It is a fine thing to be naked in joy and sensuality with another entity when awareness of the Oneness is there.

It is a screwed up affair when you lie with one another and all you can think about is the sex act and its gratification - or, perhaps, how to endure it and get it over with as fast as possible !

When orgasm results, without strain, as an overflowing of the energy which has come about from being with another in joy, then it is a thing of beauty. It will recreate for you both your bodies of light.

It is impossible that this will happen every time. Relax and let these times happen within the knowing of your spirit. Trust your spirit (which is another way of saying trust your inner energy). And have sex union only when aligned with spirit, being attuned to you higher self.

It is splendid to be naked with entities and to enjoy the trust and intimacy which body contact brings you, but never ever demand that your body should behave in a certain way. Never ever give way to the ego habit of desiring orgasm on demand. It is better by far not to have an orgasm than to push it along. An orgasm that is striven for, places an over burden of energy on the sex centres of your body, whereas an orgasm that is allowed to happen overflows and nourishes the whole body and opens up the higher centres.

Orgasm on demand will deplete the body. It will leave you feeling drained and low in vitality, even the next day. An orgasm that *happens_to you* brings you peace and a lightness of being in which you feel more connected than ever to the source of your self.

The reason that this build up of energy doesn't result in orgasm every time has to do with a number of factors. It may be that neither of you are, at the time of union, at a suitable voltage - as it were - in your vibrational energy fields. Relax. Do not worry about it. Your energy fields are changing all the time. Trust the energy. And never look to repeat anything that has ever gone before.

Many of you believe that true intimacy in a relationship can only occur when sex is involved. How wrong you are. If you believe this, you are creating a situation for yourself where sex becomes your god, where sex becomes the addiction, where without the possibility of sex you feel only half a person, empty and lonely.

This is to live in ignorance. Indeed, you can love without sex. You are love, without sex. So, do love freely without judgement and without the thought of sex, which, by being thought of, actually creates moments of no love. Why are you so frightened to give your love freely? Is it because of your thoughts of sex, the desire for it, the shame of it, the guilt of it, the fear of it? Why? Think this through for yourselves and love freely.

Love is the bounty that you are. Spread it around bountifully. Be not afraid to tell strangers you love them. They are not strangers! What gave you that idea? They are a part of you. They are a part of the Oneness. They are love incarnated. As you are. Start to validate this on the physical plane and see the light flood in, watch the old walls fall away as the rushing cleansing waters of love burst through the walls of this most ancient ego engineered dam that has stood for so long in your environment.

If you, who are reading this book and understanding it are afraid to tell people you love them, what hope is there for the remainder of humanity? If you believe intimacy means sex, what hope for the removing of this illusion? But if you are able to live as an intimate entity without sex on the physical plane, demonstrating that sex is not a requirement for intimacy, you have achieved a huge step in helping clear the clouds of confusion for all humanity around the area of sex.

A battery has two terminals, two polarities which, when brought together, create a spark of fiery life. One pole is the positive, the other the receptive. So it is with your male and female physical bodies.

What is seldom realised is that the sexual gender of your physical body is only one of the polarities (*yin* or *yang*) of your various "bodies" linked (interwoven) within your whole being - as observed in your electrical energy field, your aura.

Indeed, entities with the same sex body can, and do, form intimate unions in which orgasm is a natural electrical event of complimentary polarities. Yet, by and large, this is not the case.

The frequency of orgasms in most homosexual relationships is due more to the security that the human ego feels by being intimate with a similar sexual body rather than the more threatening situation of being sexual with a complimentary (opposite sex) body. Why is this more threatening? Because, sexually there is a great difference in the biological function between man and woman which takes some trust and understanding on both sides for true intimacy in sex to occur. But, I tell you, intimacy between men and men, and women and women, does not need to rely on sex, and nor is it useful to believe you are homosexual (which is just another limiting label to put on to yourself) just because you are afraid of being intimate (if you are a man) with women, but are still in need of sex, making sex with other men the easy option. As a man, it is better to look within you to the fears that stop you from being intimate with women, either sexually or non sexually.

When you have faced these fears, you will find that intimacy, rather than easy sex, is also possible. The opposite holds true for women. Until then, no true intimacy with anyone, male or female is possible. Thus is an intolerable situation for any entity. Very sad. Painful, and ultimately very lonely.

Love and intimacy have an affinity with each other. They go hand and hand and cannot be separated. Love and sex, as you well know, need have nothing in common whatever. Sex can masquerade as love. It can never masquerade as intimacy. Women learn this sooner than men. They are, therefore, in a position to help men to also learn the difference.

A man and a woman may function differently, sexually. But in their love nature, their true nature, there is no difference between man and woman. In truth, in intimacy, they are absolutely the same.

Sex makes them difference. Therefore, using sex to perpetuate the myth that homosexuals can only find love with the same sex is an illusion. It may be a belief system that you have taken on board in childhood, perhaps in your teens when your sexuality was rampant, or in a past lifetime, when you might have been the opposite gender and very much enjoyed it, or perhaps that the sex that you had in that lifetime was repugnant to you in that you were deeply wounded or abused in some way. These memories need to be cleared and sent into God's light so that they cease to hinder your ability to be intimate with whoever you choose.

In truth, you are an unlimited loving being. You can love anyone. Throw away the labels that condemn yourself as being *gay* or *lesbian*. They are so limiting. Just be who you are. Love whom you love. You are more, far more, than your sexual orientation! It is so limiting to experience your day to day living, and all that you do, and observe, through the spectacles of your sexual orientation. It doesn't matter who you have sex with as long as your loving presence, your higher self, is attuned to the experience, and there is intimacy present, rather than shame and guilt or the all too familiar casual *joyless-ness of being* in the act!

Men being intimate with women is beautiful. Men being intimate with men is beautiful. Women being intimate with women is beautiful. And the sex is not wrong. The error comes in using the idea of sex to limit yourself to the possibility of being only intimate with one gender. So, if you are a man and shrink away at the idea of being intimate with a man, you have some inner work to do. The same applies to a woman who is repelled at the idea of being intimate with another woman. And I am not talking about sex here, but intimacy (which, indeed, may or may not exclude sex, for in intimacy there are no rules to follow!)

There is another way to look at this. All that exists in the manifest universe exists in a positive or receptive mode. All that is created out of the Oneness takes upon itself a charge which has an affinity either to the *yin* or to the *yang*. And, depending on the relationship, this also can alter.

In other words, an entity whose energy field (mind and feelings) is positive to one entity might be receptive to another. If you are positive to a particular entity you will probably remain positive to that entity. In another situation, you might be receptive to another entity who is positive. Thus the whole of creation is held together by this intertwining of positive and receptive energy. It is truly a universe of living, loving, unions with ecstasy and joy as the living reality of The Oneness. Instinctive genital sex, by itself, purely as a body function, without awareness, without attunement to your higher self, is purely a function of physical creation. It is a means of perpetuating the species in this physical evolutionary world of ours. You, however, are not only physical in nature.

This is not to put down sex; it is to elevate it to a realistic place in your consciousness. It is there for you to enjoy when it is there for you to enjoy, which is better, by far, than being manipulated into a habit by your ego which is always telling you what you need to have, or need to do, or need to "come out" with a sexual label before you can be happy.

I have mentioned that the gender of the physical body is only one of the polarities of the various "bodies" within you. What are these other bodies?

Well, now, just as the universe is made up of a connecting lattice of positive and receptive entities, your own bodies, or sheaths, that you individually inhabit are held together within the whole of your being by the attraction of *yin* and *yang* magnetic fields.

For instance, in the physical world you have a physical body in which to function, the physical brain being a receiver of thoughts from the level of mind in the same way that a television set is a receiver of pictures from a studio which is in a separate location from the receiver. In the astral levels you inhabit a sheath of substance (a body of finer material) which is responsive to the feeling vibrations of the astral world. Similarly, you have a mental sheath in which you can operate, when out of the other two bodies, at a mental level of being.

Between the physical body and the astral body you have an etheric body which forms the energy matrix (a blueprint) out of which the dense physical body is formed. At an even higher level (I shall call it the cosmic mental level) you have a vehicle in which you consciously exist at a level where you are unified with spirit, your whole self, and the joy of your being. It is this body, your cosmic self, which gives to you the most important and over-riding polarity of your whole self.

Your cosmic self is that part of you, being the whole of you, which relates to another entity in the most real way in terms of a clear and balancing energy relationship with an other entity. It is the yin or yang polarity of your cosmic mental body that determines the results of your relationship with every entity, even down to the most dense levels on the physical planes of existence.

It is interesting to note that the polarities of all your sheaths alternate and, by so doing, neatly mesh together to allow you to exist cohesively at any level.

If your sex body is female, your etheric body will have a positive or *yang* (or 'male') polarity, your astral body will be *yin (or 'female')*, your mental body will be *yang* and your cosmic body will be *yin*. If you have a male sex body, your etheric body will be *yin*, your astral body *yang*, your mental body *yin*, and your cosmic self *yang*. This is how the sheaths (or bodies) within you are linked together, alternating between 'male' and 'female' polarities.

You can see that this accounts for the bodily stamina and staying power that women have which is due to their positive etheric body. Yet their emotional natures, being receptive, are more swiftly stirred into greater activity than in the male who has a positive emotional body; and then again, the positive incisive mental faculties that women are able to display - when they can master their emotions - is awesome, whereas the mental body of a man is receptive and has difficulty countering the female mind at the same level, hence the frustration of men who are unable to counter the logic of the female mind with the force of their own ideas. Women need to understand this and, in their own way, make allowances for it, just as men need to understand and make allowances for the emotional turmoil which women get embroiled in.

Going higher up the scale, to the next body of the male, there is the intuitive body which, when tuned in to spirit, has a positive *yang* polarity.

This vehicle gives him his strong intuition. It gives him an intuitive vision of cosmic feeling (rather than a vision of cosmic knowledge)in which he can use his will to express the joy of his being. It is for the male entity to embrace this as a vision of feeling (of love and joy and peace) and make it meaningful in the context of actual living, rather than in an eternal hunt for outer sexual love.

In the case of a woman, it is her *receptive* intuitive body which can make her receptive to God's plan, allowing her to have a vision of cosmic knowledge and the plan of her whole Self, thus becoming, as it were, "an ear unto God."

When two entities, in conscious recognition of their essence (their spirit), being of compatible vibration and complimentary polarity, have union together for the wilful undertaking of creative work (that work being the bringing of harmony to earth), then you will indeed see joy manifested upon earth. There will be nothing that cannot be undertaken. This is the great secret of the sex energy and its ultimate triumph will, one day, be demonstrated upon the earth.

It has nothing to do with penises and vaginas and your body's addictions to orgasms. It has everything to do with awareness, joy, love, peace and the creation of bodies of light. And intimacy.

As you can see, in a union such as this, it is the male (the *yang*) entity who is positive in the areas of spiritual vision, emotional charisma and physical strength. The feminine entity (the *yin* polarity) is positive in the areas of mental creativity, and energy control in the etheric vehicle. She is the master of energy and knowledge in the physical world.

The male entity is the master of love and aliveness and awareness. He is the power. She uses the power. He *feels* from his inner knowing. She *knows* what *to do*.

I repeat: the polarity of your cosmic self can differ from the gender of your human physical body. A human female with a female sex body may be a positively polarised entity (having a *yang* higher self).

A human male with a male sex body can very well be, and often is, a receptively polarised entity (having a *yin* higher self). Remember, your higher self contains all the elements of male and female perfectly balanced with him/herself. It is the whole entity, as a whole, which will have a polarity towards the positive or the receptive.

Planets, solar systems and even galaxies have an affinity to the energies of either a positive or a receptive pole. In our segment of the galaxy the Great Bear system is positively polarised to the receptive Pleiadian system, the latter being a cluster of stars in the constellation of Taurus. In Greek mythology the Pleiades is the home of Electra who wears a crown of stars upon her head. She embodies all the energy and wisdom of the feminine principle in the local universe.

Force *(prana)* flows into our solar system from the Great Bear constellation. Prana has a relationship with our solar system and the Great Bear constellation in a similar way that electricity has to the Pleiadian constellation. Prana is life energy. It is the very breath that vivifies and sparkles in us as the nourishing force, as the aliveness, in all that is.

There is a third force which enters our solar system which makes up the balancing factor in this triangle. This force emanates from the brightest star in our night sky, Sirius, which the ancient Egyptians called the dog star. It lies in the constellation of Canis Major and carries the energy of loving wisdom, the akashic current radiation. In Egyptian symbology Sirius was the dog-headed god Anubis who embodied all wisdom. The Sirian system is a system where many of you originate from. It is the system where many of your teachers come from, for it is the synthesis point for this solar system which is attempting, even as you yourself are, to balance its energies so that synthesis, and release from its present limited situation, can occur.

When a point of rhythm or balance (harmony) has been reached in a body, whether it be a planetary body or a human body, the occupier of the form is released from it. That particular personality can now escape from the environment which it has used for the gaining of experience, and return to his/her whole self and original home.

The friction between the pairs of opposites which embody the energies of attraction and repulsion and which, in turn, puts everything into motion, encouraging momentum, eventually brings about balance and light, and release, by automatic disintegration of the form through the fires of inner radiance.

Thus, sex, has, as its function at every level in creation, the goal of bringing bodies into balance, into synthesis and harmony, thus creating a greater expansion of consciousness and more light.

I do emphasise, however, that for human beings many problems around sex will be cleared up when he or she can begin to see himself, or herself, and entities in general, in terms of cosmic polarity, and in terms of attraction and repulsion and vibratory response to each other, and listen to their inner guidance upon this matter which they will get - will most definitely get - before embarking upon any sexual activity.

When men and women are true to their group affiliations, the present mis-groupings and mis-matings will, through knowledge and perceptiveness, come to an end in the world. And so will cease much endless frustration.

We are cells in the body of the solar entity which is our home system. It is truly our home. The love and wisdom that emanates from this grand entity in which we live (in our etheric life) is truly worthy of our relating to this marvellous entity as our divine parents, our beloved father and mother; for that is who he/she is, beyond even the heavenly father of our higher self.

It is their wish that you become so balanced and radiant in your being that you are released from your present cycle of limitation, and, in so doing, you aid them also in their similar quest.

Truly, as above so below. You are part of an amazingly intricate scheme, but which, for you at this time, knowledge of is the least important part of all your concerns.

All of you, however, are part of triangles and groupings which, if you were consciously aware of them, and acted upon this awareness, would benefit you enormously. All of you carry, to a greater or lesser degree, an affinity to one of the three forces entering this planetary system, and each of you will relate both as individuals and as groups to your triangles.

Simply put, these three forces are: 1. life-energy (*prana*). 2. Love-energy (*synthesis*). 3. Creative-energy (*knowledge*).

I remind you, joy (as is love) is a fundamental ingredient of all three streams of force. Wisdom is the result of the synthesis of all three.

The synthesis member of your triangle is that member who expresses no strong affinity for either polarity but who is equally comfortable (or, as equally uncomfortable, as the case may be) with both of the opposite polarities.

Remember, the sex gender of your human selves has no bearing upon this relationship whatever. In the human experience it may often be more convenient and easier to have the same sexual polarity as your cosmic self. But, if this is not the case, it in no way lessens the effectiveness of the union and, in some cases, can very much enhance it.

These are discoveries which you can make, regarding your own natures. In the course of your stay on earth, it is important to your individual well being and the finding of your place and purpose in the great plan of life, that you do so.

Most important of all, is for you to realise the polarity of your cosmic self. Your creative energy originates from this source, and, all you do, for good or ill, is a direct expression of how much of your cosmic self you can bring through to the physical plane.

Ignorance of the polarity of your cosmic body allows the conditioned ego to all the more easily dominate you with its instinctual habits. In other words, you become a slave to the purely bodily responses such as desire for food, sex, excitement, laziness, security, etc.

These instinctual responses are carried forward in the body, generation after generation, through the DNA in the genes of each physical body.

They originate from a time of evolution many planetary cycles ago. In these dim pasts the evolution of the physical body required, for its protection and its own evolution, a rudimentary survival consciousness from which today, these instincts still survive.

The importance of the evolution of the purely physical form, however, has passed. The time of emphasis upon the physical body, its control, the training of it, and the bringing of all its functions under the control of the will of the entity, by such disciplines as hatha yoga, has long ago been achieved. The physical functions of breath and elimination, and so on, have long since and very successfully been relegated to automatic functioning, allowing the entity to devote the very minimum of consciousness to keeping its vehicle healthy and operable on the physical plane.

The physical body is a magnificent instrument designed for a cosmic inhabitant. Accept its nature, accept its pains (which are its warnings to you) and its pleasures, but do not pander to its blind wishes at the expense of disregarding your mission on earth of your own higher self.

Your higher feelings are never blind. They arrive within you together with a direct intuitive awareness, a knowledge, from the source of your cosmic self, from what you may like to call the God within you.

There is a great need for you, now, to awaken to, and link ever more readily with, your cosmic self which is not as difficult or as awe inspiring as you might think. After all, you are already here, yet you are hiding behind clouds and have identified with the image formed of the clouds instead of looking behind the clouds to see who you really are. You are here already but you know it not.

The yoga of today will not have so much to do, therefore, with the training of the physical body, or of union, as it will have to do with uncovering, revealing and releasing long held fears that stop you being unified with your higher self.

You are already unified. The problem is you have unified with a few clouds as well and have fallen for the image instead of the reality.

This is not to be the age for further evolution of the body, nor for training of the mind. Just an awakening is now needed for you to see the true nature of who you really are.

Intuition, in the realms of light, is direct knowledge. But greater than knowledge is *empathy*.

Your present admiration of factual knowledge, and your acquisitiveness of it, is, I tell you, a limiting factor in your lives.

Do not reject knowledge, but neither worship it or be fascinated by it. When knowledge comes your way just let it be. Cease putting your mind to its importance. Instead, develop your intuition. Then, move into contemplation, and so into empathy. This ordered development leads you into the realm of unlimited being in which you reap the fruits of *living* knowledge. Now, this is knowledge!

Except for uncertain periods of panic and aridity, there is no way you can hinder this process except by deliberately making yourself deaf to the promptings of your inner life (your higher self).

The nature of the physical body, the sex-body, is that it is exceedingly responsive to feelings of cellular harmony (and disharmony). It is also, as it happens, and - if you allow it to be - very responsive to the feelings of joy, of love, and peace originating from your higher self, but it has no ability to originate them or control them. This is for you, with your own will, to do. And this will happen quite naturally for you when, you, the cosmic self (your higher self), is fully present in your human body without the accompanying clouds of your conditioned ego.

If you allow the cellular volition of your physical body to be the only will that exists within the make-up of your various selves, you will be lost in a stream of evolution so long past that even most of your planetary animals have passed beyond it.

Indeed, lower than the animals you can be if you fail to observe these laws of energy.

Sex is an energy thing. Everyone knows that. Closeness, respect, love, friendship, are the greatest of human qualities: but when sex is added it burns its way into the aura in a more permanent scoring - I suppose you could say scarring - where, when undertaken unlovingly, it has a negative effect on the psyche.

Sex gives union - any kind of union for that matter - of the loving, joyfully aware, kind - a huge emphasis to the current state of awareness of the entities involved; so that it underlines the loving when love is there, or, not so edifyingly, it underlines self-indulgence when indifference is there, increasing the love-less ego's impersonal appetite, turning it into addiction and sex for its own sake.

Your cosmic self, if it be in *yang* polarity is an energy which expresses itself in dynamic aliveness and an all encompassing heart. It is the energy of intuitive and empathetic "being", rather than that of vision of knowledge or "doing"'.

All of you whose cosmic selves are polarised to this energy have the potential to manifest upon the physical plane the glory of the Father principle.

Similarly, those of you who in their cosmic selves are polarised to the feminine polarity have the potential to manifest the glory of the Mother principle on the physical plane.

Those of you who are holding the energies of synthesis in your cosmic selves have within you the potential to manifest upon the physical plane the glory of man or woman, in gracious balance, peace, and loving wisdom. A Christ.

A loving heart imposes no vision upon others. Nothing is seen as particularly desirable for any one to do. Your loving father in heaven is not a member of a commune. He holds no brief for any political ideology, however wide reaching or far thinking. He holds no grand technological, or mystical, scenarios in his mind for the future as certain scientific or esoteric cults would like you to believe. He has no vision, even of harmony, in the environment. Though, harmony is the goal.

Yes, harmony in the environment will happen. But not because anyone has a vision about it. It will happen because each individual, in his or her own time, in his or her own way, discovers within himself or herself the joy of their own being.

The bringing forth of this truth within every human spark on earth, and the making of that spark into an entity free to roam the solar system as a master, will allow planetary harmony to fall naturally into place.

This world is totally accepting of your ordained right to experience this. The planet is perfectly designed for you as individuals to make this your individual reality. All of you can awaken into this freedom. And you do so desire it.

Listen to your own feelings. If you must have a vision, feel it as a feeling vision within yourself and own up to it. *You* are this vision.

Trust those feelings which give you moments of joy, exhilaration, exuberance, excitement and insight - and, especially, peace. These moments are glimpses of the doorway which I now invite you to open. And, how about running through it with all the energy of your life at your disposal!

Those entities who carry the Mother energy will help you. It is their love and their path of joyful service to do so. Ultimately, it is their wish that you should be free of their help and stand in your own light.

The Father energy is loving and joyful. His is the energy of the joy of being; as in being spontaneous, as in being in the moment, as in being without plans or thought, or any desire - not even, the desire to be helpful.

The Father energy is not concerned with what to do or how to do it. It is an energy that is in empathy with the Oneness. It has an intuitive awareness of the correctness of relationships at any one moment. It has an acute awareness of the flow of life and heart energy. Any hiatus or blockage which is happening within that flow is felt as an "ache in the heart". The Father's vision is a feeling vision a little different from that of the Mother's which is more to do with the using of energy in her creation. The energy of the Father has no desire to be creative or to channel energy. It is an energy that just likes to be. Ponder upon these words for the male role is much misunderstood.

The Mother energy expresses the energy of loving wisdom in the universe. She carries the joy of being, of the Father, in her heart yet also holds within herself the knowledge and power by which the potential Father may come about in the created universe. She then puts this knowledge and power to use. Behind her stands the Father in loving support, being the joy of her life and her conduit, as it were, to unlimited power. Thus, in balance, the male and female energies work to bring about the vision of the heart, being that of harmony, in all the levels of creation.

In the ancient days of Egypt the feminine polarity was revered as the goddess *Isis*, the all wise, the recipient of the creative function who held in her heart and mind the knowledge and power over all manifested forms. *Osiris* stood behind her, all powerful and all loving - but unseen. Thus, it was said of *Osiris* that he was lord of the underworld, lord of the dark invisible worlds.

These symbols and images relate directly to the function of these two polarities as they play out their energies within the minds and feelings, and bodies, of human beings.

The knowing of the times and seasons to assist the awakening life within the form, and the knowing of the times when to withhold that assistance, was within the province of *Isis* and, today, this is as true as ever.

It is the dual function of creativity to create or destroy, to assist or withhold assistance. It is still the legitimate function of the feminine polarity.

In the Hindu religion these two aspects of the feminine principle are known as *Laksmi* the bountiful and *Kali* the destroyer.

Other than to his closest disciples (who failed to record the teaching he reserved only for them) Jesus gave little information regarding this dual aspect of the feminine role as this knowledge would have been confusing to the crowds who followed him. They all too readily, as witnessed by the cruelty of the times, believed in the forces of destructiveness.

Jesus rightly said that every person carries within them the opportunity to access his or her spirit at any time.

It is the quiet voice (being your intuition) of the spirit within you that guides you in the ways of the Father's and Mother's heart vision for yourself and the planet. It is a vision of the right relationship of the parts of the whole to the whole itself.

The feminine polarity is that of loving mind, attuned to its own loving heart, being at one with the heart of the Father; it hears the inner voice and then sees clearly and practically what to do.

It is the feminine role to oversee, as it were, the transforming process of God's plan, and to make herself available as a vehicle through which the energy that nourishes that process can be transmitted.

This energy is the energy of love. It is the very nature and the very life of the feminine being.

It is the male role, not to create, not to know what to do, not to oversee, not to know what is the right way to do anything, but to actually *be* God on earth, to *be* joy and love extant, to *be* radiant, to *be* the power - and not to use it except through his beloved feminine partner.

It is the male role to be the shining power behind the throne, as it were. It is the male role to stand up to and resist evil, refusing it permission to take him out of his truth, seeing it, and yet doing nothing to change the nature of it. Absolute acceptance.

To those of you who carry strongly the male polarity, be you woman or man in your sex body, ponder carefully on these last two sentences because it holds much for you to think on and make your own.

It is time for male entities to stand up and shine as the gods they are and take their place with their feminine counterparts in their rightful creative functions together.

This function, I remind you, is to create harmony upon earth and to bring into balance that which is distorted and hidden behind fear.

See then, how male and female work together in this task of joy, making sacred their vehicles as pure vessels for holding within themselves the loving energy of the very life and joy of god the Father.

The sex union, my beloveds, is to enhance and balance these functions within you, so that, when undertaken with an awareness of life's purpose, you are both, as a partnership, able *to be* (as the male) and *to create* (as the female) in harmony with the great work of bringing the joy of heaven to earth. And, in so doing, at the very same time, you awaken and transform yourselves into the gods that you are.

In a practical sense, within the Oneness, the two, as twin flames, work as one. The male polarity holds, within his higher feeling nature, the heart vision of the Father, empowering it with his life. The female polarity receives in meditation the plan. She communicates it to her partner and, thus, together, upon the trusting of her guidance, they do what it is that has to be done.

The exchange of energy that results in the act of sexual union enables the higher centres in both male and female to vibrate at a higher rate of vibration. This stimulation of the higher centres only happens between complimentary polarities of a similar vibrational frequency who are acknowledging spirit as a reality in their lives.

Note this last sentence very carefully else you (the human ego) sees in this an excuse to indulge in sex at every opportunity to awaken higher centres. It will not. It will dig you into a deeper hole, and open, instead, for your fascination and gratification, the subtle doors of illusion. It will drain you of vitality and make you feel frustrated. Sexual curiosity, for its own sake, will turn your life into a charade, affirming the ego and making it ever more manipulative.

Lust is an emotion, and emotion never hurt anyone. It comes and goes. It only hurts if it becomes chronic, if it doesn't go, or if it isn't wholly cleared and eliminated. Then, and only then, will emotion turn malignant in the psyche. Then it causes general disharmony in the organism, finally disease. But first, it causes anger, deep sorrow and rage and aching feelings of alienation and loneliness, which all too readily turn into lust and perversions. Theses are the energies the grey ones need to feed off in their loveless astral levels to keep feeling alive. It is a parody of aliveness, I can tell you.

The result of orgasm in the case of compatible partners is that it enables the feminine polarity to move inward into deeper meditation, moving closer, as it were, to the ear of God. In the case of the male polarity, it enables him to experience and feel within his own being, the peace, and the joy, of the Father right through to his physical body and know the truth of the fact that between heaven and earth, and between himself and the Father, there is no separation.

He feels this well-being in his physical body and uses the vitality, and power, of the experience to empower the creative vision which is brought to him by his partner and which his partner then takes steps, with his loving support, to implement.

My beloveds, loving support means just this. It does not mean loving interference or loving desire to see any of your pet ideas or pet goals come to fruition. It means standing there in your love and joy, uncaring of the outcome - and not minding where the money is coming from!

It means giving your all, physically, then giving your mind to the solving of practical things that need to be done. It does not mean letting your mind get entangled in the rights and wrongs, or the whys and wherefores, of your actions. Neither are you to look for any particular outcome, or praise, or feedback, or spiritual fruits.

When you fixate on an outcome, you are not living in the moment; yet, the Father (which you are as the male polarity) is only to be found in the moment. If you are to be who you truly are, then, you, too, must be without expectations. So, living in the moment, living for the moment, is to be at one with the Father on earth. Only then can you be of proper use to your feminine partner who is truly the Mother upon earth.

Never be afraid of the nourishment of touching and being naked together. Much energy which finds its way to the sex centres and which you battle with constantly would in no way trouble you if you were to allow yourselves to relate to each other with warm and natural naked contact.

The sex orgies that you fear would not happen. You would find a greater peace and wholeness in your lives and you would not be constantly struggling with your sexual appetites within your minds and pelvic centres.

If you are inhibited about being naked with your friends, if you believe that the moment you are naked you are going to become, embarrassingly, sexually aroused, seek therapists who can help you unblock your inhibitions and get to the root cause of your fears. To be aroused is merely of the body. To be embarrassed by such a natural reaction is of the ego.

If you think there is something wrong about being naked or that it automatically leads to licentiousness, or that it is obscene, or rude, you have heavy clouds around your ego. Indeed, your ideas of right and wrong are obscene, and you are giving off a very rude and inappropriate vibration by holding on to these ideas.

Begin in a quiet, safe, way, when it feels right, being naked with your friends; be natural more often, and don't let anyone put you down for it.

Be joyful, and be gay. The original meaning of gay means to be care free, to be free of cares, and, above all, I would have you be carefree.

I am not encouraging you to be homosexual. Many homosexual encounters are far from being gay, often being furtive and squalid, and, even in their long standing relationships, become serious affairs where joy is an infrequent visitor. They are as much plagued - if not more so - as heterosexual relationships, by possessiveness and jealousy, and other fear generated states of being.

The disease A.I.D.S. is largely caused by the misuse of sex energy and the guilt associated with sex.

Behind this guilt is the belief that you are vulnerable creatures. The human ego that has created this belief counters it, with denial, by creating for itself a situation of pseudo carefree-ness, at the back of which lie the same old fears. It is a false gaiety.

It may appear, at first sight, to be sexual freedom. In fact, it comes about because of the human ego's slavery to sex.

Sex union, when correctly understood, is a heart to heart meeting of two entities empowered by all the bodies' energies. It is a fun, carefree, happening of exhilaration - and, certainly, of gaiety.

Be empowered by the awareness of who you are. Be empowered by spirit at all times. When you are empowered by spirit you are absolutely invulnerable, absolutely immune, to all diseases. In the Oneness there is no disease.

This is the meaning of being gay. It is not the prerequisite of homosexuals. It is to live in truth. It is to acknowledge it, and live in it, whoever you are and whatever your sexual inclinations. Gay is a wonderful word; it has a nice feel to it, and I would have all of you (setting aside homosexuality) to be as thoroughly gay as you like. You will be as care free as your beloved Father (your whole self) is care free. To be gay is to be fearless, care free, loving, intimate - and wise!

Once you have unblocked your fears concerning nakedness, which you may have released in therapy, cease the therapy and do not fall under the spell of its glamour. The prolonging of therapy beyond the time necessary for you to pin point the fear and experience the repressed emotion becomes self indulgence. The ego can use therapy just as it can use anything to hide behind (although an alert therapist will be able to see through this ploy).

Do not become lost in ceaseless exploration of the diversity of sexual experience lest you become entangled in a worse predicament than you were before.

The highways and byways of sexual enticements under the guise of healthy pleasure, or perhaps spiritual fulfilment entertained by so-called *tantric* masters, can turn out to be self-deluding indulgence of the never ending kind. Beware of it!

Sex as an energy is neutral and natural and, where there is joy attending it, is life affirming. It can, however, become an insidious energy when the mind attaches to it ideas by which to exploit it.

On going therapy, as a way of life to assuage weekly stress, like going to church on Sundays to assuage weekly guilt, is a wonderful rut to get yourself into. No less salubrious is the constant enjoyment of sexual experimentation.

Long has the human feminine ego upon this world put its trust not in the plan of spiritual vision but in the security of material things, such as the attachment to form, to human children and home comforts, thus guiding the male polarity incorrectly.

Long has the human male ego, in blindness and fear, put its trust, not in the gentle plan of love and joy but in the domination of all material forms, thus dominating the feminine polarity by the force of its emotional needs and dreams of glory upon the physical plane.

Both are equally to blame for this sad state of affairs in the world. It is not the fault of only the female polarity as some religions would have you believe - or of the male as new age feminists would have you think.

Now for another point; once you have found your life partner (aptly named because such partners, though not necessarily physically with you for the whole of your life-time, do dramatically enhance the awareness of your life), you would be unwise to seek other partners for sex during the time of your creative work together.

When a third polarity is introduced there is almost certain to be disharmony and imbalance. You cannot have three poles in a battery else a short circuit results.

Always it is two who work together. An entity on his or her own is indeed a whole entity, entire in his or her well-being, but if creative work is to proceed the two must work together as one being. One without the other is unbalanced.

When working as a team, as a unit of divine loving purpose, the female helps to ground the male's energy, whilst the male uplifts and brings light to the female. Without the male there is a tendency for joy, lightness, and play in her life to be diminished, and without the female there is sometimes little purpose and meaning in his.

However, complimentary polarities are rarely seen working together in your world in this way.

I am speaking of these things here to give you an idea of what the future holds for you. I hope to inspire you and encourage you to greater work in releasing yourself from ignorance and old conditioning. These understandings are not beyond you and the reality you create is very much a part of how you understand your reality to be. I desire to lift the veil a little.

There is a further matter that I desire to speak about and that is of those times when you are without a partner of the opposite sex, yet you have not raised the inner fires and become free of sexual desires.

The ancient symbol of the circular serpent, which is holding in its mouth its own tail, is the symbol of an entity that completes within itself a circle of its own life energy.

You, indeed, are whole beings, complete unto yourselves and sufficient unto your own well being. It is only in the creative work that you need to work together in balance with your complimentary polarity (of which there is just the one who has an equal but opposite vibrational frequency to you).

When there is an imbalance in energy potential between your physical body and your higher self, and before your higher centres are fully functioning, there needs to be an exchange, or an earthing, of this energy within the body so that balance and health can be maintained.

This overflowing of energy can safely find its release through the sex centre, and this is brought about by masturbation *with awareness.*

In this case it is the physical body which is acting as the receptive pole and your higher Self as the positive pole.

Attention to awareness must be maintained at all times during the act of self stimulated orgasm. If perfunctorily performed, or, undertaken with sexual fantasies, loss of energy, loss of vitality and loss of mental peace is the result.

This, the experiencing of your life energy, between the poles of these two aspects of your being, should be a conscious ritual of meditative beauty and one of pure and intense feeling, without the manipulative intrusion of thought.

When this is the case you will experience after orgasm a new balanced vitality, a peaceful integration within yourself and a feeling that you are happy and mentally focused.

Masturbation with awareness is a most balancing and transforming act; sadly, however, it can be - and usually is - a most unbalancing and self abusive act, as I shall outline.

Whatever you think about in your mind you create in the etheric realms around you. As you think it, so it happens. In the sex act thoughts are intensified under stimulation to an amazing degree because you are intensifying your life energy to do just this.

If during the act you are lightly holding thoughts of balance and self transformation they shall indeed occur. If, on the other hand, you are constructing thoughts of fantasy and desires of a sexual nature, these images will have, for quite a considerable time, a ghostly reality on the etheric plane, and, your life energy, instead of being held within your body for transformation and well-being, will go towards these temporarily created images and give them a most spurious and obnoxious life of their own.

This is a most destructive act for it not only creates on the ethers mindless and soulless images which further condition human and planetary egos, but these images are in turn attracted back to you. They cling to your aura, draining you of vitality, stimulating you by their presence to further lurid thoughts, and there they stay, either until you dispel them by conscious thought back into the Oneness or until they gradually dissolve on their own accord (which process can take up to 48 hours if no further thoughts are sent to revivify them).

You need to understand the powerful hold you are allowing these images and fantasies to have over you. The reason they have such staying power, clinging to you like limpets, is that it is *your* own powerful mind, not anyone else's mind, which is making, as it were, perfect tailor-made images for your own personal stimulation. So, they are perfect for you. If, however, you were to meet the actual person (the object) of your desire or fantasy, that person will never measure up to the stimulation engendered by your fantasy because they themselves are not perfect and can never be perfect. And, indeed, neither are they an object but God in manifested form, and there is always a part of you which is aware of this so that when you actually meet him or her in the flesh, in person, there is a sort of hiatus within you, a conflict, as it were, between your fantasy and the real person, and, in the present moment, in the NOW, it seems rather weird to be having sex with God!

This is the cause of the gap between fantasy and reality, and why fantasy can have such an ongoing hold over you. For the conditioned ego fantasy is actually better than reality which is why it hangs on to it. The conditioned ego's lurid images can never measure up to reality. For the whole Self, however, reality is bliss. Fantasy is the impostor!

Fantasy is a product of your mind made perfect for your conditioned ego. Reality can only be seen clearly by the still mind of God, which is at one with your whole Self, uncluttered by the personalised stuff (the fantasies, beliefs, opinions and desires) held by the conditioned ego's mind.

It is very important for you to make this distinction, for it is not only in sex that these fantasies can arise, but in all your belief systems, though I might say that it is in sexual fantasies that the energy is often strongest and therefore more difficult to disentangle from reality.

Self-control of the mind and awareness of your emotional mood as to why and when, pin pointing the exact point when the fantasies commence, is the key to ending them once and for all.

Once let loose, the best way of all to dispel these troublesome fantasies is to consciously reabsorb them back into yourself. Surround the images with love, flood them with light and command them to return into you and to go out no more. Further, you can call upon the angels of the violet flame to assist you: stand within the violet fire, feel, and visualise, its transforming violet light, flooding through you. Sound out that ancient sound which has the power to clarify the aura, the OM. Sound it out a few times, and feel the vibrations of this great sound tingle through the whole of your body.

This method is best for it establishes within yourself the recognition that you are responsible for your thoughts, affirming you as a co-creator on the earth. It is more effective spiritually and psychologically.

This cleansing should become a part of your daily life, until you are a master of your life energy. All your thoughts you are responsible for. Any you don't like, or which become chronic, or malignant, you can call back, at any time; and, with love, re-absorb them back into yourself, into your own Oneness, from whence they originated. But I warn you not to use it as a panacea, thinking you can go merrily on your way happily transgressing whenever you like now that you have found a cleansing formula. It is not like popping aspirins for a headache.

The ego will soon get you playing the game of hypocrisy if it can; then, your rituals become like a drug; you will have to keep doing more and more of them with less results. This game has diminishing returns. Life is not fooled.

The act of masturbation, being the act of self union, is a sacred ritual and I should have you partake of it as such, with as much enjoyment and with as much abandon as you like, yet at the same time retaining acute and sensitive awareness.

The physical body should be in a location where it is comfortable and relaxed and free from the possibility of disturbance. A prayer or mantra, is useful to bring poise and encourage awareness at the start of the ritual, as may be perfume or soft music. The attention of the mind should dwell lightly only upon the feelings arising within the body, no other thoughts are to be entertained. The mind is there as an observer; it is not there to monitor or manipulate the proceedings.

Immediately prior to the point of orgasm the awareness should be brought easily and lightly into the upper part of the body, into the heart and the head, and held there in contemplative awareness without discomfort for as long as seems natural and beneficial after the orgasm has occurred.

Be joyful and have no fear concerning this ritual. I am speaking of this in detail because there is a great guilt concerning masturbation in humans.

This is because masturbation is all too often a mindless self-absorbed action generated by prurient fantasies. It is the cause of much disharmony and disease for the reasons that I have given.

A friend of mine, who is an occasional channel for Sanat Kumara, channelled these words about masturbation and celibacy:

The purpose of celibacy is to pleasure oneself without the influence of another.

In pleasuring oneself the involvement of the sexual organs is usual but that does not mean it is a sexual act any more than eating food or relaxing in a bath is a sexual act, but it is still pleasuring oneself.

There are many reasons why the pleasuring of oneself is so complete and rewarding:

You know what you like.

You know when you like it.

You don't concern yourself with another's action or reaction.

You achieve peace, contentment and therefore spiritual elevation.

You are in private, where you can be expressive towards yourself.

In the achieved state of elevation, you are not robbed by another.

Therefore you can use your energy for yourself.

In being complete in yourself, you then become at one with everything because you are, at that point, in that state, completely YOU.

In becoming at one with all, you achieve peace and contentment, and

satisfaction, which promotes health and well-being, and a greater con-
nection with Source.

Remember always, you are sparks of joy. Whatever your current situation, you can be in touch with your life essence within you in the twinkling of an eye. To imagine that you can only feel most alive when in a sexual situation with another entity is nonsense.

Many of you have an addiction to sex, and are greatly preoccupied with it, because it is the only time you truly let yourselves go. It is the only time you go into the joy of abandon, into the joy of your being; it is the only time you give yourself permission to feel naked, and free, and energised by your spirit.

I tell you, pierce the illusion of this guilt and sex will move comfortably into the beautiful place ordained for it.

Every time you want to have a sexual expression, be very aware, and see if there is not another expression of your being-ness that cannot adequately use this energy.

Try moving, try dancing, try just sitting and breathing, and remaining aware; try singing or shouting, or, if you feel angry, try bashing a pillow; try lying in the grass, smell its scented perfume; try massaging a friend. But, above all, try feeling the whole of your body from head to toe, remaining in contact with the truly wondrous feeling of being here on earth in such a responsive and radiantly alive vehicle as is your physical cellular body.

Partake of your life energy with joy and zest and gaiety. Be free of guilt; but, please, do refuse to your energy outlets which are in all ways demeaning to your spiritual integrity.

Sex is a very and natural part of being human. So, enjoy it. Shame, fear, guilt, the odious expressions of denial and repression, do not serve you well.

Far too much power is both wasted and contaminated on this planet by joyless sex. I am talking here about the contamination of the sex energy by emotion - primarily emotion from conditioned ego-driven impulses such as fear, control, possession, revenge, jealousy and resentment. These unpleasant emotions sully power, so making power (which in its purity is so grand) into *force*.

Yes, there is way too much force on this beautiful planet and when it is used as such - as force - it is used in a way that is obscenely violent, being degrading and destructive, both to humans and their environment, even including, I might add - which you might be amazed at but is nonetheless true - to your patterns of weather.

Power and sex, and therefore force - as politicians are aware - are closely linked.

Sex accompanied by joy and love irradiates all the cells in your body; bringing contentment and health. It is not merely a creative act but re-creative and healing. It is as simple as that. Sex contaminated by any other emotion takes you into an ever downward spiral of depression from which spins off many an ugliness.

The issue is not whether you are married to your partner. The issue is not whether your sex has been sanctified by any god, church or religion. The issue is quite simple: when you have sex, be open to the joy of your being, both in your self and that which is in the other. If you cannot, either get some help from one of your insightful healers now on earth, if the problem is yours - or walk away from that relationship, or that encounter, and be alone for a while. It is a grand thing to vote with your legs and walk away. Being alone, after all, might open the door to self-discovery.

As I have mentioned it takes two poles in a battery to produce a spark, but have you not considered that you might already have the two poles within you. Indeed, you have. Your higher Self can be considered to be the positive pole and your human self, your personality, to be the receptive pole (that is if you allow it to be receptive!)

Sex, now takes on a new significance. It is now seen to be in relation of the lower self to the higher Self. With this awareness, sex can now be *lifted up* in order that you can reach complete union with divinity.

You will discover that sex which has hitherto been purely physical, though sometimes carried on under the impulse of love, is elevated into its rightful place as the divine marriage between your personality and your higher Self, and expressed as Self-realisation and final wondrous harmony in your whole Self.

It is this truth that lies behind the whole amazing, usually unappealing, story of sex expression in all its forms, including that of modern Tantric experimentation. Both men and women have sought, through diverse outer, physical, means, to produce this inner fusion (which all long for and crave) but it simply cannot be done this way.

Sex cannot be transcended by rituals or magic, or by any searching for glorious consummation on the outside.

The mental longings and mental images you hold in your mind which connect you to outer desires, outer fantasies and all outer scenarios of beauty and perfection, must be altered to an inner focus - simply an overwhelming desire for union with your Self.

This, indeed is the marriage made in heaven which, one day, all with achieve.

And, how is this achieved. Well, single minded intent and a longing for inner union to the exclusion of all else, awareness of mind, self-control, belief, and an insightful heart bubbling over with joy and gratefulness, having a warm non-judgemental love for humanity but a longing for God, and, finally, finding time for being *still* in contemplation of All-That-Is, are the ingredients which will make you ready for this grace to envelop you.

So, for those of you who are ready to devote yourself to the divine union, sex must be raised from a glorious outer activity to a glorious inner one. You must finally acknowledge that sex is but the outer expression of the possibility of an inner unity which cannot be achieved by rituals or physical means, but by a transcendence in consciousness.

In the long run it is all gain. I ask the human race not to compromise itself, any longer, sexually.

If you are not ready to commit yourself to attaining the inner union, enjoy sex with whomever you will (as long as they are consciously reciprocating, of course) but do not compromise yourself to anything less than sex with joy.

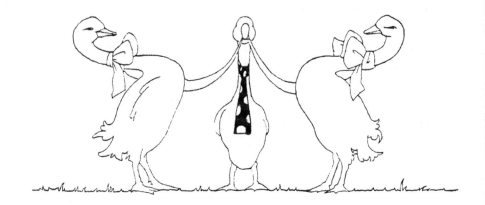

CHAPTER SIX

MARRIAGE AND CHILDREN

The relationship which humans call marriage is beset with mental agonies untold and oft times by physical cruelties.

Hear me when I say there is no such thing as marriage sanctified, either by God, or heaven, in the realms of light of which you are now to become a part. All is sacred in the Oneness. It is no more sacred to be wed than unwed, or to wed for the first time or to wed a hundred times.

By all means see your marriage as sacred, but then all relationships are sacred, are they not?

There are indeed affinity relationships and affinity groupings in this universe. Each of you have, as part of your cosmic make-up, twin (flame) relationships and complimentary polarity relationships which have been yours since the beginning of time, at your going out as sparks of individualised consciousness from the Oneness.

These affinity and complimentary relationships, through which you are working to bring about the vision of harmony in this physical level of god's heavenly kingdom, are the relationships which Jesus said are made in heaven.

There is no marriage in heaven, only beautiful relationships which last just as long as they are useful. So, if you wish to bring heaven to earth it would be a good idea to do away with marriage, solely legalised or sanctified by church or state, here also.

If you can become sensitive to your affinity pairings, your affinity groupings (soul mates), and complimentary partners, you can create heaven on earth for yourself, in a truly physical sense.

First, however, it is beholden upon you to become whole unto your self before joining with your twin flame else distortion from both of your conditioned egos will bring disruption, being vastly hurtful, to this most sensitive and exquisite of all relationships.

I say again, you cannot be happy in a relationship until you are first happy with yourself by realising that the Oneness is within you as your very self. Even more is this a truth in the case of affinity twins (twin flames) whose very breath and frequency in spirit is absolutely identical to each other.

In the case of twins flames, still having conditioned and fearful egos, they may be faced with such dramatic and accurate mirrors of themselves and their impending dissolution, that they can, and usually will, develop the most outrageous and hurtful distortions in what would otherwise be the most blissful of relationships.

It is wise, therefore, not to look for your affinity twin flame, but to look, instead, for self-realisation; whereupon you will come together again, now as two whole beings - for, in truth, you have never been apart, never can be, and never will be again on any physical or non-physical theatre of experience in the universe.

Your other important relationship, made in heaven, is that of your complimentary partner, of which you have only the one since the beginning of time. He or she will carry an opposite polarity to yourself, and it is he or she who can most help you in your task of dissolving your ego, by confronting you, by nourishing you, and by stimulating you to change.

Your affinity twin flame, having the same polarity as yourself, cannot help you in this way, though, if you meet, he or she can give you a magnificent glimpse of the energy of your whole self, which, in spite of subsequent loneliness will be of lasting comfort to you in your journey toward self-realisation. However, your affinity twin is more likely to mirror back to you your own fearful, hurting, distorted conditioned ego. He or she cannot show you the way out of your dilemma or show you how to dissolve your ego for he or she will have the identical problem as you have, and have, therefore, as little idea about the solution as you have.

You may - as I did - meet your affinity twin at a time of tremendous change in your life. However, it is usually impossible for you to remain with your affinity twin if you have (as we both did) any remaining unconscious conditioning in your egos.

In the *conditioned egos* of twin flames meeting on the physical plane there is generated inflamed desires, huge expectations, many fears, contaminated belief systems and other illusions, which you are sure to be carrying around with you. Both of you. You will both dig a mighty pit together in which you are more than likely to tear each other apart. The accompanying hurt and grief that this can cause is the stuff that great operatic tragedies are made of, yet it is the very last thing that either of you would really wish for the other.

It is not usual for twin flames to encounter each other on the physical plane for this reason, unless there are certain tasks to be undertaken which require a deep and sudden de-conditioning of the ego which can be safely handled by the entities involved. The energy released and emotion involved does quicken spiritual advancement but at a cost of potential personality loss which could, in young entities, bereft of faith and lacking the wisdom of a spiritual master, lead to self harm.

Spiritual seekers who come across and surrender to a Self-realised master who is in touch with Source will find that the master may act, in a safe environment in an ashram, as a surrogate twin flame to open their disciples to their own twin flame energy, being the energy of their higher-Self.

But, if it is your destiny to meet your twin flame, and the impossibility of continuing together arises, allow your affinity twin flame to go his or her way, however much it hurts (it is your ego that is doing the hurting); and know that, just as soon as you are whole you will be together again, once again taking up this sweetest of all relationships. This, then, is the promise of the great re-union, the symbol of the double headed phoenix; it is the reuniting of two whole beings who belong together, who, at other levels have always been together.

In this act of letting go, you are of course imitating the possibly somewhat painful act, as it may seem to you, one day, of letting go of your master to enter into your own personal responsibility for all you do, and all that you are, arising finally and magnificently with your own twin flame in the etheric levels of the universe.

You can imagine the joy that results when you and your affinity twin flame, and further along, your complimentary polarity, and his or her affinity twin flame, unite together in the realms of light. The radiance of the brightest sun is not comparable. This is the secret of the four, who are two, who are One. It is further symbolised by the four corners of the foundation of a pyramid, joined at its apex by spirit, which now makes five.

As you can see, there is much more to existence, than the three numbers of the Christian trinity. And, this is just the beginning!

This, my beloved, is the path you have in front of you. It is your destiny, for each one of you. But, first and foremost, look to your own wholeness, giving service to others and harming them not, upon your way.

It is not my intention to speak much about these (twin) relationships of yours that, as Jesus said, are made in heaven, for they are yours to experience, yours to explore in your own way, in your own time, and come to your own conclusions. In doing so, you will learn much. And heaven will come to earth.

I refer again to the institution known as marriage. It is supported by all but a few races on earth as a state most necessary for the good of society.

Yet, I say to you, if you pander to society's so called good, and look not into yourself for your own true life and well being, you will begin to die to your spirit. You will be dancing, torridly, to the tune of your conditioned ego.

The promise you make in a church to love your mate "until death do us part", reinforces the absurd belief that death is the end of intimate relationships between you and others that have existed in human bodies.

Secondly, it reinforces the belief that love can be maintained by promises; or, in other words, by making an act of mental will.

How can you make promises for tomorrow when you know not what tomorrow brings? How can you promise to be loving when your very nature is nothing else?

Would you ask your husband to promise to be a human being fearing that he or she might not really be one? Would you ask a bird to promise to sing its own song and none other?

What nonsense! These promises come from ignorance and foster much hypocrisy. They delude the ego by promising something which cannot possibly have any basis in reality.

Reality is not based upon a promised future.

Promises, which, by their very nature, are based on future hopes and projections, allow your energy no freedom to move within you.

Where there is no freedom to move, there is no life. There is no joy, and most certainly no growth toward transformation into total clarity. Frustration is the only result, and the possibility of transformation, for the meantime, ceases.

Promises to be sexually faithful to one partner and no other, to enjoy the company of one person and no other, are not only fetters to the in-dwelling entity and crippling to your spirit; they are also, of course, utterly futile.

What entity can say he or she knows of God's will, in advance, for another, or that you are only permitted to love in this way or that way - according to the laws that priests or lawyers or politicians have drawn up.

Don't be deluded. Don't listen to those who with such wonderful belief in their own righteousness take it upon themselves to sanctify that which is already sanctified, and, in so doing, place you in a straight jacket of mental agonies.

Don't listen to those who interpret God's will as a system of promises and rewards. They enjoy giving themselves the authority to curtail your freedom by dangling before you promises which only serve to reinforce the illusion of death. They stimulate fear by demanding sanctification of that which has no need of sanctity, acquiring your acquiescence to a future bound by fetters of expectations; and therefore based upon no reality of life eternal as lived in this universe.

Like unto a sun that never fails to shine, the blessings of God are within you and upon you unceasingly. And I say again, when you and others collect together, in acknowledgment of me, there I am recreated in outer glory. Do this, my beloveds, at any time of the day, if you will, but especially at the opening and the closing of daylight upon your planet.

Never be embarrassed about acknowledging God when you are with friends. This acknowledgment is not to be made into a ritual or it will give rise to dullness, or glamorous ideas, or expectations.

Be as open as if you were standing on a mountain top where all is seen but nothing is seen in detail; where nothing needs to be seen, where expectations are no more than wisps of mist in the valleys which, in a twinkling, the sun can dissolve; where, without either looking up or down, you are utterly aware of the Oneness.

When I say to you acknowledge me, I do not mean for you to make demands upon me. If you would believe that when I hear I come, this is not acknowledgment of me. It is not possible for me to come when already I am here. This idea is a barrier to acknowledgment.

Let go of your desire to call upon me or for me to assist you. Know, instead, I am here already assisting you. I am manifesting myself in you and around you as yourself and as the All-That-Is.

When you acknowledge me in others and uphold the dignity and joy of that acknowledgment within yourself you shall begin to know of peace.

Your human existence is but a blink of an eye in the scheme of existence and I would have you realise this. It is a great adventure for you but a minute part of your existence in consciousness.

I have no authority and I do not delegate any. Give not, therefore, your priests and lawyers and politicians authority over you. Are they greater than I?

In meditation and contemplation listen to my voice within, feel my presence, and in nature seek my wisdom and be refined into the purity of yours. Even I, of galactic vision, am different in expression to my galactic colleagues, but in value, in essence, in reality, in truth, we are identical you and I. And thus we share together in the nature of our being which is love.

Truly all is joy, all is love. These are words I would have you engrave upon your soul. There are none greater that these. These are the words given to me by our universal Father-Mother-God which is breath and bread to all sentient creatures in the created universes.

These words I gave to you, my beloveds, when I spoke to you through my beloved master teacher Jesus: "Thou shalt love the Lord thy God with all thy heart, and with all thy soul, and with all thy mind. This is the first and great commandment. And the second is like unto it. Thou shalt love thy neighbour as thyself. On these two commandments hang all the law and the prophets". (Matt 22:37).

I say again to you, first be true to me who is within you as yourself as the spirit of joy, and then be as true to others as you would have them be to you.

How canst thou love another if not first thou love thine very own self? My contact with you, at its most personal and trustworthy, is not outside of yourself, but within you. Is this not obvious to you?

The admonishment is not that you put yourself first in all things or disregard the feelings of others: this is indeed a way of darkness unlighted by sensitivity. It is, rather, that you are true to the spirit of truth that resides within you, at all times.

Being true to the spirit of truth within you is vastly different from the unlighted expression of being true merely to the outer personality needs of your loved ones. Learn to know the difference. This is the great learning to be done.

But this I say to you: my way is not the way of pain. When you are beset by apathy, depression; aye, and outer manifestation of physical dis-

ease, and all the debris of mental anguish, know that you are but temporarily hidden from me by clouds of your own making.

My way is truly that of joy which is your own energy, which is verily myself, and which in olden times was called the Spirit.

When others in your world refuse you permission to be this way, judge them not, neither fight them, nor explain with reason, over wearily, what cannot be reasoned but only felt.

Remove yourself from their influence. Have no fear and affirm my presence within you always. The time has come for a parting of the ways. My life, my love, my joy, my being-ness, shall be proclaimed openly from now onwards upon Earth.

Those who receive it not, nor wish to change their ways, need not fear that they are doomed or lost. Such is not the case. They wait, as I wait, for another day for their flowering. Bless them, my beloveds, give thanks for that which has been shared and go your way rejoicing.

Seek out those who acknowledge me, seek out those who shall give you permission to be true to your spirit within you.

I would speak of infants: this is a hard time for children in these times of change when the old is giving way to the new. Their tender needs must be considered but live not in fear. Release all your concerns to me and see to your children the best you are able; no more is it possible for you to do. My great plan for this world is now upon you. It shall not fail but in the changes to come your human personalities and those of your children will be buffeted and cry out oft times with fear.

This needs be for my plan has been long in the making and long resisted by the ignorant ones of Earth.

It is a time, my beloveds, for certain requirements of your personalities to be sacrificed if you are to trust in this my plan for you, which, in the last day, is to show you the illusion of past and future, and the illusion of progress and achievement. You and I are already here in our perfection together yet you know it not.

Remember, my beloveds, I AM YOUR CHILDREN. I know the times that I enter this world in baby form and, for the sake of change, I am prepared to meet my destiny in all the forms within which I manifest myself. So I say to you again, fear not for the future of your children.

Be true always to the commandment that Jesus gave you an age ago and which I have reinterpreted for you today. Fulfil this my commandment in trust and I shall lead you into a new Jerusalem, indeed, and the whole world shall be as one holy city.

It is important to remember that children, being closer to their essence, are very quick to recognise when an adult is not being real. Children are very quick to pick up, even if they don't make it clear that they do, the manipulations, the hypocrisies, the pretence, and the avoidance games that adults trot out or get involved in.

And, if by their teens you have taken no steps to change your ways, they quite naturally begin to use their new found strength to assert their individuality and distance themselves from your values because they are rebelling against the hypocrite you have become.

This agonising process can be avoided, for all concerned, if you are willing to go outside society's role model of a mother or father; if you are willing to develop spiritually; if you will treat them as your equal within the Oneness; if you will see in them the inner entity, not just the child; if you will admit to error; if you are willing to share your feelings; if you will affirm joy as being important in your family; and if, at all times, you will make a distinction between what your child may do (that behaviour which you may, or may not, not like) and who the child truly is (the person whom you love).

When changes happen within the family circumstances share the reasons for those changes with your children without pushing your therapeutic insights on to them.

Children are very insightful all by themselves. They do not need your therapy. They need your love and they need to feel your confidence that, despite its challenges, life is joyful and fun.

Never just go on automatic and join in with the outwardly comfortable demands of those around you just because its the direction in which all the other fish are swimming.

Do not justify your inaction (which is in itself an action) by pointing to the actions of others outside of yourself and using them as an excuse for yourself not taking the steps to change and grow.

Fear not for your children when, in separation, they seem to be going toward a dark future. Go you toward the light, my beloved, and leave all thoughts of darkness to me, for in truth there is none. Only your thoughts make it so. All my children, all my beings of form are in my protection; none can be lost.

Yet, in the same manner that human-kind keep pets, such as dogs and cats and caged birds, so do many humans look upon their children as pets and so become lost to their own natures.

They look to these innocents for emotional satisfaction which they feed off, which comes from having within their sphere of influence an innocent being that is totally trusting and accepting of all they do.

Many humans derive self-gratification for themselves by these means, puffing up their egos, under the pretext of being loving.

Beware of this false love. Those who truly love birds which verily are the living symbol of my song, who are my messengers to you of joy and freedom, do not cage them nor hold them in a confined space for purposes of self.

Every child is born with a song in his or her heart. It is also a song of joy and freedom. Listen and be humble. Your child can teach you much.

Love always sets free. It does not build warm cocoons of cloying safety around those you love so that they are suffocated, or, stifled of excitement, fun, initiative and adventure for fear of the great bogeyman called DAN-GER.

Of course, your children are not really children. They are Gods, such as you are, in bodies smaller than yours, having minds which are less conditioned by and less adapted to the skills of physical living than are yours. They are Gods who, like you, have also "forgotten for a while who they are", for whom you have taken upon yourself the responsibility of introducing to the physical world, so as to prepare them for their awakening as to their own true nature in the physical world.

Who amongst you, being childless but longing for a child, would take, in its place, an adult person who had reverted to a child-like state, a stranger to you, who had lost his memory, together with the ability, momentarily, to relate to the physical plane. Would this appeal to you?

Yet, setting aside the physical difference between a child and an adult, this is exactly the task you take upon yourself, in real terms, when you decide to have a baby.

It is better by far not to have children if you are not aware what life is all about. The having of children is not an automatic right of human beings.

In being automatic and following the crowd you are being like a machine, dull, rigid and purely functional. There is no possibility for you or your children to live in joy, spontaneity, and freedom, when you are on automatic. It is better not to have children, lest you and they dig deep holes together into which you all fall.

Only in awareness, only with a joyful sense of perfect rightness and with a lengthy contract to commitment is this, the most precious, delicate, and difficult of tasks, to be undertaken.

Mother-ship and father-ship is the most skilful of tasks you are ever required to lend a hand to. The caring and bringing to maturity of an incoming entity within a body as yet unreceptive to its fully conscious cosmic self is an art form of the highest endeavour. It is worthy of full consciousness from both parents.

It is not an automatic function of womanhood to build bodies of flesh for eager entities to inhabit.

In the realms of light, the feminine creative impulse, as I have already outlined, is to nurture the awakening of an entity's growth toward the light. It is to push, prod, stimulate, give nourishment, give comfort, withhold comfort, support, teach, reveal and ever to encourage the entity to look within itself in order to become the joyful, loving, independent God that it truly is. This above all is the feminine creative role.

The feminine role is vastly more than being a mere comforter, or being a bearer of babies who, in turn, hopefully, will comfort you in your old age. If this is what you want, I suggest you buy yourself a hot water bottle. It would be more honest.

Your children will take to their heels in their teens. This is natural. But, whether they stay in touch, knowing you are their friend in the Oneness, is entirely up to you; according to, whether or not, you have, as a parent, seen them as equal to you in the Oneness.

Many children at present incarnating into this world have come here determined to end denial and be true to their spiritual energy. They are usually considered rebellious or too high in energy, or unstable, but in fact they are the first wave of advanced entities who are determined to be true to their energy and live uncompromisingly to the tune of their spirit.

As yet, your education system has a poor record in accommodating these children, accusing them of having too much energy and poor attention skills. I tell you, it is a criminal act to drug and dope your children to fit in with your own beliefs about education. Most of these children find that your present schools offer nothing of real interest to them. They need to be given space and much flexibility; and, above all, *they need to be listened to*. Strange as it may seem to you, if you truly listen to them they will tell you what they wish to learn. And, what they wish to learn will be the perfect preparation for their mission on earth, which their spirit (not your education system) is training them for.

They will resist being forced to learn anything that they have no real enthusiasm for. The use of any force will backfire because these souls have come to earth to end the use of force to solve problems. They will, therefore, have nought to do with force, or undue control, except react against it in the only way they know how, by either being rebellious, or by being slow and ultra passive.

If your child tells you he or she doesn't know what he wants to do, don't panic: just give him space. Space is a wonderful healer, sorter-outer, and clarifier. It allows you to see what is real and what is just a passing fad. It sorts out all sorts of confusion in the mind, just as oil and water separate out, the oil will float to the surface.

This is exactly what your child may need: some time to be left alone (within a caring environment) and given space. Soon enough, your child will get bored with this and probably ask you, "Aren't we ever going to learn anything?" This is the time to say: "Well, what do you want to learn?"

If he says, "I would like to learn to read." You can start with that, and you will be amazed at the speed in which reading is mastered. If he says: "I want to learn how birds fly." Then teach him this.

Your high energy children are your future. They are not your problem children. They are your genius children. Listen to their vision of your future, for it is going to be a future of high energy, and of peaceful energy, of sensitive energy and joyful energy.

The energy of spirit is not wishy-washy. It is vibrant. Full on!

Do not edit it and make it comfortable. Give it space.

This may seem a bizarre way of going about things, but give it a chance. It will work. If you do, your children will fulfil your dreams - and even go far beyond them. End your preconceived notions about education. End your control, and please do listen to your children. Treat them as your intuitive equals and listen to their needs. You will be amazed. Children do naturally want to learn and they are expert at it, but from now onwards they will resist learning what you want them to learn unless it fits in with their own individual purpose in being here on earth. The end of denial on earth is imminent.

The learning that children need to do is in their timing, not in yours. The days of force are numbered.

Now, to return to the matter of partners: your complimentary (polar opposite) partner will test you to the limit. This is his or her gift to you. He or she will alternately fascinate you and repel you; be close to you one moment and, seemingly, quite alien the next.

Remember, fascination is the other side of fear. They are close friends.

Your complimentary partner may make your fears plain to you. It is a great gift, but in the process it can be confusing and frustrating, and you wonder if you'll ever get close to, or learn to trust, the other.

Trust is the bottom line here. Acceptance is the key. When you can learn to trust the other, without reservation, giving them absolute freedom to be how they wish to be at the same time as remaining true to yourself, letting go of all ideas, then you may be ready to get together with your affinity twin, and then creatively work with your polar opposite and his/her affinity twin, to reveal more of God's plan wherever or whenever it is your destiny to reveal it. This is the *Law of the Four*, for which the pyramid is the eternal symbol.

It is the yin role always to nourish the lesser ones, whether they be children in consciousness or children in bodies. But to work with consciousness is the main work. Always bear this in mind. When your days of rearing babies are over, there is a world outside where consciousness is in its infancy. Look to your service there. The rearing of physical children happens to be an extra burden laid upon entities in this physical world, though, to many - if not most - it is indeed, and, rightly so, a great joy and privilege.

The mindless ones who bring physical children into this planet by the tens of millions, are opening a door into this physical experience for a great many entities who know perfectly well that the time is coming when this planet is to move into a higher vibration, when the door will be closed to them. They are anxious to experience the least contact before it is too late; hence, the extraordinary amount of short span lives amongst entities who reincarnate as children in areas of starvation. Such entities are very happy and eager to experience how this feels, particularly those who have not previously had physical plane experience.

This may seem bizarre, but, remember, an entity, in its cosmic body, does not judge matters in terms of right or wrong; it does not look at the horror of a situation and shrink in fear from it, as does the conditioned ego. To the cosmic entity who is putting down a part of its consciousness into physical living all is already known to it to be joy, to be love; it is not afraid, it is never appalled. It looks for experience, and the means by which to awaken itself on the physical level.

Be compassionate toward these short lived entities, love them, show them that joy exists - even if it be but for an instant in a short life - but do not use their fecundity to justify your own desires for children. Be awake!

I am talking here, not to the masses, but to you who have the desire to be awake and to be self realised. You are one of those bringing light to the world. Know this. Take strength and joy from it, and place my words, as always, alongside your own highest truth.

Whatever you do in life, whether you are in or out of a relationship, put it alongside your highest truth; and know that the god of your being is joy. Let joy be your compass.

If, in a relationship, there is well being, expansiveness, enthusiasm and a joy in it, or even what you may consider to be growth, then continue the relationship; it is good for you. Indeed, enthusiasm comes from a Greek word meaning "of spirit".

I would have you put every choice you make in your life to the test of enthusiasm. It is a sure guide as to the correctness of your path. Always choose a plan for which you have a definite enthusiasm, for then you will be acting from your spirit, from your truth.

When those inevitable bleak times come, when frustration and resentment creep in, use these times as opportunities for insight into your own fears. These are times for growth. Then, give thanks to your partner for mirroring back to you that which has clouded you from your own loving and joyful beauty.

Use these experiences to change. You are always free to change . And, it is easier to change in an atmosphere of trust, in a situation where there has once been good feelings, even if they are not there now.

This, then, is the benefit of having had a loving family around you when you were a child. It gives you inner resources at times of crises. It is the same when you choose your relationships: where there has once been joy and love, there can be growth - that is, if both of you are open to the idea of growth, being the same as spiritual advancement.

If one of you doesn't believe that in the low times there is opportunity for transformation, the relationship will very quickly become stagnant; and then, no matter what sacred promises or what religious beliefs you have held, the light will go out of it, the joy will go out of it, and when these things go out of a relationship, and remain out of it, it probably needs a grand shake up on one side or the other. If it is no longer useful in terms of spiritual growth, it may mean that both of you need a time apart.

Relationships are useful in as much as they are a transforming process.

The time for using marriage for a lifetime of mutual comfort has passed. This is a time for transformation. Only in knowing that relationships are for this purpose, can you, by a process of elimination, discovery, and intuitive experience, find out for yourself who your opposite polarity is, that entity who is destined to most help you on your path to God realisation on earth.

Never be afraid of being on your own whenever you want to be. In a sense, you are only in a relationship just as long as you still hunger after a relationship; or, just as long as you need to prove to yourself that you no longer need a relationship.

Remember, you don't need something that you already have. You, the cosmic entity (your whole Self), are already aware of your truest relationships, being your affinity twin flame and polar opposite.

It is for you to become awake here on earth and know that you have no need, either, of relationships, because you already have the most perfect relationships, yet you know them not.

There is no greater purpose and none that requires greater awareness, or, that has within it the ingredients of greater adventure, or greater rewards, or greater love for your self, or, indeed - that could be more simple - than the quest for self realisation.

Indeed, I say to you, your only purpose in being here on earth in physical bodies is to transform these bodies into bodies of light. You may relax your anxieties concerning all other works. Is this not a relief!

To all of you, who, at the dawning of another age, find yourselves embattled by a thousand things to do, is this not an immense relief ?

My beloveds, to help others discover their own joy within them is the best way to reveal your own. This way, I tell you, is the swiftest and least painful way of reaching your goal, and, in the meantime, is of great service to myself which is yourself in all our manifested forms.

I am a great economist of energy. I use it not wastefully or to deliberately prolong for you the reaching of your goal. It is never in my consideration deliberately to make your path hard for you or to put tests your way. On the contrary, I constantly am smoothing your path for you for it is the nature of the human ego ever to seek difficulties where none exist but for it.

When you serve the life in others and set it free, you are freeing yourself. And, when you free yourself, to that extent the other becomes free, also. Indeed, we are One.

When each partner in a relationship, whether in or out of marriage, can take a standpoint of self responsibility for their own feelings of hurt within the relationship, and learn how to grow as a result, learning not to blame the other, then swift progress is possible.

If one of you understands this process, but the other does not and refuses, further more, even to explore its possibilities, then the relationship has become unbalanced and a "temporary" parting will probably be the only answer.

I repeat: there are no such things as husbands and wives in the realms of light, neither, therefore, are there any in god's greater plan for you on this very earth. You already have your relationships; you already have your friends in your affinity groups. All exists already for you as perfectly as you can conceive of it. Indeed, in a very real sense you are the very God that has conceived it, and, think on this: would you have considered conceiving for yourself anything that was not absolutely wonderful and perfect for yourself, that would not utterly fulfil your every desire? No, of course you would not, but your conditioned ego has distorted things so magnificently for you that you stubbornly refuse to awaken to who you really are and go deafly and blindly groping through life desensitised to your affinity relationships and oft times condemning those who, at a soul level, you are closest to.

When you feel drawn to someone, ask yourself, why? First of all, does the person have a similar vibrational frequency to you? Can he, or she, respond to you from that level of frequency which you, in your most joyful moments, are most at home with?

Take responsibility for the feeling of being attracted. What has originated the feeling within you? Where has it come from? And why?

These are legitimate questions for you to ask yourself. Is it from some mind scenario of the conditioned ego? Is it from a yearning emotional need? Is it from a need to possess or dominate? Is it a body hunger? Or, is from spirit's direction, wishing you to validate upon the earth the joy of being, with a partner?

If it is the latter, and if you are both equally drawn, let nothing - not wild horses or rampaging elephants, or dictatorial priests or parents - stand in your way.

More often, the relationships you will have will not be with your affinity twin or with your complimentary polarity, but with a member of your group soul. It will have been arranged by you and the other, and your spiritual helpers and your higher self, before your incarnation into this life-time.

These relationships are beautiful relationships. They are sometimes challenging. There is much love in them, many joyful times, great respect, and spiritual growth.

Your purpose in relating to another is not, I repeat, to create children; it is not in order to assuage the pangs of loneliness; it is not in order to have a legitimate sexual outlet.

It is, I remind you, for a journey of self discovery, together, with each of you playing for yourself the lead role. The discovery that you are a spark of joy within the Oneness as The Oneness, whilst validating this realisation with your partner, in this physical reality, is worth more than a thousand holiday homes or automobiles.

Don't be bamboozled by society's beliefs in the sanctity of marriage or the value of being faithful to your spouse. The ideas that surround these roles are used by the most intelligent and righteous of humans in this world to avoid taking responsibility for their own feelings of lack and frustration; and thus, they also miss their own salvation.

By so doing, they avoid, the conflict that would ensue were they to make any effort to be true to their own spirit. Instead they pander to the expectations of others.

These are the people who are quite happy to agree to anything as long as it doesn't rock their boat. Their agreement is a ploy to defuse a potentially explosive situation which they fear might get out of control if they were to say how they felt.

It is their ego's ploy to make life comfortable for itself by anticipating painful situations, and by knowing exactly the right answer to avoid ruffling the waters.

The soft answer that turns away wrath, when it comes from a genuine space of balance and compassion, is the hallmark of a great soul, but, when it is used, as it is, all too often, by the fearful and self righteous ego as a ploy to agree when all the ego really feels is violent disagreement, then it is a cunning and hypocritical ploy. It is dishonest disagreement.

Guilt is behind this, and lack of worth. It is particularly endemic in Christianised cultures in which it has found a fertile soil in which to flourish.

Those who sit back, letting life drift along, dishonestly agreeing to every confronting event despite their inner feelings about the matter, are suffering from moral cowardice. Meanwhile, their life energy remains imprisoned inside them, seduced into being there by their various fears and justifications, held there by the silken bars of false ease and the anaesthetising comfort of society's security blankets.

The time for change has come; but change, not for change's sake, but for change with understanding.

Change for the sake of change is nothing more than fashion. It may well become fashionable to become a "new age person"; to become an environmentalist; to become a seeker, or a therapist; to become a spiritual teacher (and to be able to talk facilely about esoteric things), yet fashion gets you nowhere. It's just another fad and just another ego ploy trotted out once again to let the ego feel it is someone worthwhile.

As a co-creator of this universe you are already worth everything. How much more worthy do you want to be? It is your ego, of course, that is ignorant of this fact, and who compels you to appropriate worth to yourself. It is such an illusion.

The change that is required is not another alternative society. Changing your society around can be as fashionable as a lady changing her hats. Being "alternative" has little value if it is but another fad or fashion.

When society accepts the idea that each individual is here on earth to undergo personal discovery, to self realise that he, or she, is a God on earth, the quality of life will alter dramatically as a direct result of the reorientation of goals.

Human children need a secure environment in which to grow to maturity. In these days of breaking up of old patterns, it is not the most suitable of times to rear children. It is a time, rather, for the using of your creative energies to give birth to your own Christ child within yourself.

Those of you who have children, count them as a blessing and a gift. Never see them as a burden. They will teach you much if you take the time to listen. They will not hinder your growth, for if you have them it is your desire to have them and, as always, what you desire is your path, and you will gain in awareness; this being the whole point of the exercise.

Spiritual growth goes very well, hand in hand, with children. In these days of change, however, it is as well to choose such a venture as child raising, with the utmost of care, and only after meditation and guidance from your cosmic self.

If you ask, you will get the answer. If in doubt, do not make long term commitments when you know not what the future brings.

It is time to learn to be a spontaneous, loving, joyful, human being, who knows that the moment is sufficient unto itself.

It is time to let go of your deep, instinctual, longing to cuddle babies.

It is time, now, to look to your glorious self who will dance in the light, as a child of spirit, which is the very essence of who you are.

CHAPTER SEVEN

JEALOUSY

I speak to you of jealousy, my beloved, as a cancer which casts its blight upon the clarity of your being-ness as does its external manifestation which gnaws away at the vital life giving organs of the outer body.

What is jealousy? Jealousy is that state of mental restlessness experienced as acute disharmony in the emotional and physical vehicles when another person possesses, or threatens to possess, that which you imagine may consequent loss to yourself.

A person embroiled in jealousy is caught in a spider's web of their own making and the spider at the centre of the web is their own deluded mind.

That which another has, which you may desire, might be a loved one; it might be riches; it might be status; it might be a state of being that you covet such as enlightenment, or contentment; it might be psychic powers; it might be some quality such as compassion, or affection; it might be some talent - as say, for public speaking, or gift of musical ability.

Jealously is often to be found hiding behind resentment, for the mind finds it sometimes easier to admit to resentment rather than jealously.

But I say to you that behind jealousy and resentment both, is desire. Behind desire is fear, and behind fear is ignorance of your true divine possibility in the physical body.

Desire is the opposite side of the coin to jealousy and it is best to approach jealousy through desire, thus:

Desire is the will of God manifest upon earth in all creatures. There is correct desire (the will to be self realised) which moves in tune to your ultimate possibility in the physical body; then there is incorrect desire (the desire to protect the human ego) which has been manufactured by the conditioned mind into its own belief systems to support its own conditioned, masquerading, self (the ego) and protect itself by every devious and subtle contrivance it can think up.

At the back of incorrect desire is the fear of loss, of aloneness, of being without love or the ability to love, of being without a body, of not experiencing, of being ineffective, of spiritual failure, of being without freedom of expression, of being without creative powers, of being helpless, of being without the ability to feel or be sensual or be sensitive, or of being trapped or immobilised, or the fear that life has no meaning.

One or more of these fears, my beloveds, are the cause of the mind's devious attempts to construct for itself a self protective mechanism. The process by which it attempts this, is what you call desire - which gives rise to jealousy. It is an emotion, stimulated by the fearful and ignorant mind of the ego.

Ponder long and deeply upon desire and the thought-seeds of desire; then, ponder upon the fruits of desire, and see both the spurious origins and the illusory nature of the fruits of desire.

For instance, the desire to be loving stems from the underlying fear of being thought of as unloving, with the possible consequences of being cast out by society or by those you love, and being alone without food, or shelter, or hope of love.

In the enlightened being there is no desire to be loving.

Just as a cat has no *desire* to be feline (after all, to be feline is the very nature of a cat), so, in your whole self, there is no desire to be loving, for love is the very nature of your whole self.

I ask you to take notice of the cat for though a cat has no awareness of its own possibilities of self awareness, it nonetheless lives in a state of grace and mental harmony which can teach you much.

Can you imagine a cat spending its time worrying how it might become more feline? Would it not become quite neurotic, and indeed be subject to viciousness, in its frustration at being unable to solve the unsolvable?

A cat moves to where it feels comfortable and at ease. It moves away swiftly from the reverse. It sleeps when it sleeps, loves when it loves, eats when it feels hungry, and purrs when it feels content.

Never does a cat confront others with mental arguments behind which there is a desire to improve its own feline-ness, or to get a relationship based on feline-ness "to work". I can assure you that a cat is far too intelligent (though acting without awareness of its intelligence) to waste its time and energy proving to itself or others that it should stay in a place where it is uncomfortable.

Become like a cat, I say, and enter a new way of being. An inner light will begin to warm you. You will begin to understand the easiness of life as it is happening in your NOW rather than desiring it to happen the way you want it to happen.

Of course, we can take this analogy to cats only so far. Cats, confronted by a threat, become a ball of spitting fury. This is a totally whole response, based on form's need to protect itself (instinct) which is perfectly apt from a cat's point of view. Humans, however, are in the process of becoming awake to something else: their individuality within The Oneness, as The Oneness. Indeed, humans, at these times of extremity, often find that surrender, calmness, or great stillness, arises unexpectedly. Fear departs. This is because the shock of imminent death shatters the mind (the ego), allowing the clarity and peace of the soul to shine through.

To those of you who have sought diligently for truth, this may happen at other times quite spontaneously.

The *desire* to be loving is often a mask behind which hides the fear of having to admit to the world a sensual need, or a sexual hunger. Deep down, this desire is unrelated to caring or sharing with your partner, being in no way tied to their needs unless by luck or by the coincidence of shared bodily magnetism.

Instead of admitting to yourself that you have a need of others for sex and sensual pleasure, your mind devises a scenario in which you need to keep proving to yourself that you love the other or that you need to work at the relationship to make it loving. This leads to a neurotic, self incriminating, and hopelessly introverted relationship, with inevitable frustration and emotional violence. Behind this devious justification is guilt at having sexual needs.

It would be better to say to your partner: "I don't *need* to love you, for my very nature is love. But I need to be sensual and at this very moment I am hungry for sex."

It is better by far to know yourself and be honest enough to admit it.

The compromise of self for fear of owning up to impersonal, sexual, or sensual needs, for fear of losing the respect of your partner, leads to a confused mind and the very pain you are seeking to avoid.

Only mental confusion gives rise to desire.

Note, I make a distinction between sexuality and sensuality. But it is not all that important. You all know the difference. They are equally strong desires. And they have the same hold over you when guilt, fear, or jealousy, is there.

On that day when the grace of the great initiation of union with The Oneness shall flower within you, sex, and the need for it, will disappear.

In preparation for this time, confusion in the mind must cease. Honesty must reign. Then, through insight, desire falls away to be seen as the charlatan that it is.

Become a momentary person. Be spontaneous. Affirm the joy of your being.

The nature of *desire* is that it is of the future, or of the past. Its territory is of vain and wondrous imaginings. In the moment desire cannot be. But, if the moment arrives and desire contaminates it, the moment is lost. You can not be total in the moment when desire is there with its murky clouds obscuring your present from you.

Give up desire; and then let go of the desire to give up desire. Do you understand?

Let me explain: your ultimate physical possibility is to have an enlightened mind with a body at peace with itself. Every physical cell in your body will be aware of the fact that it is loved, there being no possibility of being disturbed ever again by any doubt of this, whatever circumstance may arise.

This change - this great change - is a permanent happening. It is a sudden happening. Its effect upon the cells of the body is both electrical and chemical. For some people there is a fore taste of this transformation to come. For others there is no forewarning.

Your task, my beloved, as is the task of all humans, did they but know it, is to create an environment in which this can happen. It is up to you to place yourself in the right frame of mind, or even better, no mind or receptive mind, so that this transformation, this initiation (which is given to you through grace) can occur.

Prepare yourself as you would gently and lovingly prepare your garden; nurture the soil; root out the weeds; then, await the head gardener, who shall plant the rose, which rose is your own flowering.

When the mind believes it can do it by itself, this very belief creates a never ending plethora of subtle desires. They will manifest as a desire to find the answers through religion, through self denial, through good works, or self improvement, through therapy and so on; so much so, that the receptivity of mind necessary for this initiation to occur is too clogged with self-opinionated ideas and desires for it to happen.

Rather than desire, what is required is insight. Insight into this puzzle will be the means by which all desire will drop. Another way of putting it, is that you need to stop! But, again, whilst the mind is hard at work working out what insight is, or wondering how to stop, no relief is possible.

Stopping does mean stopping!

Projections of being loving, of being whole, of being alone, of confronting people, of healing relationships, of being enlightened, are still outside projections - with the mind entangled in them by some desire or other.

Let go, I say, of the desire to have better relationships. Let go of your creative desire in this matter, for, however beautiful your vision of relationship - and indeed they are beautiful, they are your stumbling block right now. They are the outside entanglements which ferment desire in a never ending circle.

There is a time for working at relationships, and, indeed, most of humanity needs be taking care in this area of development in order to learn of trust and love and create an appropriate environment in which more can happen one day, but this time for you is past. Drop the desire to be loving or make relationships work. Be honest with yourself. Be brave. Be remarkably and divinely selfish.

Desire is ever related to the outside. The great initiation of divine union is not beyond you. It will arise within you just as soon as the climate is right within your mental and emotional aura.

Let go of trying to change yourself or your relationships for the better. Let go of trying to prove anything to yourself or others. Let go of the desire for self analysis and the pressing of that analysis on to others. Analysis is a wearisome pastime and such a burden upon the joyful spontaneous soul. It shall cause you continuing and endless unrest if you pursue it so.

There is no profit in attempting, continuously, to make relationships work at the expense of your own destiny. Pander not to others, yet be not arrogant or consciously hurtful, either. Like a cat, be self possessed. Retain your dignity but do not force it upon others. Love where you will, be easy, be spontaneous, pander to none, melt away from aggression and ugliness. Be not opinionated about anything. Give hostility no energy or judgement, either for or against.

Your destiny is to become whole, to be in union with the Oneness. It is to be enlightened in your mind and alive in your body. It is your destiny to have relationships that shall constantly delight you. So, have courage. Trust, above all, that this is possible.

It is not the intention of your whole Self, nor of those who watch, to humiliate you or to leave you in darkness, or to leave you bereft of comfort, or beauty, or recognition. But it is a time for you to find out who you are and to realise your own self sufficiency. It is a time of preparation out of which you shall be re-born into your true and original nature.

Hearken carefully to what I say: you shall never find happiness in any relationship until first you be happy within yourself.

Prepare yourself. Seek a contemplative environment. Arrange your affairs. Live in a suitable environment, in harmony with yourself, which is conducive to ease in your life. If you need to be with people choose them carefully for their understanding, serenity and simplicity.

Along with this, affirm always the natural glory of nature, quietly, in the beauty around you; lend your energy to the maintaining of this beauty - yet without in any way tiring yourself, or having opinions about it.

Choose an environment where the people around you understand spontaneity, so that, when the urge comes upon you to withdraw and quietly sit, you may be able to do so without anxiety. Eat simple fresh foods straight from your garden. Exercise moderately in fresh air. Enjoy the sun and the sea, and particularly cultivate the art of walking regularly with awareness.

Live in equanimity. Observe the cat. Open yourself to your own stillness and surrender to your own inner grace and the softness of your own inner light and delight in the strength of your faith.

Become a contemplative person and make insight meditation a part of your life.

Insight meditation is to do with watching.

Make not of watching a chore, nor of meditating a rule or ritual. Be natural. Observe the hours that a cat does nothing but sit gazing.

Allow your self just to be there, allow your self to be watching without the slightest strain; allow the decision to sit come upon you, rather than you making the decision when to sit. And, when you watch, make no mental connection to that which is watched. Look without looking. Go deeply into your body and just be there.

Enter now into your own beautiful patience, as one who watches and waits.

It is time for the great preparation.

CHAPTER EIGHT

JOY

Joy is a feeling of aliveness and happiness. It is a most misunderstood feeling because human beings feel so guilty about feeling happy. There is an ingrained suspicion that happiness comes, inevitably, at the expense somewhere down the line, of a balancing bout of misery.

Yet, happiness, truly, is joy when it is not tied to the vacillating mood swings of cause and effect, when it is not, in other words, a result of ego reaction.

Little can be said of joy; so again I am trying to do the impossible; for joy is the very nature of God and who can say anything about God? A God to be read about in a book, to be preached about, to be theorised about, to be sacrificed to, to be prayed to, to be worshipped, is a God at arm's length: a very poor sort of God to have about! But a God to feel, to love, to have as friend, to experience within yourself as yourself: now, that's a God!

God is life. Your life. And life is the ultimate possibility because it contains all possibilities. Any words of so called authority upon the subject are doomed to failure. So one has to approach it by a roundabout way; and this is what self-realised teachers do when they undertake, by every trick in the book, to mirror back to you what it is without actually stating what it is or how it can be found.

Because, firstly, it cannot be found, only realised; and secondly, no one can state what it is anyway. It can only be felt - and it is you who have to do the feeling.

Feeling that it is a joy to be alive, actually feeling it, from moment to moment, is, indeed, such a joy. It is the realisation that you are a part of something infinitely greater than your self, but which at the same time is your self.

It is easy enough to agree with me that God is joy. It is easy enough to put on a knowing look and smile and say, "Yes, of course I know that God is joy, you are not telling me anything new," but, agreement, without experience, is to go to the bottom of the class. It gets you nowhere, except for feeding the ego. It is like agreeing that fresh rosy apples straight off the tree taste delicious without having ever tasted one.

There is a level at which neither you nor I can be fooled: your face, your body language, your aura, everything real about you, tell me if you are really experiencing joy or not. I don't mind for a moment if you fool me, but if you fool yourself it becomes a real tragedy.

Truly, love and joy are inseparable. God is love. But God is equally joy. One without the other is unthinkable.

That which calls itself love, if joy is not present, is not properly love but something else - perhaps duty, or obligation, or responsibility, or respect, or pity, but not love.

I cannot repeat enough times: joy and love are inseparable. Out of your very own essence (which is the nature of joy) you cannot but help be aware that love is. It is by the one that you know the other.

If you have ever had a moment of enlightenment, it wasn't when you were trying to be loving. It would be most likely when you had given up trying to do anything, including the exhausting attempts to hold everything together by trying to do the right thing.

In these glimpses, which happen without any doing of your own, you are overwhelmed and amazed at how loving you feel towards everyone you meet, and how loving the whole of creation is toward you.

During these times you are open to your whole self. The ego has momentarily disappeared. The Oneness is felt as the joyful reality that it is, in union with your personality. You cannot but help experience this as love and see love everywhere.

This understanding, that joy is of the essence and that joy is all, is to be the keynote of the age to come. From the recognition that joy and spirit are one and the same, will come a loosening of the bonds of guilt, and a replacing of these bonds by the harmonic rhythms of natural growth in a supportive environment of compassion and spontaneous celebration.

Now, here is something for you to say many times a day: "I am the life of the universe. I am the joy of the universe. I am the life of the world. I am the joy of the world. I am joy. I am joy. I am joy." You can say it softly to yourself or you can shout it out ecstatically it to the trees in the forest; you can whisper it to the stars at night; you can sing it, or you can sit in meditation and think it; you can dance it out in feeling; and, you can look in the mirror and say it to yourself.

When you sit in contemplation in nature, listen to every rock and stick and stone, to every flower and bird and blade of grass, and they will all be saying the very same thing as yourself.

Yes, we are God.

Yes, IAM. This I AM is as much *you* as it is me - as well as being every stick and stone, and bird, insect and alien flower in the whole amazing universe.

You are God, not because you are all powerful, not because you are all knowing and wise - and certainly not because you are deluded - but because you are of the identical substance (spirit) of which all *is*, all ever has been, and all ever will be.

The essence of your self is not in the least bit different, or in any way separate, from the grandest consciousness in the universe, and those of grand consciousness are those who are most sensitive to this fact.

In your personality you are unique. As an individual cosmic entity, known by the vibratory quality of your aura, you are also unique. You will remain for ever unique.

But in spirit, in essence, you are not unique, you are at one with the Oneness. The nature of your life, when viewed from spirit, when uncluttered by ego belief systems, and when freed from fear and thoughts of separation, is an amazingly simple, and peaceful, joyfulness.

Out of this peace arises love and joy, and out of love and knowledge arises wisdom and compassion, and the strength and courage to do all things.

Joy is particularly a quality of aliveness and a feeling of absolutely spontaneously celebrating aliveness. It is a resonance of the I AM within you to all your thoughts and feelings. I AM beautiful. I AM loving. I AM alive. I AM joy. I AM harmony. I AM peace.

It is a feeling of being alive and being present, in the moment, right now.

When you join with others in the recognition of your whole self and your spirit, the group acts like a magnifying glass, focusing spirit into an explosion of fire within all the entities present. Hence the Christ's observation: "When two or more are gathered in my name there I AM."

The ego-mind will have you running around looking for happiness, flitting like a butterfly from activity to activity. Soon you will be exhausted.

Now, there is nothing wrong in being like a butterfly: to be free, to keep moving, to keep tasting, to be spontaneous, living in the moment, it is a wondrous way to be.

If it comes from the mind, however, it will soon be exhausting and there will be the mood swings: the highs, the lows, the moments of creative genius, then the crashes into depression.

For joy to be there within you as a constant, it must come out of stillness. No hard work is involved. All that is needed is the willingness to stop the earnest mind which is forever thinking of what has to be done, and listen, for a moment, to those other feelings of yours which are trying to surface from underneath.

It takes a little practice. The mind, having made a separate ego for itself to deal with what it conceives to be the dangerous side of physical living, will not take kindly to interference in its (by now automatic and habitual) activities. The ego is not about to let spirit usurp (as it thinks of it) its place as master of your self.

It is useful to reassure your ego-mind that nothing dreadful is going to happen to it. It is not going to be forced to go away, or to abdicate its creative role; to lose its memory; to go mad, or be dissolved into empty space. It is just going to be still for a while.

If it feels under threat it will fight tooth and nail to stop you being still enough to feel your real feelings. So, reassure your mind that nothing is going to happen to it; that on the contrary, it is going to be immeasurably strengthened and fulfilled by allowing itself to be open to spirit.

This is what meditation is all about: the practice of being still so that you can get in touch with your whole Self.

Meditation, as I am proposing here, is not a way of life, though a part of your life it will become. It is a practice. It is a means to the discovery that you are life. It is a means to the discovery that you are joy, and love and peace - and that you are in harmony with All-That-Is. It is who you are.

And then you can get off your bum and be it!

When you have found the knack of living in the joy of your being, when your spirit and your ego have come to terms with each other, this kind of meditation in which you are endeavouring to be still in order to find out who you are will no longer be of such importance.

The other side of joy is peace. When in joy, you are in peace. From peace, joy arises.

Now, you are ready for contemplation.

Contemplation, as I have mentioned already, is the art of being present whilst you are watching all that is happening, inside you, and around you, without your mind pushing along any of its own pet fantasies or pet schemes that give it a feeling of satisfaction, or of worth based upon value judgement or opinions.

Contemplation *is* a way of life.

Beware of the spiritualised ego which fancies itself as being worthy of enlightenment. It will try and make meditation into a way of life. It will work really hard at meditating and keep meditating and meditating, thinking that it really is getting somewhere, but all that is really happening is that you are meditating your life away and getting a numb bum.

As always, the ego delights in taking hold of something that is vitally useful for you and making a meal out of it, and, in the process, completely and successfully obscuring the truth you are looking for.

Meditation, though, *is* important for you. It is a practical and useful discipline. At any time of the day, be still for a moment and recognise who you really are, then move out again and *be* who you really are. But don't let the ego make a big deal out of spiritual practice or you will end up being made a meal of by your ego.

Meditation is not hard work. It is just giving yourself time to be still. See to it daily. There can be no enlightenment without this smallest of disciplines. Is it so much to ask to be still a few times a day?

Joy does not arise within you out of any desire to be spiritual; it doesn't arise out of religious or shamanistic mania, or esoteric discipline; no person of spiritual dignity or authority, however pious and holy, can give you a secret key to joy by any so called transfer of power.

Those who make of life a heavy task of religious observances, who arrange around themselves a structure of authority, dignity and piety, mean well, but they are missing the simplicity of life which is in need of none of these. To be joyful is to be spiritual because that is the very essence of God. It is a very simple truth. The clutter of religion is all ego clutter which loves to feel important or worthy in some way or other.

The ego will work particularly hard at being humble which is when it feels most worthy of all!

In all this hard work and in all this knuckling down to the authority of religious doctrines and observances, life, and its simple spontaneous joyfulness becomes hopelessly lost and contaminated by beliefs which rob it of most of its precious love and joy and the peace which profound relaxation brings.

Perversely, and sadly, those of you who most long to be at one with the Christ, entrapped as you are in such religious straight jackets, are denying your own Christ within yourself, by adhering to these beliefs and allowing them to run your life for you.

Take the time to really feel how you would like to be if you were really free to be how you would like to be, then be it.

You are free. Have courage and take steps to be free.

Humans who work hard at religion are working hard at something that doesn't need to be worked at.

Can you work at being joyful? Have you ever been joyful when you tried hard to be? I suspect it turned out to be a real flop. You cannot plan joy in advance. Joy is not like a smile you can switch on and off when it suits you. How can you work hard to find something the very nature of which is neither in work nor as a result of work?

It is not possible. No, it is not possible. Joy arises when there is surrender to what is there. It arises out of nowhere that you can pin point. It is a child of spontaneity and arises, not from trying, or, from discipline, but from relaxing, from letting go of trying, of letting go of trying to be this or trying to be that, and letting go from trying to do it this way or that way.

Don't be afraid that in relaxing your disciplines you are going to get lost in a sea of emotion or that you are going to become a raging maniac.

In meditation, stillness creeps up on you. You begin to be aware of peace within you. Your spirit, being in harmony with the Oneness, has an awareness of its own. It is not going to hurt you, neither is it going to hurt anyone else.

In contemplation peace is there, full stop.

Do trust this. You are going to feel very much more peaceful and you are, at moments, going to be capable of feeling intensely alive. And remember, you always have your observer which monitors, in a flash, faster than thought, your mind, which can instruct it to respond appropriately to any situation that might occur.

It is true that others around you, having a vested interest in you remaining how you always have been, for the sake of their comfortable status quo, may begin to get a little upset. This is their problem. It is not yours. You have not caused it. They are hurting themselves by not accepting your need to change.

In these cases, be compassionate but don't try and do anything to take away their hurt for them. They won't want to stay in their hurt for very long. Who does?

If you attempt to alleviate their pain, you will most likely fall into the old habit of trying to make things all right, and, whilst there is nothing intrinsically wrong in this, it is not useful if the main impulse for making things right for others comes from the desire not to be hurt oneself. This is an old pattern of the human ego. It loves to pander to the egos of others.

It may be best to remove yourself from their influence for a while in order to crystallise, as it were, this new realisation within yourself, and your new commitment to the unusual experience of living for the joy of being.

The well known phrase: "A prophet in his own country...etc" is very appropriate to this situation. You should never be afraid of leaving those who have supported you, spiritually or otherwise, in order to move into the independence of your own being. Love is not lost, and neither can entities be lost. Physical plane separateness does seem so real, but it is the greatest of illusions. Your need to be your whole self is paramount.

Pursue this goal for yourself ruthlessly - that is to say: with compassion, but with single minded determination. Letting go of ties is setting them free, as well.

When you weave around yourself an intricate structure of strong moral beliefs which, through thick and thin, you are determined to live by, you probably feel that it is a very solid, upright, thing to do. It may give you a sense of belonging. It may give you a sense of identity. But it will not allow you to be open to your spirit except at those rare times when, possibly at a crisis in your life, you let the ego's defences relax. You, then, find yourself being shaken to your core by what you may well interpret as a religious experience (associating it with the beliefs of your church).

If you cannot find your own Christ within your self how much less are you going to recognise it in another ? The fact is, you won't, and this is the tragedy upon relying on a religion to lead you to the heart of the Christ. Religions fixate on an image. But the Christ is not an image, and neither are you. The Christ, so called, is outside of all religions. Therefore, to focus on any particular religion, including Christianity, as being the door, is to look in the wrong place. True, the Christ embraces all religions, but this great energy embraces everything. And I mean everything - even to the most deluded of satanic cults - even to every impersonal atom in the solar system. So, by focusing on a part, you are being too narrow. It should be obvious that a narrow minded person, focused on a part, cannot hope to become self-realised when the outcome of realisation is that everything is part of The Whole.

How much better to rely upon yourself. How much better to allow joy to be your compass, rather than your settled religious beliefs, to guide your way home.

The peace that "passeth all understanding" is not something that is beyond you, attainable only by Christ. It is merely that *understanding*, per se, (being of the mind) is of a lower vibrational frequency than peace. Peace, like joy, is also a quality of divinity prior to mind. Out of peace joy arises when the moment calls for joy. Our message for this age is that joy be honoured. When joy is truly honoured, the conditioned ego has a hard time maintaining its defences and its denial. Joy is both very stimulating and destructive to the ego. It is confronting to the ego. It brings buried emotion to the surface very quickly and, when real joy is present, emotion is discharged easily. Then, harmony results through the whole organism.

This is the bringing about of harmony through conflict. Laughter is the end of karma. The laughter of *insight* is the end of fear.

Where the will-to-good is present, conflict will result in harmony. Be assured, however, that the will-to-good is not a mind ego-driven desire to do good, rather it is a decision to live uncompromisingly to your spirit and the joy of your being. In other words you don't go about causing conflict just to stir up people in order to heal them. But you do look within your self to the cause of conflict and bring harmony to your self, allowing others the freedom to do the same.

Many of you will know that harmony is seen in the aura as a radiant apple green colour. It is the Ray colour of the Fourth Ray and is strongly influencing this world at present.

Peace will come to this planet - and to each individual - when joy is firmly established in the hearts and minds of men and women as being a divine quality worthy of acceptance in their everyday life.

I promise you that peace will one day come to this world. And every individual will experience it. This planet is not destined to be one of those that on the surface seems peaceful, yet, the inhabitants remain frustrated and dissatisfied.

A peace that is imposed on entities from without by government, or by well meaning social engineering, is a joyless peace. It will eventually wither the spirit - or, better put, it withers the will so that it can no longer access spirit. Such a civilisation is going nowhere but into a quiet well ordered grave. Some worlds have taken this path. They can learn from you, and will do so. Sometimes a blockbuster of a shake-up is needed in such a situation so that life can move again. So, you can see that conflict, from the soul's point of view, need not be negative. It goes without saying that, of course, we all abhor the pain of conflict. But if it has to occur, it has to occur. It is, we know, always a stepping stone on the way to a vibrant joyful peace, which goes together with an understanding of who we are and our place in the scheme of things.

I must remind you that there are two basic discoveries to be made by everyone. They are both to do with who you are.

You have to find out who you are *twice*! Firstly, you have to know, without any doubt, that you are an aspect of God and that in essence you are not in one iota different from the essence of The Oneness and everything in it. This is who you are, fundamentally.

Secondly, you will discover who you are in terms of your role in the planetary, or solar, scheme of things. This is who you are from your whole Self's perspective. It is the role your whole Self has accepted to play in the universe, for the moment.

To imagine what the role of your whole Self might be without recognising experientially that, fundamentally, you are the same in essence as everything in The Oneness, can lead to amazing arrogance which can give rise to grandiose fantasies and unleash demonic and destructive forces upon the world. Many dictators and religious leaders have fallen into this trap.

This is why, first off, it is important to know who you fundamentally.

On the other hand, dreaming away your life, believing in The Oneness without having actually experienced it, gives rise to benevolent harmlessness. This is the conditioned ego's ploy to accrue good things to itself by pretending to be The Oneness or to have experienced The Oneness when it has done nothing of the sort. It avoids any confrontation, which might unmask its hypocrisy, by a show of piety.

Harmlessness is a most divine quality. Yet, it may not lead to much personal satisfaction in your life or be of any great service to the world unless it arises out of your truth. The dream of union with The Oneness must end and the actual experience take its place.

This is why so many teachers say that the greatest question of all is to ask yourself: WHO AM I? And so it is.

So, first find out who you are fundamentally. Then find out your role. One will lead to the other very naturally, without you doing anything about it, anyway.

Of course, there comes a point when all searching has to drop. The very search will one day become an obstacle to self-realisation. But, don't anticipate this. You will know it when it comes. So, don't stop searching before the searching ends. For, indeed, it will end. And it will not be you who ends it. It will be the end of hope and the end of you regarding anything as an end. The search creates the environment for the end to arrive.

Do not despise disciples or the journey that disciples undertake. They are on their way, just as you are on your own journey. Remember that Jesus said: "Knock on the door and it shall be opened unto you." He was correct.

A peace that each entity finds for itself, which comes from within, is a peace that starts from inside and moves outside, embracing all, loving all, and *enjoying* all.

I can never stress enough that to live in the joy of your being is to own the vibrational frequency of who you are. It is as simple as that. There is nothing more you need do than to live every moment honouring the vibrational frequency that is yours to own. All else shall follow.

When I say that joy is the key to self discovery I am not speaking of a joy that necessarily expresses itself as constant joviality, dancing all day, hugging everyone in sight and laughing outrageously at the slightest thing. This happens when it happens, especially amongst those who carry a strong yang life energy. But there is another aspect to joy which people who express the yin polarity will feel more at ease with: it is a feeling of connectedness, a feeling of calm strength, and peace.

These are the two faces of joy. Both of them have as their main characteristic an intense sense of being at one with life and being vitally alive. Both these faces of joy are always within you whichever cosmic polarity you happen to be expressing at the time.

The self-realised person can be at peace within and dancing without, or be dancing within and calm without. It is no matter. All is one.

So much ritual, dogma, structure, organization, and such a welter of called sacred beliefs, have contributed to the clutter of the search for truth that the whole boat is in danger of sinking.

All the established world religions of today are anti life; they do little more than perpetuate the myth that their priests have some sort of special link with God that no one else has.

The sad fact of the matter is that sincere men and women live according to a set of beliefs interpreted by priests instead of being encouraged to trust in their own sense of love and joy. Any unusual display of independent aliveness is treated with suspicion. No one is encouraged to explore and honour their *own* feelings or create their *own* reality or live uncompromisingly to their *own* spirit and none other.

To a greater or lesser degree, all religions in the world are repressive rather than liberating, of the human spirit.

And here, with these words of mine, is yet another book being written about spiritual matters. More clutter for the mind to latch on to!

If this book is ever considered to be special, or a definitive treatise on joy - or the words of the planetary logos, it will have failed in its message. It will have become a millstone round the neck of you the reader. So be awake!

Look to your own uncharted territory, within yourself, for that is the only place you will find speciality. It is the only place you will find God's teachings and they are very specially yours and yours only. You have your own map to get to joy. Is that not something! Does that not make you feel special! Does that not make you feel powerful! Does that not make you feel free! Well, it should!

No one - no priest, no bishop, no saint, no Christ - has ever trod your path, and no one ever will. It is your territory. It is your map. It is your experience. It is your life. You have a niche which was created specially for you and no other. It is yours to celebrate. It always has been and always will be unique to you.

It is for you to find the one and only original you.

At the moment of self realisation you will, indeed, realise that all is one, and you are at one with the One as the One.

When this happens you still remain you. Your personality with its outer expression remains the vehicle through which the sweetness of your truth touches the world from now on.

Embraced by this sweetness (which may, on occasion, even have a fierce face) you will be faithful to your own unique expression and place in the universe.

Your truth doesn't depend on how others behave towards you, and neither does it depend on whether or not they live up to your expectations. It can never depend on whether or not they support you or co-operate with you in your latest scheme.

It may seem hard when those expectations, for support or cooperation from those close to you, are not met. Nonetheless, the joy of your being is dependent on none of it.

Joy doesn't depend on external factors such as what you do, or what others are doing. It arises, rather, from your deep trust in your own natural life impulses and a trust in your own rhythms. It arises out of your freedom to be assertive, or withdrawn, or contemplative when you wish to be, rather than being forced into these positions by external pressures due to your own lack of confidence and lack of self awareness.

It arises out of your loving acceptance which allows others the right to be as they wish to be, accepting them as they are right at this very moment.

Accepting people as they are doesn't mean you have to agree with their ideas.

It does mean you accept their right to be treading their own path, to be learning their own life's lessons and experiencing for themselves the results of their own thought processes in their very own way, which is perfectly right for them to be doing; which means you hold off from worrying (and showing it).

Worrying about others is a pernicious form of ego activity, which, from the worrier's point of view, goes under the more acceptable term "compassion". But, worrying about others is not compassion. It is anxiety at its most stressful. And behind anxiety is the double headed dragon of pride and fear: pride, because you think you know best and fear because you are afraid of letting go your role as the great helper - behind which is your fear of losing the love of the one you care for, fear of doing the wrong thing, and fear of being alone.

Whenever you worry about anything or anybody, you are identifying with your manipulative ego. It has wrapped you up in its woolly clouds of illusion and absolutely no amount of convincing yourself that you are really being compassionate or considerate is going to fool yourself or others in the long run. Your body language, your face and your aura, say it all.

When all the well meaning worriers in the world get together and have a mighty good grizzle together, it will occur to them how ridiculous they look. Then maybe they'll start laughing. What a day that will be!

Whenever you condemn someone for (as you see it) wrong behaviour you are actually saying to that person: "I don't like you because of what you are *doing*". All your attention is on what the other person is *doing*. You are not seeing the magnificent entity (the being) behind the doing. If you were, whatever that entity did to you or did to someone else, nothing could topple you from your centre of equanimity.

Whenever, in your mind, you focus only on a person's actions, it all becomes a murky business because you have lost your clear sight of the causal entity that stands behind its experiences. You identify instead with the transitory nature of those experiences. All you see is a general mish-mash of cause and effect to which you react with confused horror. And if you refuse to accept your own responsibility for your refusal to see clearly, then you are most liable to project this onto the outside world as worry for the other person.

Worriers dig deep and subtle holes for themselves, refusing tooth and claw to accept they have any problem to look at. The ego is very satisfied with its ploy of being seemingly compassionate and involved in another's welfare: it takes the heat off itself, so to speak.

Whenever you judge another's actions by giving them anxious worried looks (even if you are doing your best to hide them), you are not seeing matters clearly, and the result of this is that in your mind you are separating yourself from that person, creating a gap across which it will be difficult for real communication to happen.

If, on the other hand, you say words to the effect: "I see that you are a beautiful entity, but the way you are going about things fills me with horror"; this is clear and it is honest; it allows freedom to be there, and respect for freedom to be there. The other will feel that you really do care, and they will always remember that there is one person in the world they can turn to who is honest and compassionate and can see clearly.

When this happens, there is no separation between you and the other. There is, in fact, agreement: you are agreeing to disagree and, more importantly, there is now a link between you both, and, who knows, there is always the chance you may one day walk arm in arm.

When there is clear sight and recognition of the transitory nature of all experience, then what people do will not in itself lead to separateness. What people do will be seen merely as activity in which men and women (entities) indulge themselves in order to test and reflect back to themselves their own reality at the physical level.

To a self-realised person it isn't what is done that gives rise to joy; it isn't even *how* it is done.

Pure joy contains an awareness that nothing deeply truly matters, and nothing needs to be done, because everything is already perfect just as it is.

On the other hand, there is no joy unless you also accept yourself to be naturally yourself and do naturally what you would like to do. Naturally, you are a human being. Human beings are creative beings. It is natural, therefore, for you to be creative. It is natural for you to use your creativity as a means by which to test out and experience your present reality.

It would be unnatural, therefore, just because you read in a book that it doesn't matter what you do, to get stuck with the idea in your head that you are never going to do anything ever again; thereafter, living the life of a passive sloth.

So, we seem to have a paradox here: it is not what is done - or the doing of it - that is the key to self-realisation, yet neither is it natural, or useful, to do nothing. The real key to this is: that it is important not to do nothing, but it is not important if anything is done.

Do ponder deeply on this paradox. If you at least take on trust the illusion of separateness, you will see what an amazingly liberated statement this is. Take heed.

It is now up to you. What is it you really want? What is your deepest urge, your deepest desire? What do you really want to create around you? If you were free to do anything you wanted to do what would you do? Do you want to paint a masterpiece? Do you want to become a political leader and feel the power in that experience? Do you want to care for people who you consider to be less fortunate than you? Do you want to go on a spiritual search? Do you want to create a happy home for your family? Do you want heaps of money? Do you want a beautiful and eternally fascinating woman to be married to? Do you want to be a wise guru? Do you want to dissolve into the Oneness?

All these desires are fine. Any one of them is your true path if the desire is truly your desire. None of these desires are greater or lesser than any other. It is *you* experiencing what *you* really want to experience - that is, if it is truly your desire.

Ego comes in to muddy the waters when desires get mixed up with other desires. In other words, your truest desire might be to find a beautiful woman and get married and experience the adventure of married life on the physical plane with such a partner. But, then, you hear of a guru and a part of you begins to think how nice it would be to be with a guru and become self-realised; so now you are confused and don't know what to do. You have lost sight of your deepest wish, and, try as you might, being with a guru doesn't seem to be very satisfying. So, maybe, you try being the guru instead. But, of course, being a guru, now you have no one to turn to for help because you think to yourself that gurus should be beyond the need for being helped, so things go from bad to worse and you are in a big hole.

On the other hand, your deepest desire might well be to be a guru, but if you get side tracked into marrying a beautiful woman, again your clash of desires will dig you into a hole.

Everyone has a life plan. It is the plan that your cosmic self (whole Self) has for you. This plan shows itself to you by the strength of your desire to do whatever it is that you really want to do. No life plan has any more merit in it than another. The question is: have you embraced the life plan that you planned to have when you came here or have you become side tracked and chosen another. When you choose the plan you planned to have, you are opening out to spirit; this is growth. This is spiritual advancement. The alternative is a wasted opportunity.

By avoiding the experience of your life plan you will probably have to have another adventure with it at another time.

Do not avoid looking at your desires in the belief that desire is a sin. On the contrary, your strongest deepest desires are a signal for you to look at them and acknowledge them. They are like flags on a distant hill waving in the wind for you to go and put your hand to. Desires which come from the conditioned ego can also wave quite strongly in the wind but they do not have behind them the same deep strength, the same sense of exuberance, of expansiveness, of enthusiasm, of commitment, which the desires of your true life plan have. Take the time in meditative stillness to feel out the difference and then go for the desire of your life.

Your truest desire is God's message to you from within yourself and it is the key to your path. If in doubt, put your choice to the test of the enthusiasm you feel when thinking about the desire. Enthusiasm and joy are close partners. The very word enthusiasm comes from the Greek, meaning *with spirit* or *in God*. When choices have to be made in life, let joy be your compass. You cannot go wrong.

No one can tell you what your life plan is. Don't go round looking for other people to tell you what it is. Just have the confidence to sit still for a moment, gather yourself together, trust your feelings and go into the joy of your being.

Remember, also, to live in the moment. Your desires can change. The nature of desires is that they can change. They can change very fast, so just try holding on to your hat, and take a courageous dive into life. Just try it!

Not only will you be taking your life positively into your own hands, but you will know that you are creating your own reality (your own outward reality) rather than believing you are at the mercy of some fate outside your control.

In fact, nothing you are presently experiencing is the result of another's will unless you allow it to be so; and, if you allow it to be so, then it is your will that is doing the allowing. Consciously, or unconsciously, you are always responsible for the situation you find yourself in right now.

There is no fate or destiny capable of taking you away from your connectedness with spirit. Nothing can take you away from joy unless you give it permission to do so.

If it is your deepest desire to do nothing, then do nothing and do it to the very best of your ability; but make sure it really is your truest desire. Doing nothing out of the conditioned ego comes from a lack of confidence, a fear of being hurt, or a fear of being unmasked or becoming vulnerable or whatever.

Doing nothing *positively* becomes contemplation. It is a most positive action. It is *doing* without the ego being present and without attachment to results. From the outside it appears that nothing is being done, yet from the point of view of the cosmic entity much is being done. It is great doing!

The Hindu religion comes close to recognising joy as a divine quality when it says that the universe is *lila*, or play.

Some people play games seriously and others play them light heartedly. Whatever seems appropriate at the time is, of course, the appropriate choice of behaviour. It is not wrong to be serious but neither is it wrong to be playful or light hearted. Humanity has over balanced on to the side of seriousness because ego has a vested interest in keeping matters subdued and weighty lest they get out of control or beyond its understanding.

However, over-seriousness, behind which is a desire to see a course of action realised to the satisfaction of the ego, carries the seeds of worry and anxiety in it.

It is not in the nature of the cosmic entity to be worried about anything. It never has had and never will have anything to worry about. It is not interested in results. It is interested in experience and reality. Experience can be profound but it needn't be a serious matter.

I would like you to know that your ego can get great mileage out of mood swinging. It can go from playfulness to seriousness, from suffering to happiness, from deprivation to satisfaction, and so on; but your realised

Self exists ever in a state of grace, being that of profound peace and joy, and love.

Playfulness is, in a very real way, a quality of (for want of a better word) the Godhead. It is a quality of being. It embraces laughter, mischief and a light heart. It recognises that all is a game, *lila*.

The important thing to remember is that the game soon loses its fun if the fact that the game is a game is lost sight of. When players of a game lose sight of this simple fact, their behaviour becomes seriously compulsive. The game may take a few nasty turns outside their control!

This feeling that the game is getting out of control is due to you hanging on to an *idea* of how you want the game to end. Probably with you as the winner! These desires get you so entangled in the game that you begin to put value judgements on the game and on the results of the game, rather than just being in the experience of the game. You lose your relationship to the game as both its creator and impartial participator - plus your sense of fun and well being.

A person who finds it difficult to let go into play and laughter, yet who fancies themselves, perhaps, as a deeply spiritual person, will find, at the end of the weary trail of dutiful love and religious practices, a cliff with a seemingly bottomless abyss over which they have, apparently, no choice but, in an agony of frustration and loneliness, to fall into.

This psychological state of affairs, this so called abyss, this dark night of the soul, means a point has been reached where all has been tried, and all has been attempted, but nothing appears to have any meaning anymore.

To the personality this apparent meaninglessness is the dark abyss. To the higher self all is well. It is merely the conditioned ego that is fighting for its spurious life. It teeters at the edge. There is no more any hope. It feels it is falling into a bottomless pit of hopelessness which is a final end to everything. It is correct. It is an end to the conditioned ego.

Playfulness has no meaning. Joy has no meaning. To those of you who find it difficult to play, the dark night of the soul may one day catch up with you. You will create it for yourself. For those of you who can play there need be no dark night. Not ever.

Only egos believe that abysses exist. Only egos are afraid of meaninglessness. Only egos are afraid of dying; and, whilst any of these unconscious fears are still there, of course they have to be met in order to show the personality that there is nothing to fear after all. In other words, whatever you (the ego) fear, will, one day, be drawn to you so that you can pierce the illusion, unmask the mask that your ego has put on, and blow away the fog that stops you from seeing who you are.

Whatever you fear is also what fascinates you. You will be alternately drawn to it and repelled by it, until, one day, it holds no more entanglement for you and you see it clearly for what it is, neither rejecting it nor being lured by it into its illusions, either consciously or unconsciously.

The ego creates a spurious role (a mask) for itself by thinking in a certain way. Thinking about yourself in a certain role strengthens you in acting out that role. Your thinking reinforces your role and your actions in your role reinforce your thinking.

The result of this is a personality that may bear little relationship to your whole self. The ego sets itself hard into its role like a mask, covering the real self, and the mask seems to be real. The work to be done is to crack open the mask and let in the light. Sometimes a good shaking is the answer.

The light is there behind the mask, just waiting for the ego to surrender. And this is what happens when the ego finally confronts its fears of annihilation at the abyss of its own making.

The mind lets go of its defences and its false identity, the soft warm light floods in and all is well. All is seen and felt to be One. The vibratory note of the self, now at one with All-That-Is, is both joy and peace, and love is experienced as being all that there is underneath all outer distractions. Death and meaninglessness hold no more fear. Play and laughter, and sensitivity, reign supreme.

Standing before the dark tunnel, no light is seen. After the tunnel, the searcher no longer strives towards the light. He or she *is* the light. She or he relaxes. There is total acceptance. All resistance drops away. There is no longer any desire to alter that which has no desire to be altered.

A new state of being has arisen in which there is grace and balance, and a naturalness like the naturalness of a bird singing its own song from which all distortions have been eliminated.

The world needs to understand that joy is not only an acceptable feeling but it is a feeling that is the very nature of God. As the world as a whole enters a finer vibration, joy must now take its place in the affairs of mankind.

When joy is permitted to enter the consciousness of mankind through enlightened individuals, and through groups of enlightened individuals, it will have an amazing quickening effect on the whole. All that is not of that vibration will shatter which will cause all that is of the old to fall away.

Joy is of the very essence of *being*. It is role-less. When you have no vested interest, or compulsion, when you are not being driven by some addictive idea about keeping up your role, joy arises within you so very naturally.

Right now you can send your self some kind thoughts, telling your self that it's all right to be joyful.

Repeat this many times a day and before you go to sleep at night. Your conditioned ego will begin to dissolve. You will allow meaninglessness to be more acceptable. Gradually, you will begin to feel the joy of your being and trust it. This will bring a turn about in your life: thinking about joy will open the door to accepting it as a valid and useful part of your life, and your actions will reinforce your determination to trust it.

You are changing your belief systems. You are recreating your own reality. You are bringing light into the fog. And you are doing all this without threatening, over-much, the vulnerable ego - and without needing to face a dark night.

A dark night of the soul is merely the ego's reluctance to accept meaningless as a possibility within the Oneness. This does not mean you will live aimlessly without meaning. It means that you accept that all possibilities are possible within the whole, including meaningless.

Accepting meaningless removes from all achievement, from all doing, the underlying ego charge of expectations which puts such stress into your activities. *It is not so much a question of there being no meaning in life but of you being attached to the fact that there either must be meaning or there might not be meaning.*

Of course, your life has a meaning, and all you do has a meaning. But being attached to that meaning is another matter altogether. The paradox is that all that you do has a meaning but, in truth, none of it matters.

Within this statement are the ingredients for the dark night. Yet, when the paradox is accepted, when all the concepts around it are released, the dark night is never again a reality.

Remember, it's not necessary to give yourself a hard time, and don't give others a hard time. Affirm the joy in your being and tell yourself a hundred times a day, I AM JOY. I AM JOY. I AM JOY. Say it and really believe it. It is a great mantra, because it happens to be true. It is the greatest mantra in the universe - and it works!

Here is a song:

I AM JOY

1. Singing, singing, singing all the day, singing all the day, singing all the day.

    It can't be cloudy if you're singing all the way, singing all the way, with me.

    I am the joy in the heart of the winter, in the heart of the summer, in the heart of the spring.

    I am the joy in the heart of all nature, I'm in every colour. That's why I sing!

2. Flying, flying, flying all the day, flying all the day, flying all the day.

    It can't be cloudy if you're flying all the way, flying all the way, with me.

    I am the joy in the heart of the oceans, I swing through the trees,

    I soar through the sky.

    I am the joy in the roll of the thunder, I fall with the lightening.

    I know how to fly!

3. Dancing, dancing, dancing all the day, dancing all the day, dancing all the day.

    It can't be cloudy if you're dancing all the way, dancing all the way with me.

    I am the joy in the heart of the mountains, I dip in the creeks and leap through the plants,

    I am the joy in the heart of a tiger and I love every mouse.

    That's why I dance!

4. Playing, playing, playing all the day, playing all the day, playing all the day.

    It can't be cloudy if you're playing all the way, playing all the way with me.

    I am the joy in the heart of creation, at one with the night as well as the day.

    I am the joy in death and hereafter, love, life and laughter.

    That's why I play!

142

CHAPTER NINE

EVIL AND SUFFERING

Evil is an idea manufactured by the ego to justify to itself the hurt and suffering which causes it pain and opens it up to fear. Evil only appears to exist on those levels where distorted mind (the ego) can make for itself a separate identity and believe that it is separate from God.

The consequence of this alienation, whether deliberate or from ignorance, is suffering.

In all the countless levels of experience in the universe, only on those of dense vibration, as on this physical plane, can the mind make for itself such a false identity, surrounding it with such protective devices that the soft warm radiance of the eternal light nourishes it not.

Evil is not opposite to good. Good is the nature of God and comprises the whole. Evil is merely an idea thought up by ego. It has no reality as such. Suffering has a reality. And there is, indeed, much suffering on Earth.

There is only suffering on the physical and lower astral levels in the universe.

Religions on Earth have made a big song and dance about evil but, as you can see, when looked at in its proper context, it is merely an anomaly of ego which occurs as a result of the friction between spirit and form on the physical plane, which makes up a minuscule (yet no less important) part of the universe. There are as many non material levels of existence in the universe as there are stars in the sky.

There is no evil or satanic force which is malevolently and intelligently, on a grand scale, in opposition to God's will except for those sadly deluded individuals who deliberately set themselves apart from The Oneness on the physical plane and on those astral levels close to it. They seek for themselves transitory powers.

Whether it be from resentment or from rebelliousness, it is always, fundamentally, from fear itself that they behave thus. They are terrified of relinquishing their desperate egos. These can egos only exist on the material and lower astral planes of this universe. Their influence is only limited to these planes and they are terrified of surrendering any influence that they do have. Anyone so frightened is to be pitied, not feared.

These egos shrink from contact with spirit. They occlude (hide) the joy of their being (even, on occasion justifying it by calling it *occult*). These entities can easily be felt by their cold logic, by their lack of compassion, and by their lack of genuine humour when confronted with a situation which is out of their control.

These sad and lonely egos are not evil; they are merely ignorant. The masks of their egos have set hard due to their fixated mind-set. They are not opposing God's will because God is the Oneness, and within the Oneness the will of God is supreme, being the only true will there is. They are like the fly on the wall of your kitchen, believing it is the master of the house.

So accepting is the Oneness, that it even accepts the possibility of ignorance of Itself being ignorant of Itself, and all the suffering that arises out of that ignorance.

There is nothing outside the aura of The Oneness so there are no outside forces of evil. The only thing that imagines it is set apart from the Oneness is the ego mind that fabricates for itself a false identity.

The false identities that so distort your life on the physical planes are like hail stones which fall out of the sky on a summer's day. They hit the earth with a cold sharp impact but are short lived and soon dissolve back into the elements from which they came. It is the same with ignorance or resistance. It cannot last. The energy to sustain it becomes too great. When faced by the light, over a period of time - which can be instant or prolonged - the conditioned ego self-destructs, returning all its elements to the light.

Evil, therefore, is an idea which is man made to serve man's vision of how there comes to be suffering in the world. Believing in evil takes the heat off the ego from assuming responsibility for its suffering.

From now on we will discuss this question of suffering which is of profound importance. Laughter is, indeed, the reality standing behind suffering, but suffering itself is not a laughing matter. It is a painful reality, but it needn't be the reality you have to choose. You have the power at any moment to change your reality from one of mental and emotional anguish to that of joy and peace. This will flow through to the physical body amazingly fast.

Physical body damage can cause the most excruciating pain but even this does not have to be tolerated unless you so will it to be.

Physical pain is a direct result of you being unaware of the nature of The Oneness while being in a physical body, either in this life or from a past life time. This has given rise to disharmony, and expresses itself as physical disharmony on this physical plane of demonstration.

When the ego dissolves, when the personality is illuminated by the clear light of spirit and full awareness is achieved, balance is restored to the whole organism; all frustration, mental, emotional and physical, ceases.

Around your physical body you have a highly charged energy body: your etheric body. It is the blue print for your physical body. Within its electrical matrix it contains a true knowledge of the perfect design for your body. For however long you live, and however disabled you become, your etheric body still holds for you its perfect design for a perfect body.

This you can access to renew and regenerate your body. There is no physical ailment and no disease that cannot be cured. The perfection in your etheric body guarantees it.

As ever, the great work to be done is to bring to your awareness that which you have previously been unaware of, lying beneath the threshold of your consciousness.

However, *a holistic approach is needed.* It is not enough just to do emotional discharge work. It is not sufficient just to go on a nutritional programme. It is not enough just to alter your beliefs by doing affirmations. It is not enough just to embrace a so-called spiritual life and meditate for prolonged periods. None of these in isolation, though they may help, will bring you freedom from disease. Your physical body is a part of the whole. Indeed, the whole of you, together with your body, is a microcosm of the macrocosm. For healing to occur, the whole must be harnessed. Hence, the holistic approach, embracing all the above modalities, is essential (being of the will of spirit) for healing to happen.

When the physical body is *correctly mineralised*, when the electrolytes in the body are balanced (through correct nutrition)- being hydrated with pure water - the electrical energy within the body itself (being the *kundalini or God's energy*) will move to do its healing work, reasserting the perfection of its design when, and only when, there is an accompanying inner or outer emotional discharge from the patient which both verbalises and brings to full awareness in the mind the original cause of the trauma, at the same time as dissolving and taking full responsibility for the belief that caused the disharmony in the first place.

When this individual work is done within a group of people of good will and skill, regeneration and healing will occur. I repeat, regeneration and healing *will occur in every case.*

It is certainly true that you can become self-realised within a diseased or wasted body. Many have, and they have had to deal with considerable physical pain which has severely limited their ability to function in the physical world.

However, would you not prefer to have both your cake and eat it: to be both self-realised *and* to have a perfect physical vehicle? Of course, you would. And, you can!

Suffering is the result of the misuse of creative power. It is often exacerbated by the disregard (non-acceptance) of the ethical or moral laws of the society which the entity is currently living in.

Misuse of power is the use of force to achieve your aims, either at the expense of your own body (mind and feelings) or that of another's.

The ego cannot see clearly; it always desires to change matters according to its limited vision. The force it uses is ego force. This energy does not arise from unconditional love, and, as such, does not have the infinite capacity of limitless energy from which to renew itself. It must sustain itself more and more from the material world and, in so doing, it cements itself into its limitations ever more deeply.

As you can see, this progression is eventually self defeating. It ends, either - in a few very rare cases - in the total destruction of the whole personality, returning all the elements to the Oneness, or, as is the rule, in the timely dissolving of the conditioned ego, allowing spirit to illuminate the personality, thus uniting the personality with its cosmic entity (its whole self).

Ego force is not a natural power; it is a manufactured force held together by a strong idea about the rights and wrongs of life and, as such, is inevitably expressed through a personality in conflict with itself.

This results in mental and physical disease.

Disease is a violence done to the personality self by the unaware thoughts and acts of its own conditioned ego. In the ego's refusal to wish to accept responsibility for its own acts of self violence, it connives with other like minded egos to shift the blame to outside causes, and thus you have a fruitful environment through which spread the diseases which so proliferate in the world as epidemics.

As a force manufactured by ignorant minds, the ability to use this force for disharmony is severely limited to the environment in which these egos dwell and have their creative influence, yet it is, nonetheless, a potent force in this reality.

Many egos which think alike reinforce the manufactured thought which thus takes upon itself an increased vitality and power. The power in a thought can only be diminished by those responsible for thinking it, and in this they can be helped by those of compassion who are prepared to confront these thoughts, fearlessly, with the gentle power of their love and spiritual integrity.

This is the work of the teachers of compassion who enter the arena of suffering: they confront those who are suffering with the sufferer's own thoughts in order to show him or her that it is the conditioned ego that is entirely responsible.

The confronting of these thought forms manufactured by ego is the responsibility of all those of you who would be world servers.

It is spiritual truth united with a desire-less mind which brings forth a cosmic entity into manifestation on Earth. This is true for everyone; thus everyone is a potential world server.

There comes a point, when all has been done that can be done to eliminate the ego. At this point, rededicate yourself to service as a world server and the ego will finally disappear as if it had never been. You will forget about your preoccupation with the ego (being the ego's preoccupation with itself) and light will flood into your being where before all was confusion.

To do this requires utter commitment to God's work and nought else. The service of confronting the thought forms of the world's massive human ego and the releasing of the imprisoned life of the world is of great service. Social service to the needs of personalities is useful but not comparable.

If you would dissolve your own ego look to your service as a releaser of life in the world, trusting that every word you utter and every thought you think is God's word and thought.

This is the key to freedom and the dissolving of your own ego.

The dissolution of your physical body - what is called "death" - is of little account compared to the confronting of the illusory thoughts of ego on the physical plane.

The confronting of illusion with a calm loving mind is the task of all entities who live on the physical plane.

Fear not physical death. It is merely the shedding of an outer garment - and a very limiting one at that. Better, by far, to stand firm to your own principles and die rather than submit to your own contamination by a repressive force or a repressive idea, living, thereafter in a murky frustrated compromise

Do not pander to those who would organise you or socially engineer you at the expense of your own inner light, your spontaneity and the joy of your being.

Stand against repression but do not fight aggressively for the downfall of illusion else you lend it credence, justifying its existence and giving it energy to continue fighting you.

The answer lies, not in the destruction by you of egos or their thoughts or systems of beliefs, but in the encouragement, and stimulation, by you, for each person to take responsibility for his or her own thoughts so that they see the merit in dissolving them by him or herself.

It is only the conditioned ego that fights for a cause or desires to wipe out what it sees as obstacles to happiness. Do not fall into this trap. There is much truth in the saying, "It takes two to make a fight".

Whenever egos oppose each other, they both think they are in the right. The massed egos of warring nations even have their war machines blessed by their respective priests. It is the height of delusion to imagine that God has favourites.

The illumined mind, at one with truth, has not the slightest interest in being right. It sees the suffering of others as needless, and gently and lovingly points out that this is so. Joy is its reality and joy, therefore, is its teaching.

The illumined mind is not interested in *trying* to be joyful. It has no need to try. Whenever you are trying to do anything - especially if it has become a compulsive - the chances are you are covering up some movement of energy within you that you are afraid of looking at.

The self-aware entity is an expression of joy. It actually cannot teach joy; the teaching comes in being close to the aura of such a one and allowing yourself to become infected by the desire also to melt into the Oneness and the Oneness to melt into you.

Don't try to be something that you are not. Don't try to be joyful when you don't feel it. This seems such an obvious thing to say but humans become so addicted to the feeling of energy coursing through them that when it's not there they feel something is wrong, then do their very best to hide this fact, even from themselves.

Your life is attuned to the breath of the planet, the sun and the stars; everything has rhythms, times of breathing in and breathing out, times of quiet and activity, and times of dormancy and times of bursting forth. Don't put yourself down because you are going through a quiet space. Don't make it into an issue. Just watch and observe, and allow anything to be there that wishes to be there. Surround it with love and watch it pass. All is constantly changing. Don't make such a big deal about feeling different from day to day. Play with all your feelings, good and bad, and don't take them so to heart. Don't take them personally. They are only feelings; it is only energy passing through your aura to which you have attached thoughts and upon which you have passed value judgements.

You don't have to do anything with so-called negative feelings except to become aware of them. And, by this, I mean, not just being casually aware of them but accurately aware of them.

When you feel in a safe and suitable environment (which might be away from children) let any emotion arise and come forth freely. Do not, at this point, try to will away or love away your feelings. Be like a hollow bamboo, let it all flow through you. It is, after all, only emotion. And, believe me when I say, emotion never hurt anyone!

You might ask, then, of what use is emotion? Basically, emotion has two uses. Firstly, positive emotion charges or infuses a thought with the energy which the thought needs in order to be created in matter as a form. The thought originates in the mind, then is stepped down through emotion (feeling) into the form desired.

Secondly, so-called negative emotion signals disharmony and, at lower levels, severe limitation. This is a wake-up call that something needs doing! When negative emotion - especially that which has been repressed for a long time - is released in a safe environment it brings about a very positive result: it brings about healing at all levels.

The release of emotion heals!

When the emotional charge has been totally released surround yourself with all the love you are able, then just stay there and keep watching, and be very present.

A wondrous warmth fills your body. Your aura expands and you feel good again; another bit of fear has gone for ever.

During the throes of releasing emotion, whilst you are crying, and being angry or doing good work with some fine primal screaming, please do remember that laughing is also a very applicable emotion at these times. It has a potent healing frequency. *Never ever repress it!*

In fact, it can be said that when laughter spontaneously arises, rather than arising from the self-conscious ego, it is a sign that the healing work has been done!

In order to truly experience the so-called negative feelings, it may be helpful, to begin with, to emphasise them by putting yourself actively into a simulated situation which brings the fear up for you. But don't reinforce the ego by actively doing anything with the fear, such as blaming it on an outer cause, or by attempting to set to rights what was once a hurt in your life.

Some of you will be holding an emotional charge from something that happened to you in a past life-time. It may be deeply buried, but your life-plan will confront you again and again with this emotion until you have faced it, felt it, taken responsibility for it and been healed of it.

It will be necessary to re-experience the emotion that you may be holding around situations from your childhood. *All of you, without exception, carry some trauma from your childhood. It cannot be avoided. It is part of the sacrifice you have accepted in coming to this world.* Feel it as totally as you are able, then surround the memories with all your deepest love, and then be still and watch.

The cellular memory in your body holds the memory of all these traumas, *until you release them.*

It is a futile exercise to go and rage at your parents. Unless they are very understanding, it will get you nowhere. You are not looking to change matters outwardly; you are looking to your own inner transformation. Your parents didn't put those feelings there inside you, you did. It is true that you had no choice in the matter; but it was still you who put them there once long ago when you were weak and small; and now that you are strong and big and worldly-wise it is up to you to release the energy locked up in this fear so that you can become the warm loving joyful entity that you really are.

The preliminary work is done by re-experiencing the fear, bringing it to the surface of your mind from the unconscious, where it has been lurking, unconsciously controlling your life in compulsive patterns of behaviour not to your liking, which result in even further troublesome emotion.

Yet, the truly great work is in being *still*, with the mind as the observer, allowing the emotional discharge to release the fear. It is not necessary to do anything about the fear. On releasing the emotional charge totally, the fear will release on its own. The cellular memories of your body will alter on their own. The healing will occur on its own.

Now for a warning: when you release emotion into the daylight of consciousness without there being present your disciplined will, that is, when you are unable to resist releasing your anger upon others, you will cause much confusion for yourself, and you will deepen the mistrust between you and previous loved ones who may not be as ready, as you are, to explore their own fears.

In this case, healing cannot happen because you are still connecting your emotion to an outside source; you are still delaying the time of meeting up with the original fear and taking responsibility for it, by getting caught up in some ego orientated activity which may give you the idea that something is changing, whereas nothing is changing. You are merely transferring the emotion to a new location or a new person or a new situation. This is also called projection.

A feeling of relief, of having got something off your chest, doesn't necessarily lead to inner healing. It is temporary relief, at best. At worst, it fools you into thinking you are on top of the situation. Actually, you have burrowed more deeply into your conditioned ego!

Do not delay the day of confrontation between you and your fears. Sit still, with great love for your self, feel the feelings which arise, and discover for yourself who you are.

You can call this therapy if you wish. *Therapy* comes from the Greek, meaning *to go into God*. So, why not call it *God's* work (or *good* work). It would be more meaningful by far!

Using therapeutic techniques, as above, to look for and expose the deep feelings beneath the unconscious is essential. But it has a partner. Meditation. Meditation is also essential and becomes increasingly so, so long as it is not fixated upon as being the final answer to enlightenment.

You can go on getting relief and insights through therapy until the cows come home, and valuable they are, indeed. But without meditation you might as well have not gone to the trouble or wasted your money.

We are talking here about a person who may have been cleared emotionally, but who has no further interest in self-realisation.

Therapy, without meditation as its insightful partner, can result in producing powerful egos who may become highly successful in getting their outside life together, yet who may remain spiritually impoverished. They know all the tricks of the ego and can talk the language, but the ego remains, and becomes, more skilful at hiding its fears than ever.

An entity who maintains this state of affairs in its psyche is in danger of treading what has been called the left hand path. Now, the ego is powerfully trained ego in the ways of therapy. It has been cleared of all obstacles, emotionally, that would inhibit or sabotage its creative powers. It may even be able to talk the language of spiritual knowledge but, sadly, it will have little connection to its spirit or to the joy of its being. This entity will be more interested in controlling a situation to its benefit, keeping the status quo and developing material acquisitiveness or sensual gratification (albeit for so-called spiritual reasons).

Such an entity is known by its inability to retain its equanimity and its sense of humour in a situation not to its liking. If you feel this describes yourself, do not worry. It is a stage along the path that all, sooner or later, have to face. Just accept it and know that you have more work to do. This is called humility. It is a divine quality. But, please, do not stay stuck in this place over-long. It will cause you grief if you do.

So, do allow yourself time to stop, to sit, and listen.

Give yourself time-out to resist being manipulated by your compulsively driven active mind (the ego). Allow yourself to be vulnerable enough to be a watcher rather than a doer. In this space, in the facing of your deepest fears inside yourself, in your own solitude, is your salvation.

Meditation combined with therapy will avoid the pitfalls of the so called left hand path. Healing and transformation will happen beautifully, naturally, and easily.

During meditation you will be assisted and surrounded by many beings of light who watch and wait, who will help you and who will make their presence felt when the time is appropriate. But you have to want to do it. I repeat: *you have to want to do it.*

In your every day life try to avoid being false and putting on a pose. This is hypocrisy. When you are confronting a situation you don't like be honest enough to say so. Don't try and be peaceful when, in fact, you are feeling angry. And, as a corollary, don't try and whip up anger to suit a situation which you think deserves it when, in fact, all you may feel inside yourself is neutrality - or indifference.

There is nothing wrong in being angry unless you reinforce your ego by blaming the outside situation for your anger, believing you will be happy again when you make it right. This is your ego trying to control the situation to its advantage.

Before allowing your anger to erupt you always have a split second in which you have a choice as to how to allow that anger to emerge or, indeed, whether to be angry at all. Use that split second, not necessarily to stop the anger, but to contact your observer. Your observer is aware that your anger is not, fundamentally, directed at anyone outside of your self even though you might think that it is.

Watching how anger arises will, after a while, give your anger a different focus; it will come from a more whole space and be less personally directed.

It is better to fight when you have a desire to fight, rather than pose as a spiritual person when, in fact, you are feeling anything but spiritual. It is better to fight than passively submit to what you feel is evil or wrong; for otherwise fear gains a stronger foothold, increasing its influence by stealth and guile.

It is best of all, however, to be self-realised, when all will be seen clearly, when there will be, naturally, no energy or inclination to fight because the ego has dissolved into the Oneness.

The most important thing is to be real and not be a hypocrite. You cannot be expected to behave in an enlightened way before you are enlightened. If you attempt to, you reinforce your ego and make it even more difficult to become enlightened.

Enlightenment is about being real and owning up to your real feelings. How else can you look at the fears entangled with these feelings?

Pretending to be enlightened when you are not is a great role for the ego to give itself. No one can put their finger on you. Anything anyone says you have an answer for. It is a great role for the ego to play. Enlightenment can mean many things for the ego and the ego revels in all of them. It will get its money's worth and try every trick in the book to remain in this space of pretence enlightenment. This can go on for a long time and is the cause of much inner pain to those who are close to enlightenment but are still ensnared by the games and manipulations of their ego.

Never allow illusion to take you away from your own reality if you can help it, for every time that you do you are pandering to its false life and reinforcing its strength. At times of crisis, when you feel anger arising, know that anger is like a wall of water that has been building up behind the concrete dam of your ego which can no longer resist the pressure of its bursting through and getting your life flowing again.

Watching in meditation pin points the feelings behind the fear, and stops you putting back all that energy into rebuilding the dam. That energy is now available to be integrated into the whole organism in which there must be balance before the union of the inner and outer.

When you are self-realised, no crisis can occur without you immediately seeing the ephemeral and illusory nature of it, so no anger is possible.

'Evil' has gained a fine sphere of influence amongst religious hypocrites who profess peace and sweetness and harmlessness but who, within their minds, are hiding behind their religions and their cults. They scheme, grasp, and manipulate, fearing loss of prestige and power, and loss of spiritual authority and influence.

These unhappy priests would gain much by admitting to their fears, by admitting to their longings to be loved and have joy in their lives. They would be better off by being real, by ending the denial of their hidden pain and shame, and by facing up to their personal experiences of abuse done to them, rather than piously submitting to an outer evil or aggressively fighting evil under the pretence of humility or a conjured-up spiritual identity.

They enjoy the authority of swaying the masses, and they perpetuate the myth of evil because they have not done their own inner work. They know not the truth that all teachers have taught: that all is within them, including all evil; outer evil being merely a fabrication of their ego; a useful projection by the conditioned ego to deflect attention well away from it!

Do not hide behind new age ideas and make them into a religion lest you fall into the same trap. Many new age gurus will jump merrily on to the new age band wagon and you will need to keep wide awake to avoid the pitfalls of allowing them to become your new age priesthood.

I wish to tell you this: it is not the mind that is the cause of suffering, it is the ego. It is the ego which has appropriated for itself some mind stuff, as it were, to wrap around itself. This mind stuff is a cloud of its own ideas, the chief idea, the chief 'evil', being the idea that it is separate from the whole.

You are fooled into believing you are this ego. You are fooled into believing you have a separate mind. I tell you, though, that mind is not separate. Mind is a unity and exists quite perfectly as the total mind of God. It is only humans that believe in the separation of mind into its countless human parts.

Humans who are searching for a way to dissolve the ego, recognising that the ego and mind have got tangled up together, often blame the mind and seek many ways to try and rid themselves of mind by spiritual practices or by living a mindless life, allowing their feelings to wash them around in the sea of life like a jellyfish at the mercy of every current.

The ego is very happy if you spend your life trying to eliminate your mind. It gives you something worthwhile to struggle against. But you will be like a dog chasing your own tail. Even if you bite it off where is it going to get you; you will still be the dog!

The answer, my dear ones, is not to rid yourself of mind, but to combine your mind with the mind of God - where there is unity of mind.

Mind, as such, you can never be rid of for it is a unity within The Oneness. Only by allowing your mind to drop into this unity (in harmony) with The Oneness can you find your joy, and regain your peace from your machiavellian ego.

Do you not believe that the mind of God has a function? Indeed, it has. It is to express the will of spirit, which is life's will *to be*. Mind itself has no will. It is a medium through which will can be expressed.

The mind is a very mobile and fluid medium; anything can be created out of it, yet it has no will of its own. The conditioned ego has a "will" but it is far removed from your spirit's *will to be*.

The ego's will is a puny manufactured will which is mainly concerned with its own separate existence and its defence of that existence.

The mind of the whole (the Oneness) exists as a medium through which the essence of God, being the will of God, can be made manifest and be demonstrated to be the truth behind all creation; which is, that love and joy and peace be the realised expression of the whole throughout the whole. Truly, this is returning everything back into harmony - with awareness.

Mind and essence (spirit) work in perfect balance together. Spirit encourages mind to free the life imprisoned within form wherever illusion is found to be keeping it in limitation. If you like, God's mind is ever at work freeing life from limitation wherever it encounters ego in the universe.

It stands to reason therefore that if you wish to become at one with God it might be a good idea to become at one with the mind of God, for then ego has no foothold: it is no where, and spirit quite naturally fills the vacuum, taking its rightful place as your will, your guide and your inspirer. It is also your nourishment, your joy and your peace.

This is a simple way to dissolve the ego. It is the path of a server of the light. It is the way Jesus exemplified as being the easy road, the great road, for mankind.

This is the path of a world warrior, a world server, and all of you who are now reading these words are world servers else you would not have come to this world.

Don't struggle, therefore, with your mind. Your struggle is to do with your ego and its belief systems. There is a great difference; and you need to see this difference else you end up disowning mind as the culprit, bottling up your life energy even more than you are presently doing.

Your meditation to still the mind is essential; but, only still it long enough to put you back in touch with your spirit and, only long enough, so that you can renew your confidence and listen once again to that small quiet voice within you that is always at one with the mind of God. Then go and be the server that you are. Use that energy you have been given.

Keep meditating, and often sit in contemplation, for, whilst you are on the physical plane, meditation will be your life line to your whole self which is truly at one with the mind of God, and ever at one with universal spirit.

In conclusion, regarding the mind, I repeat, and this cannot be emphasised strongly enough: the mind is not evil. It is the ego that brings up these thoughts. The mind is a neutral medium which serves whichever master activates it.

We can say that ninety nine point nine percent of the universe is unified mind; the other point one percent or less is made up of frightened egos all believing, in their own way, that they are separate. Where they gather together, en masse, they create suffering for themselves.

Each ego that decides to open up to the mind of God, placing its mind in the loving hand of God unifies instantly with the greater mind, and, in a warm flash of light, the ego dissolves, never again to cast its shadow upon the world.

I wish I could show you that the task in front of you is not to become enlightened, but to dissolve the ego. Enlightenment is always there. You are the light already. When the ego goes, enlightenment is automatic; nothing, absolutely nothing, can possibly stop it happening for you. Get rid of your conditioned ego and you are home.

Now, the ego messes up your chakras, those whirling vortexes of energy that bring light into your bodies. And, the enlightenment you have been waiting for necessitates the clearing of the 2nd and 3rd chakra. For thousands of years you have been longing to free yourselves from the fears that have lain deep within you. Your 2nd chakra holds your blame and guilt for which its outer expression is control. Your 3rd chakra holds your fear for which its outer expression is force (please note, *not* power which is a separate thing all together).

In your 2nd chakra you experience *lack*. In your 3rd chakra you experience responsibility. It is now time to take responsibility for all your feelings at a core level, be it at a genetic level, DNA level or a past lifetime level. When these two chakras are fully cleared and aligned, the imbalances that caused you such suffering over ages of time will end. The conditioned ego will be no more. This is the great work to be done. And, as individuals are cleansed, so will nations become peaceful.

Ego is not false mind, rather it is mind that has been given false programming. Remove the programme that is all. When you wipe mind free of its programme it automatically regains its pristine condition. The ego will have automatically disappeared. Then life becomes easy: its like you are on automatic, choices are so natural and easy they don't seem like choices at all. Everything seems so obvious and spirit's will so pervasive that all you have to do is harness your mind to do its bidding.

The ego has many ways in casting its illusions over the minds of men and women, so there will be just as many ways of helping to confront it. Your path of service will be unique to you and you will have no difficulty discovering your particular path as long as you remain in touch with your true feelings and use your whole mind for whatever service is yours to give.

Say to yourself; how can I help this entity feel more loving about himself, then you are on the right track. Could nothing be simpler?

Don't consider the problems. That is ego stuff. The ego is for ever fascinated by its concern with how things are to be done. Just look at the life within the person, see the love that is really there, which has been hurting for so long, see the joy that is there if only they would let go of this or that idea; then wisely, compassionately, with a clear mind, help them *to set themselves free*.

It will also set you free. Service in this manner will help to dissolve your ego very quickly. Nothing else is needed. The light will follow, for now you are in harmony again with the one light which is enlightened mind. And where enlightened mind is, ego cannot be.

Of course, you cannot make someone to be free like you make a cake. Each person must take the steps to free themselves, it is true. But you can point the way. You can show how it is done. You can inspire. You can nurture and maybe even assist in the birth of one who desires to be born again. Your whole self will know, quite perfectly, how to act in every situation. Each person is given the optimum opportunity of seeing for themselves something which is really going to help them. This is great service indeed.

For those of you who believe that you can't help others, I say nonsense! That is your ego talking. It is afraid that if you align your mind alongside the enlightened mind of the Oneness, in service to the light, its days will be numbered. Yes, they will be!

Teaching is a service. All the great teachers have demonstrated, in their own way, a life of service: Krishna, Buddha, Mohammed, Jesus - to mention only a few.

It is true that you can take a horse to water but you can't make it drink. But at least you can take the horse to the water. And you can show kindness to the horse, and you can create an environment where the horse feels safe enough to approach the water. And, by drinking from the water yourself, you can show, by example, that there is nothing to be frightened of.

You are not exactly horses but the principle is the same. Drink deeply of the waters of life and encourage others to do the same. Your encouragement, your inspiration, your example is needed.

Look around you. Be alert. The next person you meet treat a little differently. Be there for them with a little more awareness.

And, when you get discouraged, and when your ego starts to put your emotions through your habitual mood swings, stop a moment, be very still, and go deep, and stay in that place for just as long as you need to observe the fear, feel the feelings associated with the fear, then feel them move through you and be transformed. Recognise the feeling of joy that arises, allow your mind to see clearly once more. Then arise and be the server yet again.

You say to me, I live alone or I don't see many people in my life; I am old or crippled; I can't get about; I'm stuck at home with the children; I have to work to pay the bills, and so on and so on. These are all excuses from the ego mind. The ego loves to jump ahead of itself and keep jumping about like a mad jack-in-a-box which mesmerises you. But it is not a huge step that I am asking you to take. On the contrary, I am asking you to start exactly where you are, in the moment, right now, so that each moment leads to the next moment, perfectly naturally, without any prior compulsive thought or drama.

Making yourself at one with the mind of God (being that of your whole self) and being a server doesn't mean you have to actively rush round the physical world being the great teacher. It means being at one with the mind of God in such a way that your every thought is one of service, and not a hindrance, to the greater plan of harmony. It means you keep awake. It means you are mindful of your thoughts.

Thoughts are powerful creative effects. A thought is either an effect of ego or it is an effect of spirit. Which are yours? Which *will* is motivating you: that of spirit or that of ego? When you think thoughts which are in harmony with life's great plan, and none other, you are constantly recharging yourself with life energy and dissolving your ego into the bargain. And you are serving greatly.

When there is nothing to think about, don't do any thinking. Just be there, just be present, with nothing going on in your mind.

You don't have to be in meditation to be without thoughts. You can be sitting with no thoughts or you can be dancing with no thoughts, you can be driving your car with no thoughts, no matter. You can still be awake, alert to everything going on around you. It is a fine way to be. It is better by far to have no thoughts going on, than to allow your mind to be the recipient of every stray and random thought which comes through; not that there is anything wrong in having stray and random thoughts, but there is nothing very right about it, either, for it makes it very easy for you to start chasing a thought which, before you know it, has taken you away from the moment. Then your ego has got its claws around you once again, negative feelings arise, your aura shrinks and depression and lack of confidence set in. The familiar pattern.

Being of service, watching the mind, being true to your feelings, together with meditation and contemplation, is the sure way to dissolve the ego. It is the five fold path. Each one of these five is vital. If you leave out any of the five you will become unbalanced and there will be needless suffering in your life. They are:

1. Service.

2. Watching the mind.

3. Acceptance (ending the denial) of all your feelings.

4. Meditation.

5. Insightful contemplation.

I am sure you will remember these five headings easily because they add up to SWAMI. And, you are definitely going to be your own *swami*!

This is a path of balanced activity. It is the royal road to freedom.

Do not be over passive. It leads to sterility. There is an ultra passive state in which the ego indulges in the belief that enlightenment will happen when the mind is still. As I have said, enlightenment is already there and you will observe that it is there just as soon as you allow your mind to be at one with the mind of your whole self. Your whole self is in harmony with all that is. This is self-evident to it. This is its plan for you. Align yourself with this plan. It is the great plan and purpose of life.

Be considerate of the laws of the society that you live in, and apply to all your dealings the ethical laws of the universe which are simply that of justice and fair play for all, and which demand that all sentient creatures, being at one with the life of the Father (spirit), are permitted to tread their own individual path without interference, being permitted to seek their freedom in any way that they wish as long as it doesn't hinder others from also realising the truth of their own being.

The ego loves to talk and show off its knowledge. Don't permit others to filibuster you with their knowledge lest you fall into the same trap of re-plying in kind, so losing your spiritual integrity and well being. Speak only when inspired, otherwise listen.

Never try and eliminate so called evil, else you end up playing the same game that evil plays. When you try and wipe out evil, you fall, uncon-sciously, into the stance and position that the evil force has taken: namely, that it is necessary to protect yourself from some outside force or otherwise suffer loss. The very thought that you need to protect yourself is an illusory (or evil) idea.

What is this ego? This is very difficult to say: it is easier to say what the ego is not. The reason for this is that the ego is a phenomena of motion but has no real substance of its own. It is like a mirage in the desert which arises when the climate is right and dissolves again just as quickly. The ego is like a whirlpool within the fluid mind of your whole self which is aware of itself only within the confines of the whirlpool. It is like a wind whirl-ing around itself that collects more and more debris as it goes, sucking up debris from the ground, strengthening itself at every turn, creating havoc wherever it goes and having to spin faster and faster to keep itself alive. It is aware only of its immediate frenzied activities and very much resists its dissolution back into the calm air of the whole from which it first arose.

It seems to be very easy to convince the ego that it has a separate iden-tity, and difficult for it to stop its motion long enough for spirit to unite with mind to produce a clear and balanced personality. Whenever there is compulsive doing you can rest assured that your ego is whirling you along on a merry dance. It is called the dance of suffering.

Nothing can be killed in this universe. Only the form changes and you, being a god, can take any form you wish. You are form changers. There are entities in this planetary system that can, whilst in deep meditation, be in many different forms at the same time, and remain actively aware and in contact with all of them, all at the same time. If you are the human personality form of one of these great entities, you have much to draw upon. Rid yourself of the ego and allow your grand self in. It is you, after all. Your ego is an aberration which is all that stands in your way of being here in all your glory.

Each of you is a cosmic entity in your own right. You are this entity right now and always have been. Stop still for a moment and get off from the merry-go-round of the world's massive ego distortion, listen, hear and act, and heal this magnificent world.

Just as nothing can be killed, neither can you kill or wipe out ideas (beliefs).

You can, however, by resisting their manipulating influences, show them up for what they are: spurious forms, holding no energy of their own, being ultimately self protective devices for deluded egos.

When seen, when lovingly confronted, they self-destruct. You have done nothing. You have merely brought them to your attention. You have switched on the light. The shadows, which at one time seemed so real, which at one time seemed to have such a powerful hold over you, which gave your life some important meaning or some belief about your identity, disappear; and, once you have unmasked them as such, will not reappear.

Affirm always your positive nature, affirm your spiritual integrity, and do not give your energy to ideas which you have discovered form the habit pattern of thoughts which come from your ego.

Do not, on the other hand, try to eliminate, or deny, the ideas or the feelings that are associated with them. Only the ego denies anything. But don't reinforce them, either.

Your beliefs, and the feelings associated with them, are your areas of transformation. They are valuable to you for this purpose. But they are not there for you to be proud of; they are not there for you to do anything with; it is true, that the more negativity is present the more transformation is possible, but if in some sort of perverted way you become proud of negativity and look for more and strengthen it so as to make more transformation possible, you are falling under a spell; this is the height of stupidity or, maybe, from the ego's point of view, the height of cunning.

Accept your negative feelings, be aware of them: for, when you do, they are automatically transformed, releasing energy into you that has previously been blocked. This is the third vital ingredient of this five fold path: it is the acceptance (ending the denial) of all your feelings.

Non denial of feelings means just that: you don't deny them, yet, neither do you strengthen them by *doing* anything about them. You allow them *to be*. You accept them. You watch very carefully and you keep very awake. Be still, and be very accepting and the transformation will happen.

Remember, it is only the ego that desires negativity to be present so that transformation can happen. The goal is not transformation but *that the need for transformation is no longer there!*

Be aware of your negativity, but worship it not; be not involved with fear like women who wrestle in mud for the sheer thrill of its sensual fascination lest you get sucked into the mud and drown in it.

Non denial of your feelings opens for you the door of transformation and healing in your astral and physical bodies. A mindful affirmation of your divine nature opens the door for you of union with the mind of your whole self. Service is the key to a natural life in tune with The Oneness. And from this point it is a small jump to self-realisation.

Meditation holds all this together, creates a synthesis, and contemplation brings to fruition the final transformation.

Don't go chasing negative feelings to transform. This is an unlimited universe and you can create as many negative feelings as you wish until the end of time, with the aim of transforming them!

If you believe you have to experience something negative before being self-realised, you will create that reality for yourself and spend many happy hours creating amazing negative experiences for yourself just so you can have the pleasure of transforming them. This is chasing your tail. This is wallowing in the mud.

So, I say to you, deny not your feelings, but neither go looking for negative feelings. Observe them accurately when they come. Feel every iota of them, then let them go and get on with your positive life.

If your positive affirmations are tinged with ego, negative feelings will arise soon enough for you to look at. They will arise without any doing of yours; and that, then, is the time to look at them.

If your positive affirmations are not tinged with ego, negative feelings will not arise, so give them no thought and onward go. It means your mind is at one with the mind of your whole self and the mind of God. Hallelujah!

Let your old ideas and beliefs, the ones that you know reinforce your ego, dissolve back into the Oneness from which they have been manufactured. When you give them no thought, you give them no energy and they will soon dwindle and dissolve from lack of nourishment. The feelings that have been associated with them (you now being aware of them) will no longer have any hold over you.

Each of you has your own sun within you. It is up to each of you to call upon that sun to dispel your own clouds. Know it and trust it. It is the path of positive affirmation: that the glory of the Father, your own individual father in heaven, does exist within you.

Look to this sun. Do not look for an outside sun as a solution to your problems, else you wait for eternity.

Your conditioned ego would have you wait: it is quite happy to wait for all eternity. It has no interest in change other than to avoid suffering (or to avoid admitting to suffering) which it can become more and more skilful at doing; yet, it cannot end suffering. However much it tries it cannot end suffering. This is a point to reflect upon.

Some of you believe that you cannot help others because it would seem to be meddling. Yes, the ego can meddle and often does so under the guise of showing concern which is a rather subtle form of worry. I am not asking you to meddle. I am asking you to be aware of your own inner life which is calling upon you to validate that life in another. I am asking you to be aware and sensitive and to look to freeing the inner life wherever you find it - even if it be the slightest response.

I say again: this would be a sorry universe if no one helped anyone. This universe, you are going to discover, is one of co-operation, sharing, and helping. It is not a sorry universe, it is a joyful universe.

Krishna said that life is *lila*, a play. It is indeed. Have you considered, when you go to the theatre to see a play, how all the different people involved, the writer, the director, the actors, the designers and the stage hands, together with the audience, all have a part to play in a great creative synthesis, producing a play for the entertainment and elucidation of everyone. And how, at the end of the play all the actors go home, happily aware that in the play they have only been playing roles. Now they can return to being themselves.

This is very like life as we know it, except that in the world today everyone forgets they are merely playing a role on the stage of life. Instead, they identify with the role they are acting out. Whether it be as a housewife or a Prime Minister, a Muslim or a Christian, rich or poor, diseased or healthy, no matter, they latch on to the role and identify with it to such an extent that it becomes their fixed identity. Confusion reigns. Rights and wrongs become entrenched. Beliefs and ideologies take on importance. Fear and death seem real. No wonder there is suffering and fighting between all these spurious role-playing identities. Everyone has forgotten who they are. Everyone has forgotten they are in a play. Everyone keeps acting out the same tired old play - believing it is the real thing, unable to let go of it. How boring. How stupid. How ignorant. The conditioned ego keeps the belief going that this role you happen to be playing at the moment, in this life-time, is the real you. BUT IT IS NOT.

You are greater by far, and, indeed, less by far, than any role you ever have played or ever will play. You are The Oneness in manifestation playing this role for today. It may produce a great play and great excitement to have wars and suffering being acted out but, in truth, we need it not in this world any longer. Surely, your fascination with limitation and suffering has begun to pall. It is time to step aside for a while, end this part of the play, recognize who you truly are, and go home. Let harmony reign.

Know that: to meddle in another person's life is an ego inspired activity in which expectations of results, usually for the benefiting of the helper, is the general rule.

To help free the life within the form is spirit inspired. No expectations are demanded. There is only the joy of service.

It is possible to help others and at the same time allow them to be free. There is no greater service.

Try it, and be amazed at how you grow in stature. Be amazed how concerns and worries fall away and how you feel, all of a sudden, that you are on your path.

Beware of gurus and teachers who hold out before you the promise of spiritual fruits upon the fulfilling of certain conditions. And be careful you don't do the same. They are to be avoided like the plague.

No one, and again I say, no one, has the authority - either god or the masters or pope or priest or anyone - to insist that you lead a certain life style in return for spiritual benefits.

There is no greater way of progress upon the path to self-realisation than that of service to others to the very limit of your spiritual integrity.

Upon the path of service you will come face to face with many illusory ideas that you are holding on to, especially concerning right and wrong. In service, you will find it easy to let go of them. You will cease giving them energy which you unconsciously may have been doing to manipulate others for the satisfaction of your ego.

Those who help others out of ego satisfaction, fostered and conditioned by religion, do sadly retain their manipulative ways, and, by so doing, do nothing to lessen the power of ego or diminish illusion. The great majority of religious hierarchies have fallen unconsciously into this sorry state of affairs. Some perpetuate it consciously. If we are going to use the term evil, we would call this evil.

It seems obvious enough but it has to be said: beware of those who say to you, "Now that you have joined us, you are special, and if you do this or that you will be specially blessed." This is blatant manipulation. In their next breath they will be saying to you: "If you leave us or talk about our teachings to outsiders you will be damned for ever."

What nonsense this is. You are not special because you belong to this or that organization; you are already special because you are what you are. And you can never be damned because you are God. How can God be damned?

Yes, I say again, you are God on your way to realising that you are a god, as God, in a human form. You are on your way to being a Christ which is a realised god in human form. Jesus the Christ, indeed, showed the way, but in their frenzied excitement to spread the word about the great new teacher his disciples lost sight of the truly great part of his teaching which was, as he said: *"You, too, can be as I am."*

Never put a value judgement on an action. One individual may act in a certain manner which, in its time and place, is entirely appropriate to the outer situation. Another may perform the very same action at another time which has no merit in it whatever. How, therefore, can religions and so called spiritual organisations lay down rules of right and wrong for their "flock". You are indeed a flock of sheep if you follow them at the expense of listening to your own God within.

There are no greater clouds of illusion to be found than in religions, and no greater egos to be found than amongst the priestly castes both male and female.

Keep awake and keep free of the sticky fingers of priests and popes and mother superiors and their good intentions; they are floundering about in the comfortable glue of ancient ideas and familiar habits. You have out-grown these games, so remove yourself from them lest they become such a burden to you that you die in despair.

It is better to let go through insight rather than be forced to let go through exhaustion.

The coercion of independent intelligences by the method of holding out to them so called "spiritual fruits" is a cardinal outrage. If ever there was an evil this must be it.

No greater sanctity exists than the sanctity of the individual. Anything that prejudices or restricts the individual from gaining full knowledge of himself or herself is worse by far than the deliberate murder of the physical body. It is the deliberate denial of the loving life of God.

Sadly, if this is the only way in which the ego can prolong its existence, this is the way it will choose. Realisation can be delayed for long periods of time.

But I repeat, there are no cosmic conspiracies or dark gods in competition with a greater God. *The cosmos is a vast inter-penetrating network of planes of being. Only a minute fragment of it exists at the physical level.*

In the very looking for conspiracies mankind creates the idea that they exist. This also creates the fear of them. And this perpetuates the myth of duality and the illusion of inimical forces in the universe.

It has been maintained that you are being duped and misled by unscrupulous beings who are cultivating humanity as a source of psychic energy - in short for a kind of grand scale vampirism.

This is utter nonsense. The blaming of the world's problems upon the fantasy of outer scenarios is irresponsible rubbish. Hollywood movies of evil aliens intent on world domination do you no service other than to give you an adrenalin rush. They only generate fear where there could be respect and grateful thanks to these wonderfully helpful entities.

Again, it is avoiding the need to go within and get close to home where both the responsibility and the answers really lie.

It is so much easier to point the finger and blame, is it not? It is the ego that does not want to take personal responsibility for its woes.

Blame and criticism of anybody, whether it be false masters or dark gods or the uncongenial neighbours down the road, originates through fear of them. Fear always creates a gulf and generates more fears, thereby deepening the division and strengthening (though it be but an illusion of strength) that which is feared.

In medieval times it was fashionable to blame the devil and witches for the wrongs of the world. This has been upgraded, in this new age, to cosmic or planetary conspiracies where aliens and grey men are out to control the world. Don't get hooked in to this. It is not real, and it is not true, and it is not a reality you want to make real by believing in it. The ego loves to blame anything and everything outside of itself. Don't give it any energy.

When you know that you are at one with the Oneness, there is no gulf between you and others: there is no *other* which you can blame. All must come from you because you have experienced yourself as One and therefore you are also the original will of the One. This is the only reality. The reality of Oneness.

When you fear things outside your control you are, in effect, saying that you are afraid of being trapped in an irreversible situation. In fact, the only irreversible situation you will ever experience, if you allow it, is in Oneness. All else changes constantly. And, the paradox is that in Oneness lies your real freedom.

Letting go of your ego can feel like dying. The ego doesn't like it at all. In fact, it is the ego that believes in death. It would prefer to blame anything, or anyone, that reminds it of its vulnerability, and call it evil; then get as many other egos to support it as it possibly can so that everyone can then believe in "the power of evil".

Then it can become a leader and lead other egos in a crusade against evil. Now it has something *to do*. No one can really say what the evil actually is, so, a bogey man is made up that no one ever sees but everyone is convinced is there, waiting, to get you on some dark night.

When your ego dissolves it is a surrender into your own rediscovery of your spirit and the Oneness. Your personality, your individuality, is not lost but merely fulfilled. Only the manipulative ego, that part of your mind which has believed in separateness, is no more.

Upon experiencing this, it becomes illogical to fear anything, or even be critical of yourself. So guilt completely ceases. There is nothing outside of yourself, anymore, to fear.

Now no one can affect your state of well being. No one can psychically vampirise you because you are recreated in your totality and there is nothing superfluous to yourself to vampirise. Self identification with the One has, as its corollary, absolute indestructibility of your individual personality.

In fact, the great outrage committed against any independent intelligence is not so much their coercion by another, but the belief that such coercion is possible.

The belief that coercion is a possibility, allows a climate to evolve in which coercion (by egos in the dense levels) can occur.

This is the point I am making: if you think it can happen you will create the happening, and perpetuate it.

When you refuse to believe in this belief, believing instead in the freedom and unlimited nature of yourself, your belief that coercion is a possibility, and fear of it, will completely disappear. The energy contained in this thought will disappear from your orbit of influence - not because the coercion has been got rid of - but because its existence was never possible in the first place. It was merely your illusion.

A belief in coercion creates it for you. This may seem hard to believe but it is so. Fear of suffering is, in the final analysis, the only painful reality.

That which you see and then interpret mentally, you create; and it is attached to you.

You may believe in duality and conspiracies if you wish. It is your choice. But, by so doing, you give fear and its illusions an everlasting reality of its own.

That which others hold out to you as their truth is their truth. It is not yours. Any truth, other than your own truth, is irrelevant to you who stand in the light of Oneness. This is as true today as it was yesterday, and will be true tomorrow and for all eternity.

You create your own reality until you find that the perfect reality is already there within you, having no need to be created, and this you must affirm with courage. You are a unique entity and you know in your heart what makes you feel buoyantly alive and loved and connected to life. Affirm these heart and gut feelings for yourself and don't give your power away to others.

You may explore, through therapy and self analysis, these feelings and put them to the test of your own reality but always be on guard that a belief in therapy does not take the place of a fundamental belief in your own wholeness.

You will create a truly magnificent reality for yourself; and why not? You deserve it. *And, because it is already there!*

This reality will have no space in it for the poking your nose into conspiracies, lending them a power they can gain no other way other than by trading on fear.

Be as wise as those three wise monkeys. Hear no evil, see no evil and speak no evil. Monkeys can behave very foolishly, but, I say to you that those that seem foolish are often the most wise.

CHAPTER TEN

RELIGIONS AND SCIENCE.

I have already touched on religions and the illusions they generate. Science also generates its own illusions, but science has in no way been such a deluding factor as has religion.

Many religions have made of their religion a science with a proliferation of observances and rules to learn, yet scientists, no less, tend to make, of their observances, their analysis and their research, almost as great a religion. Both miss the essence of life.

Seekers of knowledge who place their trust in the analytical process of mind, in knowledge and in outer discovery, are exploring matter. This is fine as far as it goes. The search for knowledge is useful. But does it lead to happiness? Does it lead to peace? Does it lead to a true understanding of the nature of the universe, and the underlying truth of why it exists? If it does, well and good. If not, it is possibly nothing more than wasted time.

Matter has infinite possibilities because it is the expression of an infinite spirit. To exhaust them all is an impossible task. Energy and matter are inter changeable and ever changing. To examine the ever changing for clues as to the source of that which never changes is useless. At best, it teaches you where not to look and will provide you, at the end, with a belief in an absolute creator. But it fails to show you where to find the Oneness which is within yourself.

There is no ultimate particle. Spirit is the ultimate and it is not a particle. In fact, spirit can make infinite particles, each smaller than the next, until nothing is there to be seen or measured because nothing *is* there!

Oneness is the ultimate mystery: as I have said it cannot be understood. But it can be experienced; and the only place where it is ever going to be experienced is within you. It is going to be a totally subjective experience for you; you'll never be able to prove to anyone else that you have solved the secret of creation; but once you experience it, you will know without any doubt that you have the answer. If knowledge is truly your goal, inside is the place to look. If you wish to be recognised as a knowledgeable person, by all means continue to look outside, but you will not, I promise you, find the solution there.

Do not search for an ultimate *non-changing* point, or particle, by analysis of the *ever-changing* universe lest you fall into delusion which, more often than not, expresses itself as agnostic cynicism.

Exhaust not your energies in pursuit of the outer. Searching for truth in the outer universe of ever changing energy is like a man standing upon the sea shore searching for the perfect wave.

Eventually, you will become embittered by not solving the mystery; or you may become arrogantly proud of your research which you must then call "truth" in order to justify your work and existence. Frustratingly, though, your truth will soon be superseded by another truth and then by yet another, and so on, and so on. Oh dear, it does get tedious !

The danger of science is that it can so easily become like a fascinating drug which men and women throw themselves into with fierce mental energy, delighting in the thrill of anticipation of the next discovery which surely lies over the next fence. It is rather like going to the races and putting your money on the horse you fancy. You just can't wait to see if it's going to be a winner!

Despite this, scientists have brought great benefits to the world, not the least of which has been to break the stranglehold of inane religious beliefs, and superstition, which have manipulated the minds of men for so long.

To this end, they have striven mightily and have often given far greater service to the upliftment of mankind than the fanatics of religious zeal who proclaim so roundly that they do God's work.

From the standpoint of the one life, beliefs, knowledge, science and even the politics of community relationships, is seen to be such dry nourishment from which to draw your life and your inspiration. You are now ready to enter *the heart of being* where life alone is sufficient to be your nourishment and your joy.

There needs, now, to be a drawing together of innocence and science, and to this end the so-called native or aboriginal peoples of the world can teach you much about innocence, though, from another aspect, they are riddled with superstition.

Your scientists can teach you much about pure reason though they, in turn, are bedevilled by scientific dogma and closed minds. Each can learn from the other. Superstition cannot stand in the light of pure reason. Dogmatism cannot stand in the light of natural innocence and spontaneity.

It would perhaps be useful if scientists were a little more religious and religionists a little more scientific and, yet, as practiced today by most people, both science and religion are merely opposites to each other which give human beings a multitude of intriguing excuses to explore ever more fascinating research material, always looking outside of themselves. How much more satisfying to do your own inner work, meet your own inner fears, and realise the truth that lies behind every other truth.

It is strange, is it not, that those of religious inclination who profess to love and follow the master, worship the master yet often fail to follow his precepts.

I am sure you have noticed that those who trust in science and worship medicine as the solution to all humanity's ills have a characteristic similar to that of priests: they can be amazingly closed to anything new.

How stubbornly, scientists and doctors resist change. And how proud of their orthodoxy are those vaunted followers of the faithful towards their religion. They become so puffed up with pride and self importance that little do they realise how hard and unyielding their nature has become.

Pay careful attention that your new age teachings do not so get you into their grip and dominate your thinking that you become as hard and unyielding in your desire to be spiritual, or unorthodox, as those orthodox ones whom you disparage.

Truth cannot be found, or tested in any manner, by relating it to a scientific premise, nor by relating it to religious texts, for at the very time this is being done the moment is being lost; it is, as it were, being glossed over for some future reward to satisfy the ego. When the moment is lost, spirit is lost. The moment is all there is. Spirit, the Oneness, is here this moment. Feel it and jump into it. It is only in the moment that you can catch it; only in the moment you can feel it; only in the moment that you can be in the joy of your being.

The ego's reward is in believing it is right. It is a satisfying feeling to be right. And when you have put your theory to an outer test you can say to yourself, "I have put my theory to the test and now I know I am right!" Very satisfying indeed!

However, truth cannot be tested against anything for there is nothing outside of itself to be tested against; so, whenever you think you are testing out truth you are again chasing your tail. There is no duality involved in truth; nothing relates to truth. Truth is. Truth is in this moment, *now*.

Wherever you are reading these words, *right now*, standing, sitting in a chair, or lying in bed, being aware of your feelings and the physical sensations of your body, this is your truth.

Truth is not about being right or proving anyone else wrong. There are no opposites to truth that can prove anything wrong. In short, truth is about being whole, and being whole is an experience - a feeling beyond all feelings.

Those who would relate or measure their behaviour against a doctrine, or against a theory, or logic, or against the life of a saint or of a master, are being deaf to the whisperings of their own true nature. You are not here to model your life upon the wonderful examples of other teachers. If you do you will become like a model and all you will be good for is sitting on the shelf. Life will pass you by.

Belief in the "Word of God", and belief in the "marvels of science", amount to the same thing: you are building models and falling in love with the models.

Some people will run after anything new, new religion, new teacher, new therapy, new discovery, new medicine, yet their characters remain little altered. Many who run after anything new only do so because of their esteem for the teacher or the discoverer.

Reverence for a teacher is natural and beautiful and all very well but it can well become a high road to self delusion. Truth is not to be found in the worship of the words of a teacher but in putting *your* every experience and *your* choices of action to the test of your own inner life, your own intuition, and your own pure reason and common sense.

Worship of teachers, be they religious or scientific, engenders laziness of mind.

An all too ready acquiescence to teachers will lead you into indiscriminate nonsense which will have you doing actions against your inner feelings and against all practical ethical common sense. This will put you into the position of repressing anger. One moment you will be flying high, the next you'll be crashing; or, worse, you might become a monastic zombie, going through the motions of your duties with a prayer on your lips but murder in your heart. At the very least, you will be lost to the sparkle and joy of your being and lost to the love that you are both to receive and give to the world.

When a number of people get together and worship a teacher their combined laziness of mind creates an organization. Organizations, especially religious organizations, thrive on lazy minds. They exist only for lazy people who soon conveniently lose sight of the teaching but still keep gathering together because it gives them good feelings to do so.

Further, no organization can tolerate spontaneous people. Spontaneous people are liable, at any moment, to withdraw their support and walk away. This is the case, without exception, of every organised religion - and they do not like it!

Teachers do come to awaken you to truth; but human beings love to organise truth. They organise it into a belief and then bask with others of like mind in the warm cosy glow of their belief system which is fed by the auras and energy of all the other people in the organization who believe the same thing.

Organised religion is like a drug: in this one respect Karl Marx was correct. It does buffer humans from their reality. It is, indeed, opium for the masses. And those masses which are spoon-fed by religions are a mass of drugged individuals. This is serious ego conditioning. En masse!

Religions usually start with an out pouring of love, with great enthusiasm and good intentions. At first, hopefully, they preach freedom of thought and encourage differing opinions within the fraternity. But, in the passing of but a short time, woe betide anyone who takes a line other than the official one!

The might of the organization in all its pompous self righteous indignity descends upon the poor unfortunate's head!

The godless religion known as Communism is as much an offender in this respect as any of the other organised philosophies, religions and ideologies. They are murderers of the spirit all.

There is a strange idea, held - especially among various new age fraternities - that technology and anything scientific is not conducive to, or useful for, spiritual advancement. Science is disparaged.

This is lazy thinking and arises from a fear that the pursuit of material things will swallow them up into the mire of personal illusion and the suffering that goes with it.

There is some truth in this, yet they are very much over reacting in the same way that one who has just given up smoking cannot abide other smokers being in their presence. They are still very sensitive to the dangers they have just escaped from, and need a while to distance themselves from every association with the habit.

Of course, there is nothing wrong or evil about technology. Any judgement in this area needs to be looked at closely. Humanity has derived very much benefit from technology and will continue to do so. It is all a matter of wisdom. Just as there is no right or wrong concerning money, there is no right or wrong concerning technology.

The invention of the hand plough, the wheel and the candle, aeons ago, were the technological discoveries of the ancients. They were the scientific breakthroughs of the age which lightened the load of humans upon Earth, giving man more time to ponder upon his experiences and the nature of himself.

These discoveries were no more and no less good or wrong than the combustion engine, the aeroplane, nuclear energy, or the computer sciences of today.

To those of you who abhor science and its discoveries, I say to you that the knowledge this world possesses of science is yet in its infancy - a mere drop in the ocean of knowledge that is to come.

The martyrs for science, I can tell you, have done more for this world than the martyrs for religion and philosophy.

Technological advances do not have to be the polluting hazard that many of their applications have become. That this is so, is due, mainly, to overpopulation and corporate greed, together with a general ignorance about spiritual life. This has erased much of the beauty and usefulness of technology for you. The biggest disease in this world at present is the cult of materialism and the lust for attachment to form in all its aspects which includes the appalling clinging of humans to subtle but pervasive mental thought-forms, those ideas of religious beliefs and diverse ideologies, which bring so much suffering to the men and women of this planet. It is encouraged by your educational institutions and supported by your media.

A dependency upon technology, to the loss of your spiritual integrity and awareness, is, of course, your own personal responsibility. Be aware indeed! But do not take away from others the benefits they enjoy or the things they think they need to be happy for their life here on Earth.

Scientists tend to fall in love with knowledge. They like to play god, with knowledge as their magic wand. But those who are against science also fall in love with knowledge. They play god as well but they put their faith in beliefs.

I am asking you to drop all knowing and become God by dropping into God; then you can play as much as you like without making self righteous pronouncements about right and wrong and other anxiety forming nonsense.

Those that have the amazing audacity to say that they know God's intentions are enmeshed by their own delusions of right and wrong because they live in fear of spiritual loss - as if there could be any such thing!

Many men and women of goodwill are trapped within organizations which they should long ago have withdrawn their energy from.

Many of these entities have done much helpful work on Earth but it is time for all men and women of goodwill to confront the beliefs put out by these cradle organizations and reacquaint themselves with their spiritual integrity.

And what is this spiritual integrity? How do you know it? It is, I remind you again, your own joy and your own peace. You know it by the joy of your being.

At every age, new teaching is given. You would not teach your five year old daughter the lessons of a ten year old, would you? So, also, are new teachings given to humanity from age to age, the teachings chosen being appropriate for the times.

These are new teachings. And you will find them being given out in many different ways the world over at this time, for it is time for the Earth's enlightenment.

The old ways, the old teachings, are no longer appropriate. This world is now to enter, as it were, a High School stage of learning and growth.

You no longer need the old style religions or esoteric brotherhoods which hold out to you rewards like the carrot before the donkey. And, you need to be very discerning in the way you use your science.

Ideas and beliefs, be they of science or religion - or new age teachings - no longer apply to you. They are liken to a mill stone round your neck. They develop a power of their own and become a suffocating influence. Distance your self from them.

See to it that you live uncompromisingly, in each moment, to the tune of your own spirit.

Then, and only then, will you enjoy all the future marvels which science will, in its own beautiful manner, and in its own perfect timing, bring you.

CHAPTER ELEVEN

GOVERNMENT

In ancient times the entities that chose Earth experience became lost and blind to their purpose in taking human form.

Desire, not for the experience of life in matter, but for the things of matter itself became so strong in the minds of these entities that they lost all knowledge of who they were; they lost their connectedness with the Oneness and, in consequence, they lost their joy and discovered fear.

They became afraid to die, ignorant of this quiet process of change from one state of being to another; becoming, instead, anxious and jealously protective of their own bodies and the bodies and affections of their loved ones.

This led to bands of humans gathering together for protection against other marauding bands of humans. This led to rules and regulations, initiation rites and ceremonies so as to weld together the group and keep the members loyal to the group by intricate mesmerising rites of entry or by fear of punishment for transgressions of the group's maxims.

These bands threw up leaders who thrived on the power and self esteem that accrued to them in their positions of authority.

Thus were governments born out of ignorance of the divine nature of the Oneness, for the self-serving and self protective blind desires of form (this being its intrinsic and instinctual nature) rather than for the freeing of life within the form and for the dissolution and transformation of form into its light components.

At other levels in the universe you inhabit bodies of light components and you live in these quite happily, without losing your integrity of being - which is what the body of flesh has such a strong tendency to engender.

Yet these tendencies were at one time not so strong; they have become so through habit, through ages of conditioning, and by the imprinting of fears upon the unconscious psyche of the race through the DNA of the individual body matrix of every human being.

Government, then, was introduced for the purpose of protecting human beings from other human beings. It originated for this purpose and has gone on, as you well know, to extend its authority to almost every act of human living.

It is the most insidious of self protective devices that the conditioned egos of human beings have created for themselves. Yet, as individuals, you are more than ready to blame those to whom you have given away your power, for all your misfortunes. When you have delegated your personal power of choice to another and you don't like the choice that they have chosen for you, it is rather convenient, is it not, to be able to turn round and say, "It's your fault, not mine."

Certainly you have the right to delegate and allow others to make choices for you, even to protect you (if you wish) from the attentions of thugs and war lords, but then you must need take responsibility within yourself for doing so.

If you choose someone to look after your interests who you know has an unconscious fear of loss, how can you, in your heart, truly blame this person when you find out he has been stealing from you?

In other words, when you choose leaders who are blind to the true purpose of life you can't start getting upset when they fall into a hole and drag you in with them. And if you choose leaders who are trying to become awake but who are still working through a whole heap of unconscious fears, you must accept that you and the group, or the nation, are going to be in for a roller coaster of a confusing time.

Politics should not be about power: it is truly about service. It is about creating an environment in which others can grow and find their individual freedom. The spirit of service lies at the back of all true service to others. The act of smoothing another's path by providing him or her with basic facilities and opportunities, or by looking after basic services, is, indeed, a loving service. It enables the other to devote their time to personal growth and, hopefully, to the discovery of their own individual destiny - and possibly even to their self realisation which would be rendering them a great service indeed.

If you are deaf to the urgings of spirit you are going to choose leaders who are also deaf to spirit, and you and they are going to have a fine old time, wallowing from one mud hole to another, under the delusion that this is progress. This is not government. This is lunacy.

Loving and wise government would be a possibility if you were to choose wise and self realised entities to make these basic choices for you, which would, in fact, make life easier.

These entities would not be there to govern, however; they would be there to serve.

Now, the ego enjoys power for its own sake. It enjoys the feeling of having power and using power; moreover, having a powerful feeling delays the day when you have to look at fears. The ego will put off this day as long as it humanly can.

There is a world of difference between helping your country in a spirit of service and helping from a mere liking of service. The motivation of spirit is to set you free; but the ego likes to serve because of the goodies it gets back.

Enjoyment of the esteem of your fellow men, the marvellous feeling of wielding power through your voice, the exclusive feeling of detachment from the common herd, and the many material rewards of money, mobility and the power for sex and security gratification, arise, not out of love, but out of a liking for service, out of ego.

Love is always that which sees the need of the inner life and serves its need.

Every entity in creation is a free entity, ungovernable by any other. Those who, without awareness, give away their freedom to make choices to others are conditioned by ancient and well established ideas about society and its myriad conventions.

The eternal political arguments about the pros and cons of different systems for human beings to live by presuppose that human beings are objects to be packaged and processed, be wrapped up in the same pretty paper, and thereby be comfortably nestled together under the warm umbrella of the State. The idea of most politicians is to mould, manipulate, organise and generally to become as skilful as possible at ordering people about without them resenting it, making them believe it is for the sake of their own good or for "the sake of society".

But how can you possibly know what is good for the whole unless you yourself are whole? You cannot.

Unless you are whole you are blind to the outer and deaf to the inner. Smooth talking politicians, social philosophers, priests, lawyers, in fact anyone who says they know what is good for people, are deluded: they are the blind leading the blind. They have no idea what they should be looking at in themselves let alone knowing what is good for a nation.

Their true inclinations have been so overlaid by conditioning that they have lost all sight of their joy; they live in denial of their deepest feelings, being empty vessels mouthing clever words, but which are stale and musty with the smell of their buried fears ever present.

The masses who they seek to rule soon sense their lack of authenticity; respect disappears and contempt arises. And, unfortunately, when people are frustrated violence is then easily redirected back toward the ruler. A skilful ruler, knowing this, will often use his or her charisma and silver tongue to divert this energy to an outer imagined threat; and so to war and killing.

When leaders act from wholeness they'll be taking themselves out of the limelight. They might even be doing themselves out of a job. Leaders must have followers, but if you follow how can you be authentic unto yourself. Peace can only happen on this planet when everyone is being - and allowed to be - authentic unto their whole self.

Leadership, as the term is understood today, means responsibility for others and if you believe this is good (or of God) and that this is the way life must be you are in error.

If you think that responsibility is your lot in life and that this is what life is about at all levels, then you are in for some surprises - and probably your ego is in for some sorrow, as it attempts to hang on to ideas that one day it will have to let go of.

No one can say what life is, and even if I say that life is not about responsibility, then I am in error. It is better to say that if you believe life is restricted to this behaviour or that behaviour, you are in error.

Therefore, perhaps we can say that life is responsive but not necessarily responsible. Life is responsive to the needs of life. It is like water flowing downhill to water. It will seek its own and come home and be at one with the ocean again.

Of course, the ability to respond, the urge to respond and the joy of responding lovingly and wisely, and maybe making a sacrifice to do so, is the very nature of the gods, but these same gods know that, in the final analysis, every entity is responsible for their own well being just as they are for theirs; and yet, as we are all linked, are we also not, in the final analysis, all responsible for each other? Indeed we are. And here is a paradox about the nature of life. It is a paradox, like so many others, which just has to be accepted.

Distortion enters into responsibility when you believe, to the point of fanaticism, that only you have the answers for the welfare of others. By believing this, you are, in the same breath, denying that each human being is a spark of God in their own right; because, of course, if they were god they would presumably know what was best for themselves.

Whenever you know what's best (or think it) for another person, you are denying them their divinity.

When you deny others their divinity you are certainly not going to be happy yourself. And it is only when *you* find out who *you* truly are that you will know that every other person is God, too. It must be so, and is so.

It is not so much a question of "owning your own power" as *owning your own integrity of being*.

The phrase "owning your own power" has implications of being a powerful person. Yet, when this phrase is turned round to the more truthful "owning your own integrity of being" it takes on a vastly different implication: it means keeping yourself open to the still small voice of spirit (which may entail laying yourself open to being vulnerable) and resisting the power of others that would try to cut you off from your essential self.

Wondrous entities who lovingly watch you, encourage you and assist you in so many ways, most of which you are totally unaware of, do so because it is their joy to do so. It is not their responsibility nor their duty. It is the role they have joyfully chosen to play, and they do play it so beautifully.

Any time they feel you are in danger of being obligated to them through your desire to worship, or through your desire to be dependent upon them, they do withdraw for a space.

It is the joy of these helpers to assist you to connect to the joy of your own being. It is their only joy; it is their only desire and it is given freely without any "hooks", without any expectation of return payment in emotional satisfaction or its kind. This is not regarded as a duty bound responsibility to look after you, pamper you and generally make sure you make the grade. Rather, it is a response from the very heart of life to life itself. It is entirely without ties or thought of results. Who can be tied? Who is there to tie? Will God tie God?

The greatest joy of entities who live in the realms of light is to assist others, for they do at all times spend their lives within an energy field of such high frequency that they are constantly experiencing God inwardly (but not exclusively) as themselves.

Out of compassion only, which is indeed an outward growing branch of the tree of life, do entities draw to themselves the mother creative energy and assist others to awaken to the inner life.

And so it should be with service upon this plane. But, sadly, no governments yet see themselves as providing this kind of service.

It takes two to form a government: one to give orders and another to obey them.

There is nothing wrong about agreeing, voluntarily, to obey the directions of another for a while. This may be very necessary for you if you wish to learn a particular craft or if you agree, for a while, to take upon yourself the role of disciple to a master.

But these are roles, they are acts you are playing out for your own enlightenment or sense of adventure or life experience. There is no authoritarian government in the realms of universal light which imposes its will upon the beings of light that live within its circumference. The very idea of separation from God is punishment enough as is seen in the suffering that is caused by the separative ego.

Indeed, human beings who believe in governing sooner or later gather to themselves a barrow load of sorrows. It comes in the form of intense feelings of rejection by those they most try to govern. The black despair of wounded pride, of abandonment, of feeling unloved, is the classic case of the conditioned ego taking a severe knock.

A free man is an ungovernable man and a free woman in an ungovernable woman. A free man will allow government to exist without allowing it to dictate to him what he should think or how he should behave. He will tolerate it for the sake of others who still need it.

Those who believe in the ultimate need of government have, within themselves, the seeds of desire to be governors. It is merely the other side of the coin. And, those who would govern have, within them, the unconscious desire to be governed.

The masses on this planet live in such ignorance that relaxation of all government would lead to chaotic anarchy. Without any government whatever, conditioned egos come face to face with fears that are deep rooted in the human psyche, the fear of abandonment, the fear of being cold and lonely, the fear of non-achievement, the fear of non-existence, the fear of dying. These are black fears which egos will do anything to avoid recognising they have, even to the point of pillaging and plundering and murdering off any opposition to keep themselves safe.

These fears are too much for most of the masses of this world's egos to face at present (though, for you, who are reading this book, they are not too much for you to face).

By now you will have realised that, though this book is applicable to everyone; in point of fact, it is aimed only at those of you who are now, at this very time, responsive to this message, being already conscious servers of the light in the world today.

These teachings will, in fact, be of most use to those of you who are already conscious of being teachers.

In this present day world, the anarchy that would be generated, without just and fair government (with laws based on ethical justice), by conditioned egos held in thrall to the instinctive demands arising from the reactions of blind cellular life, would(and does)lead to the most horrific chaos. Better by far to have democratic government than this.

A form of government such as democracy, which has within it adequate checks to resist exploitation by the elite or by the power of vested interest organisations, is an excellent form of government for the world's nations of today, for it brings together many different viewpoints in a spirit of sharing and creative cooperation in which dissent and opposing opinions are tolerated and, indeed, actively encouraged.

This is definitely a great advancement from absolute monarchies or dictatorships which provide (in most cases) a most impoverished environment for the spiritual growth and enterprise of individuals.

Democratic government does provide for a minimum of interference, hopefully, in the freedom of choice its citizens have in which to express their own individuality. It provides for more opportunity for ego transparency and dissolution. Further, the leaders of the nation have an opportunity, in a far safer environment than in a dictatorship, in which they can explore and face the illusion of power, and admit to its inadequacies: namely, force, as the great solution.

Democracy should not be thought of as the perfect government. There is no such thing. It should not try to be moulded into a perfect utopian social system by a few in the name of all, the few believing that they have been chosen to have a mandate to lord it over all their citizens. It should, rather, be the ideal of a democratic order in which the goal of life is sensed, and to which end leaders commit themselves to serve; and in which freedoms of expression of varying richness can be embraced.

You, who are to be the teachers and healers of earth have little need of governments and little need of the lessons that political affray affords the egos of politicians. It is your being-ness, not your good ideas, which will be as an enlightened example to other individuals upon the earth. Your light will shine with such simplicity, with such integrity, with such love and joy, that many will flock to you to ask you for your secret, and then will be the time to tell them.

You can also allow governments *to be*. Do not fight them or take issue with them with aggressive intent. But, neither allow them to compromise the truth of your being.

The time when government does not need to exist will come but it is some ages away on this planet, and it will not happen as a result of a decision but as a gradual changing of its form and an even more gradual falling away of interest and energy for its perpetuation. So, I say to you, relax and do not try to hasten this time. In truth, a time will come when no governments exist as you know them today. It will not take the form of one great central government, or of a theocracy run by priests in control of all, though there will be a centre of light to which (or to whom) all will look. Neither sterile control or chaotic anarchy will be the result. But, there shall come into being the flowering of a beautiful living organism wondrous to behold. The fully enlightened earth.

You are to resist government pressure to model you into mindless and comfortable functionaries, but it is not for you to battle for change and entangle yourself in the mire of the life of the political ego which is a formidable ego indeed!

Perhaps the most important function of government is education. And enlightened education is the foremost service of those who would be helpers and leaders.

Behind all the acquiring of skills for human achievement and survival, it should never be lost sight of: that self-realisation of The Oneness and thus the true enlightenment of the mind is the goal of every person.

Enlightenment of mind, which is the realisation of the role you play within the Oneness, brings about such focus and good will within you, as an individual, that it acts upon the environment in ways that are so far reaching that even the rocks and crystals in their rudimentary consciousness are affected.

The impact of a person's realisation of Oneness and the enlightenment of their mind is of far greater benefit to the world than, say, the impact upon human consciousness of peace workers who, despite their useful and worthy efforts, are often quite aggressive and far from peaceful in themselves.

You too easily compromise your spiritual integrity, being your ability to live authentically and vitally in the moment, by embracing various causes and giving away to them your sovereignty of being. Outer causes are legion. They are always springing up like mushrooms after the slightest shower of summer rain. Be wary of them.

When, out of fear, human beings act together, in a group or in a government, they are looking to retain and sustain their power in equal proportion to those who would take it away from them. Again, it is the duality of the ego that is being mirrored here; and in so doing the ego of these power brokers cements itself into a permanently altered state, shutting out the inner life - in fact, paradoxically denying it the unlimited power it so desperately craves.

The greatest denial of truth is the belief that being vulnerable is dangerous, or against the best interests of the individual: the opposite is true.

Firstly, no one can take away your power to be your sovereign joyful self unless you imagine they can. If you believe they can, your ego will set deep foggy clouds around you. You will live in a distorted ego reality in which you will probably find yourself accepting the social security of the State on the one hand whilst railing against your frustrations on the other.

Secondly, there is the fear of death. This is so universal that it is hardly worthwhile commenting on, yet it is so absurd this fear. Galactic beings do not have the concept of death in any shape or form, so why should you? And why do you so compromise your joy and your sovereignty to this bogey of non reality? I shall speak more of death later.

Fundamentally, human governments have always been about protection and power. They thrive on the belief that someone can take something of value from you, which basically comes down to the belief that they can take away your joy and the independence and freedom of your being. When you believe this, you allow it to come to pass and you will start to build a power base around yourself which is at least equal in power to the imagined threat, before you can first feel good about yourself.

So whenever you find yourself accumulating lots of comfortable things around you, yet you sense frustration and boredom in your life, it may be an indication to you that you are suffering from a deep belief in your own insecurity and immobility.

As is the case in any of your relationships, you don't have to like the relationship you have with your government. You always have the choice of coming out with your feelings and inviting a change. If that doesn't work, or if it isn't appropriate, you can always invite them to leave. And if they won't, then *you* can. You always have a choice: if not physically, at least in consciousness.

You can do all this without blaming; for, as I have said, blaming is a judgement from the distorted viewpoint of the ego. But you can always act. Not so much talk and more action! It matters not so much what you do, only that you act with clarity and with the awareness of your connectedness to your source, the Oneness. Act when there is enthusiasm to act.

Holding on to power, trying to match power with power, is admitting to a belief in your own intrinsic vulnerability and, if persisted in, will lead to loss of power, loss of immunity, loss of psychic energy and loss of peace of mind, and it will inevitably lead to premature ageing and many illnesses.

Have you ever seen two stags with their heads down and their antlers locked together, trying to match power with power; it's heads down, eyes to the ground and, to be sure, neither of them has any idea of where they are going except to try and push the other off the face of the earth.

For human beings this is a futile way to behave but so many do just this in their relationships: it is mental head butting all the way.

Never fight with another unless you have a prior agreement to explore with each other the origin of your feelings of resentment or frustration. In these cases of mutual agreement, the emotion released can be greatly beneficial.

Without this prior agreement, though (which is, between loved ones, an expression of the will to be) it is not helpful to involve yourself in fighting for the sole purpose of relieving yourself of anger; it can only strengthen the ego which can soon justify its need to be angry in the belief that your sovereignty is able to be compromised by the outside imagined threat. And, of course, this belief is further strengthened if the outer threat does give way, temporarily, to your blustering strong arm tactics.

This matter of power and vulnerability, again, are two sides of duality. It is not a question of deliberately making yourself powerful or of deliberately making yourself vulnerable; both these are opposites and undue emphasis on either must lead to illusion. It is, rather, that having an awareness of who you are, being aware of The Oneness, a natural power arises in you which is the power of being in your joy even when physically you might appear to be at your most vulnerable. This is to live in harmony with The Oneness and all the components of your personality.

When you open up to your own spiritual integrity there is no desire in you to try to be powerful from any defensive ego stance and neither is there any desire to make yourself vulnerable from any other ego motive; for, as you know, making yourself deliberately vulnerable or passive is a cunning ego ploy to defuse a potentially dangerous confrontation by behaving un-naturally defensively.

The secret is to open up to your *natural* power; which is to live in the moment as a spontaneous and very alive joyful human being, through which spirit (your whole self) will surely govern you in all your actions. Yes, politicians can do this. Indeed, many do already serve with fine intent and goodwill. It is great service. Know you that power can be wielded - and often is - safely and wisely for the good of all.

So, do not be cynical about politicians. Look for the best in them. It is a valid path of service, and oft times not an easy one.

Blessed is the day when nations serve and love each other according to their abilities; they shall uphold and make straight the great way for every sovereign individual; whereupon the ideologies of self-serving politicians shall be dismissed as the ravings of lunatics.

CHAPTER TWELVE

HEALING

It could be said that healing is the great art of making a person whole. Yet, I ask you again: how can you make whole that which, in one sense, already is whole?

Indeed, you may, if you are self-realised, trigger off within the other his or her recognition that within them wholeness has always been there, eternally, original, pristine and immutable.

This recognition can effect instant healing and it can well be permanent if that recognition is maintained and crystallised into the personality of the person, by them, as self realisation.

By this manner, the conditioned ego loses its conditioning and realises that it is not only an expression of the whole, but at the very same time *it is the whole ITSELF.*

Thus, personality is not lost, but illuminated by its realisation of its wholeness both in the part and in the whole, together within the Oneness.

So, now, understanding that healing is not, fundamentally, the art of making a person whole again, we can rephrase our first sentence and say: healing is the great art of helping another to remove their beliefs that they are separate from Oneness - God.

There are many ways to help another return to this inner recognition and dissolve the beliefs of their ego. As I have said before, the devious ploys of the ego is more than matched by the many skills of helpers, all of whom have had ample experience in many lifetimes of the deviousness of their own egos and who are thus very qualified to be healers and helpers on the physical plane.

Depending on the character and personality make-up of the person to be helped, he or she can be approached through therapy, religion, art, music, philosophy, not to mention the vast field of medicine, both alternative and orthodox. Any of these, and countless other avenues such as films and television, and even war, can be, and have been, of use in reaching egos and giving their beliefs a shake up. In rare cases, a self realised man or woman will arrive upon the scene and dramatically confront egos. In these cases, the events surrounding these teachers are often stormy and turbulent; the egos involved will make a final stand. Their ploys are unmasked and they either have to dissolve them, releasing them to the light, or stand and fight - or run for their spurious lives!

This creates a lot of confusion for onlookers. But their day, too, will come!

Healers, teachers and helpers have, in this way, achieved much and if it wasn't for their selfless and magnificent acts of sacrifice and service, this world would long ago have fallen into anarchy and blown itself apart. Do love your teachers, they have given you much under immense hardships, over many lifetimes, asking little for themselves. They are about to step on to the world stage and reveal themselves, with some reservation, I might say, for they are entities of great sensitivity and relish not having to deal with the murk and flak of generally desperate egos. But, above all, they do love you. Their compassion is boundless and they deserve your love (but not your sentimentality or your worship).

Of course, there have been short comings and the occasional hiccup in these wonderful streams of effort, but the overall result has been one of patient and steady achievement, *and success is now assured.*

In religion, emphasis has been on outer worship and on an outer saviour. This emphasis is now changing. New age teachings are proliferating and will, very soon, be appealing to the masses. Orthodox psychology has traditionally gone no further than the treatment of personality problems. After treatment, the person is encouraged to return to the same life style and value system from which he or she is, unconsciously, trying to escape from. But, this, too, is changing as more and more psychologists open to the Oneness and look to their spirit and come to trust it.

Philosophy has got lost, being bogged down in a love of words, and a love of meaning and analysis for its own sake, but here, too, there is a new wave of thinkers who are prepared to look a little further than what is inside their brains and their dictionaries.

Twentieth century medicine has done well in curing the effects of illness, but seldom has it thought to look at the causes of frustration or the denial of feelings that lie behind it. Yet, medicine, too, is upon an avalanche of change.

There is a time coming when all these activities will be complimented by direct spiritual power, the agents of which, by the grace of their own impeccable being-ness, by their own magnetism and psychic energy, and by being attuned to the Oneness - or God - will be so able to stimulate and stir the inner life of an entity that that entity's life will come forth and effect its own healing. Then shall healing be seen for what it really is: not the making better the unwell, but the unwell accepting with sudden joyful insight the self realisation that they are whole, that they are God - as a part of God.

I have touched on this method of healing in Chapter Nine (*Evil and Suffering*). Here I will add to it. Forgive me if I am repetitive, but there is an antidote to suffering, and this is it. It is nothing less than ending the denial of all those feelings which lurk behind the camouflage of so-called evil. It depends on the release of old locked-in emotion, of the emotion lying behind old hurts and wounds. And this means all of them, wherever in time and space they may have originated.

It depends, further, on you yourself retrieving responsibility for the hurt or the wound, both for the original wound itself and for the healing. It depends on you taking full responsibility for any healing which eventuates, gratefully acknowledging the help of the healer and divine grace.

It finally depends on you letting go of old belief patterns and old mental programmes you may have long held on to which no longer serve the new enlightened you.

In this work, it will help to have a physical body that is sufficiently mineralised, having a medium of correctly balanced electrolytes and being sufficiently hydrated with pure water. This will assist the spiritual (kundalini) energy in its healing work.

Remember again, the discharging of emotion heals. Removing old belief programmes and sending them to the light, heals. Doing both together heals permanently!

This work automatically clears the 2nd and 3rd chakras.

Fundamental, strongly held, core beliefs held by your conditioned ego concerning the truth - as the ego sees it - about your separateness from God or the Oneness, is the cause of all your suffering and disease.

By removing these internal (usually unconscious) mind programmes, by allowing the discharge of emotion - if there be any - and by releasing these old negative programmes (by sending them to God's light) and replacing them with new positive life-affirming programmes, and in believing once again in the Oneness or our Father-Mother-God, or Great Creative Spirit (however you wish to call the Oneness) you are creating the environment for healing to happen. And it will happen. In fact, you can command God to make it happen! Remember you are God, as an aspect of God. As a co-creator, now affirming this, now knowing this, you can command healing for yourself *as long as you do your part.*

This is what co-creation is all about! You do your part. God does His/Her/Its part. A co-operative venture. Don't leave it all to God. That never works! God needs to know you are serious about any kind of manifestation by seeing that you are going for it. And I do mean really going for it first!

There are four levels within your mind body that hold old (sometimes very ancient) ego-conditioning beliefs. They all need to be cleared.

The first is childhood conditioning. These crippling beliefs are held in the front region of the brain. The second is genetic conditioning. These are beliefs that over the millennia of the evolution of form upon the earth have found their way into the DNA of your physical body. They are to be found in your pineal gland in the centre of your head.

The third origin of deeply buried beliefs come from your past lifetimes. They are to be found at the back of your head. The fourth area to be cleansed is in the area of the heart where deep seated emotion such as grief, despair, terror, loneliness, betrayal and any amount of hurt and wounds may be lodged. These feeling-scar-memories can even be lodged as memories in your higher self (your soul). They are at the deepest level of all.

All these four levels have a profound impact on your 2nd and 3rd chakras, both in your etheric and physical body, providing and qualifying the energy for your day to day activities in the physical realm.

When you are replacing your old mind programmes (sending them to God's light) with new ones, it is *important to imagine* all these four areas, front of head, back of head, pineal gland and heart, releasing their old programmes into the light *and being replaced with light.*

This manner of healing allows you to work with the very core of your being in such a way that healing may happen instantly.

To begin this method of healing, you first need to enter into meditation, affirming with God your intent to command a healing in order to be healed. Having made your intent plain, you command (*not ask!*)the Oneness to make whole that which is in dis-ease or in disharmony in your body. In your mind, *now using visualisation,* you go to that place in your body and *actually see (or imagine) the healing take place.* When you are satisfied that it has, you affirm that all is done and you give thanks to God that all is done. Don't forget this last part. It is important.

In this manner, you co-create with the Oneness and you command God to effect healing on yourself, or, indeed, upon others (*as long as you have their permission first to do so*) which can change their life for ever.

In the case of others, first, you will look inside the body of your patient and identify any problem areas, including the four areas in the head, and then, *with their permission,* you will command the creative forces of the universe to perform the healing. Yes, miracles do happen!

This type of healing is in its infancy in the world at present. After some predictable opposition from entrenched medical academics, this method of healing will evolve into the greatest and most efficacious healing system ever known, and for the very reason that it works!

Drugs will have no part to play in this type of healing.

The kundalini fire, the all-wise Mother Fire, as it has been termed, being the body's own energies, attuned to God's light, and being complimented by that of the healers' energies, will do the healing work. It will become standard healing practice. It will become as ordinary and as matter of fact as going to the doctor today. Except, there will be, in this mode of healing, a radical change of emphasis from reliance on the doctor to a reliance on yourself.

Orthodox medicine will still have its place, but its emphasis will be more on diagnosis, emergency repair, virulent infection control and convalescence.

Another type of healing will begin to make itself known. We shall call it cosmic healing. It will occur spontaneously around self-realised men and women. It will be increasingly seen in the world.

But, first, I will speak of an important aspect of healing which, though it applies particularly to cosmic healing, applies equally well to all healers: it concerns *desire,* and *the will to heal* - in other words, the motivation of every would be healer.

Relinquishment of self and the concerns of self, the abandonment of all concerns to The Oneness with acceptance and surrender, is being in that state of grace which is termed wholeness.

It is a total elimination of self-consciousness (desire) from the act of healing or of desiring to be healed. Even the desire to be instruments of service to The Oneness needs to be eliminated (which is misunderstood by even highly developed entities of the higher planes). There is a fine distinction between being of service as a result of *being in the authenticity of your wholeness* and desiring to be an instrument of service to God from a well intentioned personality desire.

There is a vast difference between service from a state of wholeness, and having the conditioned ego desire to serve selflessly.

Service according to God's will (as when you are in your natural and spontaneous wholeness of being) necessitates total relinquishment, and moment by moment surrender and dedication to The Oneness.

The relinquishment of the conditioned ego is none other than the relinquishment of the self conscious will of the individual.

As I have said, the time draws near when cosmic power (which is the same power that Jesus demonstrated) will again startle the masses into recognition that God is still "ruling" His/Her creation. In other words, that the Oneness is still around to be remembered and embraced!

This cosmic power will only be channelled by those who have disassociated self from all desire and all expectation of the results (most especially subconscious desires) of healing.

Those channelling cosmic power will be permeated with cosmic energy only in proportion to the degree of selflessness demonstrated by themselves.

Cosmic healing is totally unconditional upon any human condition, especially upon receiving money or any so called "exchange of energy".

Those who insist on payment, either as a means by which to make their livelihood or as a condition of a concept of "exchange of energy", are not living in a state of grace or wholeness, totally surrendered to God, relinquishing all material concerns. They will not be recipients of cosmic power.

Cosmic healing is of the nature of purification which not only cleanses the physical body but also the conscious mind, leaving in the recipient only the desire to live impeccably connected to the truth of his or her being - in place of any desire to possess material things or mental attributes.

The ultimate healer is LOVE. It doesn't matter whether you are physical on non-physical. It doesn't matter where you are in the cosmos, love rules everywhere and everyone. No one, and nothing, can escape it! It is the motive power which empowers all life, human and non-human.

Please do remember that the non-humans (the aliens) you shall meet are love in manifested form, such as you yourselves are.

If you have a problem on your mind which, by the way, is where all problems originate, you can solve it when you surrender your mind to the universal Christ spirit. When you do this you will find the problem will solve itself. Your mind will regain its peace.

Indeed, this is such a simple way to effect healing that it is often overlooked.

The universal Christ spirit, which in non-Christian terminology can be termed the universal mind of God, is not to be seen as being exclusive to Jesus or any other religion. It has been termed the Cosmic Christ. It is universal to everyone.

I have not spoken in this short chapter of the truly legion of healing activities upon this world for they are well documented and, moreover, the time has come for the recognition of the wholeness of your being and the recognition that every individual walking upon the earth today is indeed a supreme god in manifestation, and that this is a demonstrable fact.

Recognition of God as the whole, and as the whole within each and everyone, will eliminate myriad intermediate steps of present day healing in the seemingly complex procedure of the restoration of imbalance encountered by the healing professions in their approach to the ills of mankind. And also of the seemingly endless meanderings of therapy.

Those who have ears to hear, hear now that only those who have great courage and lack not faith in the outcome of their act of relinquishment, shall be the redeemers of mankind.

Relinquishment is faith in action. This assignment is given only to those dedicated individuals who are ready to relinquish all the remains of selfish desire. It is so utterly impersonal an act that few accomplish it. It is to the few that I speak.

You are the flowers of humanity. You shall heal the world.

So be it.

CHAPTER THIRTEEN

OF NOURISHMENT

All in this wondrous universe of ours is nourished by love. It is this fact and this fact alone which brings to the enlightened mind that peace which passeth all understanding.

Without striving and without understanding the whys and wherefores, everything in the universe is constantly and naturally and easily being nourished by the continual and eternal stream of love-thought-nourishment rays which beam from the source of our Father-Mother-God to reach every single particle of The Oneness.

It is this knowledge which brings to the enlightened entity the sparkle in the eye, the laughter in the heart, the strength in the bearing, and the peace upon the brow which permeates also to every cell in the body.

Without the awareness that your real source of nourishment is the loving rays of light, your bodies will become more and more dense as you believe in your conditioned ego separateness from the light and fixate more and more addictively on dense food.

In this sense, and in this sense only, you are what you eat. If you believe it is your dense food that keeps you alive, you will increase your density until you are a very dense and materialistic entity. If you are aware that it is the rays of living loving light which are, by far, the most important part of your nourishment, then you shall clothe yourself in your body of light whilst still in the physical body, and that physical body shall also then undergo transformation.

It matters not so much what you give the physical body to eat as long as it is healthy and appropriate to its optimum functioning.

Concerning material food, it is untrue to say you are what you eat: you are not going to turn into a banana or a coconut if this is all you can find to eat (and very fine foods these are, too, for the physical body). You will not turn into a brute if you eat animal products and neither will you turn into a weak minded layabout if you eat only vegetables.

An entity who is aware of and consciously acknowledges in his life the source of his or her true nourishment cannot possibly suffer loss of consciousness by eating food to the degree that eating that food would change him or her into something else. It is only the ego that changes. It shuts itself off from the rays of living loving light which then leave it at the mercy of the food that it eats, for it sincerely believes it is dependent upon that food for its life; and, of course, as you believe, so it will be drawn to you.

It is far truer to say that you are what you think you are: if you believe you are an entity of light and you are nourished mainly by light, then light you shall be and it will pour out from your being (your aura) and nourish others. If you believe you rely solely on physical food for your life, you take it in, nothing goes out, and you sink like a stone into density.

Any food that you take into your body should, therefore, have as its aim the keeping of your body in perfect balance and at peak mechanical efficiency, at the same time as assisting in the transformation of your body to a vehicle of greater light, being a type of body suitable for your cosmic self to use.

In other words, every time you have a snack you need to say to yourself: "Is this chocolate bar, or this cup of coffee, going to keep my body more fit and healthy? Is it going to allow the cells in my body to hold more rays of light?"

These are the two questions to ask yourself before you eat. So, eat with awareness and resist the unaware and compulsive grab for the cookie jar. I know that this seems to be asking a lot and that it is very much easier said than done, but it is vitally important that you act with awareness in this area of your life, especially those of you who are here on earth to be teachers and healers.

You will have to discipline yourself to become aware of the times when your ego tries to remove you from your awareness of eating. You will learn so much about your fears and ego manipulations in so many areas of your life just by watching your impulses to eat. Look at the times when you remain aware; look at how, and when, you override your better judgement and feel guilty afterwards.

If you keep watching and keep confronting the ego and keep having insights concerning those times when you eat compulsively, you will learn many things about yourself concerning inhibitions, lack of confidence, frustration, loneliness and lack of love, and so on. The most important thing of all, however, is your discovery concerning your beliefs. At one time or another you have bought into the belief systems of others, making them your own, and your food has become a way of giving yourself the love that you felt you didn't get (or couldn't give), and then, of course, the food has become an excellent compensation for feelings denied and deeply buried in the cellular memory of your body.

So, here we see the importance of observing the mind once again. Watching your mind in the area of food is of the greatest importance. Food and love, together with sex and love, are entangled with each other in deep and archetypal patterns of ego confusion, and the way out is not, I repeat, so much in the discipline of what you eat but in the disciplined awareness of *how* and *when* you eat.

If you are having difficulty in this area of food, do not be depressed; it is one of the last barriers that ego puts up. You are well on your way to self-realisation.

God is love.

The ego says God is food.

You are at present swinging in the middle, but the days of the ego are numbered. You know its game and it is weakening. It is only a matter of time. Keep watching and keep meditating, keep feeling, keep validating the joy and love that you see in your friends, and help them own up to it. It shall set you free. Never give yourself a hard time over food lest you strengthen ego guilt.

And now to another matter: know you that the plants you eat which enable you to inhabit a flesh and skeletal structure suitable for the earth plane are nothing less than the loving rays of living light crystallised (with the help of the angelic stream of evolution) into living loving food for you.

How seldom do you acknowledge this fact when you eat ? How seldom do you acknowledge this fact when you plant your seeds or when you harvest your food ?

You will always draw into yourself what your thoughts dwell upon. If it is your greatest desire to be a living expression of love and joy on earth, and indeed why not, then it is beholden upon you to hold in thought that the food you eat is an expression of that same love and joy energy, which indeed it is.

You should know that you are a spark of God in manifestation and that your plants, which are your food, are this also. In essence, you, and plants both, are an expression of the loving joy of the creator which is yourself.

The only real difference between you and plants is one of consciousness. You are awake to the possibility of knowing who you are and you have the ability to alter, if you wish, how conscious you are. The plant has to alter its form if it wishes to alter its consciousness; you do not.

In plants, abundant provision has been made for your body - for its perfect nourishment and for the delightful experience of feeling good in a physical body. The union of the two, physical body and plants, is more than stoking a body with fuel. It is the merging of two loving life forms. It is a marriage, a relationship, every bit as sacred as any other. And in this there lies a profound truth.

The merging of plant consciousness with that of the physical body of human beings is paralleled by and resonates to the merging of the angelic stream of consciousness (for the angels do imbue plants with their very own life force) with the human stream at another higher level of consciousness and this is of profound moment to the growth and awakening of this planet which is moving from a planet of darkness to a planet of light, as witness the renewal of global environmental concern.

It will also, by the way, see a large increase in vegetarianism which will even become fashionable as humans everywhere, albeit unconsciously, begin to resonate to this truth.

Awareness of this merging of the two streams, angelic and human, and the positive affirmation of it, however, will bring to the world a great blessing undreamed of by even those who are already dedicated vegetarians.

Whenever you eat, recollect that these streams of light and colour are also nourishing you. They are directed to you by the angelic streams and are, indeed, a part of their very own consciousness and being. Thus you unite with them at a moment's thought. They are not there to serve you, though serve they do, but to unite with you and to bring to fruition a wondrous plan of light for earth.

At any moment you can send a thought to these wondrous ray angels and ask to be bathed through and through with their rays of colourful loving nourishment and energy, but, in order to change your compulsive and unaware habits concerning food it is particularly useful to do so at times of eating.

Have you not heard it said that the Christ was ministered to by the angels? Well, it was so, and remains so to this day. You, also, are to be a Christ and this is how you will be ministered to. Be aware of it and begin to allow it to happen.

The symbolic story of Satan tempting Jesus with food in the desert was really an interpretation of the strength of Jesus' desire to remain awake to his compulsive eating habits and get to the root of the fear behind the unconscious desire to eat. When he had done so, when he had confronted the illusion, and affirmed that he was a being of light, then he recognised the angels of living-loving-colour, merging with them in consciousness. They were to become an important part of his life in the area of his nourishment and vitality, both physically and spiritually; and so great things began to happen. And so it will be for you when you can confront your unconscious fears and compulsive habits and know that you are a being of light, to be nourished by light.

I am bringing to you here a great truth which can revolutionise your life if you allow it to. How you eat is an indication of how you see yourself to be. Don't starve yourself to death or weaken yourself by going on strange diets or by trying to prove to yourself that you don't need food: anorexia is another ego ploy which would prefer you to starve rather than look at the denial of your feelings and the fears that lie at the back of them. Eat sensibly from the plant kingdom. Eat joyfully. But, KEEP AWAKE. Then you can experience the feelings which arise, pin point the fears, discharge the emotion behind them, and, having confronted them, then you can change your old habits into new ones. You will reaffirm all that is positive in your life, knowing that you are indeed a being of light and that your etheric body (your true physical body), is one of pure living-loving energy and always will be.

Such a simple thing. Can so much change happen to me just through watching my eating? I hear you ask.

Yes, it can. I cannot emphasise this strongly enough. All of you need to watch this area in your lives very closely, for it holds much for you, and you will not be given the keys to your kingdom until you have done so - as was the case with that great entity born in Bethlehem.

When you eat, feel the joy of life within you. Never eat at a table where there is likely to be disharmony, and do not get dragged into frivolous or boring or aggressive discussion which will take you away from your awareness of the profound relationship between you and food, between you and the angels.

And, by profound, I don't mean solemn! Beware of the holier than thou demeanour! Eat with joy. Your relationship with the angels is one of joy. Affirm it always.

By all means say a prayer or a blessing at the beginning of a meal, but mean it!

Never let a prayer become a perfunctory routine. It is the worst of ego ploys, and don't shovel food into your body whilst sitting in front of the T.V. The awareness you retain through the meal is the all important matter. An attunement together, perhaps holding hands, at the start of a meal is beneficial. It can help you be aware and receptive so that the blending of these two wondrous streams of consciousness, the human and the angelic life, within you, can give rise to what every union should: greater joy, greater balance, greater peace, and greater energy.

The problem with television is that whatever you watch, for the time you are watching it, becomes your reality. It very effectively takes you away from your own divine moment and the awareness of your Self. For those who have strongly conditioned egos, or who are not yet able to disassociate from their egos (as in the case of children), television has a subtle and malign influence on their lives.

Television is responsible for much distortion because it subtly alters your perception of reality. It is a cause of much confusion in young minds, and the cause of much apathy in the masses. Its easy seductiveness all to easily obviates the need for personal relationships, allowing you to bury feelings which would be far better confronted and released. Relationships are all important mirrors for you. They are absolutely vital for your lessons in this world. They mirror for you the joy of your being and they mirror for you where you are blocked from experiencing the joy of your being. And, practically, they teach you how to share, to play and how to co-operate with other human beings in a world where sensible compromise is often eminently useful and, indeed, loving and self-sacrificing when undertaken in a spirit of service. Television mirrors back to you absolutely nothing. It is not usually very educational and it is never recreational. It recreates nothing. Watching it for many hours a day cannot but help to reinforce the ego's belief in the pointlessness of life. Thus, it is a fact that television (and compulsive computer addiction) is a contributing factor to suicide amongst young people.

Another damaging aspect about passive television watching is that it numbs the imagination. Now, imagination is the spark behind all innovative and original creative thought. Television reduces the need for any thought. Television brain-washes you in to believing you have no imagination or, that, if you have, it is not worth much. This is an appalling error. It is certainly in the ego's interests to keep you ignorant of this otherwise you might have enough imagination to start believing that you might be a free and powerful, and joyful loving being - or that you might even be God in incarnation!

Your imagination, being unique to you, is your spirit's way of communicating with you. When you disown it or take no interest in it, you are disowning your spirit. Through your intuitive link to spirit, imagination opens the doors to vistas you need to experience.

Imagination, also, is the key to psychic development. So, whichever way you look at it, anything that tends to stupefy or negate imagination is a blight upon the light. Television and computer excesses are a going to cause many problems for your society unless individuals wake up to these dangers.

However, your concern with food is perhaps your major, in your face, on a continuing day to day basis, ego-conditioning factor. When you consciously (and lovingly) acknowledge the rays of loving nourishment that beam towards your planet, you will find to your astonishment how little food you need. How much healthier you will be and how much easier it will be for you to achieve translation into your light body.

From a cosmic viewpoint your etheric body is, in fact, your true physical body; it is a body of vital energy perfectly suitable for moving about in and experiencing life on the physical plane. Your dense physical body is a further densification, a fossilisation if you like, of your vital body. This hardening of the etheric body happened in the dim past of human history due to the merging of two streams of consciousness which were not meant to merge but which did merge. There were those who experimented with this long ago unnatural union, hoping to assist the evolution of earth. Unfortunately it had the reverse effect. The experimenters lost their awareness of their divine origin and came to know fear. Scientists of today who are experimenting with the exchange of body parts between humans and animals, cloning, and the like, should take note.

The entities of those ancient times, whose desire it was to experience physical plane existence whilst at the same time assisting earth, instead of remaining in their true physical forms (being their etheric energy bodies) became trapped, as it were, in dense bodies of flesh. They lost their mobility, and they lost their ability to move from the physical plane to higher planes without "dying." Further, they lost their ability to solely depend upon the nourishing rays of light for all their energy, so that, from that time onward, they had to work by the sweat of their brow. This has caused much confusion and imbalance among the different streams of evolving consciousness on earth, not the least of which has been the apparent elusiveness that seems to have arisen between you and your planetary teachers and planetary guardians. This has been as a direct result of this unusual experiment. However, this *apparent* distance between you and your planetary guides and guardians is about to end.

Your teachers have, of course, never left you, for they have all this time been living in the etheric levels of this world. There, they have been extremely busy, encouraging you, supporting you, and stimulating you; even, from time to time, taking dense physical form as Krishna, Jesus, Buddha, Mohammed, and many others have done.

It so happens that the veil between you and your teachers is now thinning very fast. Moreover, many of them have again taken physical incarnation at this time in order to hasten this thinning of the veil and to reveal to you once again both the glory and the reality of the Oneness.

I might say that this long ago experiment of unnatural union was also in the way of a grand adventure, for no experience is ever wasted. To the entities involved it has brought much richness and insight into the nature of creation; and the entities, despite their suffering, have gained much, even being "envied" (if that be an appropriate word to use) by many in the universe. Do remember that nothing is wrong and that nothing ever was wrong. There is only experience, and if the experience has been one of suffering for you, then it has been your desire to experience suffering, and there is nothing wrong in that.

Most entities, however, and I presume that you are one of them, would now prefer to undertake their experiences without suffering. Indeed, this was supposed to be the plan on earth but (originally with the best of intentions) another experience was chosen.

In hindsight, it is easily apparent that doing things with the best of intentions is no guarantee to harmony. Only in surrender to The Oneness is harmony to be found as a constant living truth where joy and love and peace are yours eternally.

It is now time accelerate the cells of your physical body and tune them to a higher vibration so that you can undergo a physical transformation and regain your etheric body of energy and light which is your true physical form. To do this you need the help of the angelic stream of consciousness and their wondrous rays of colour. This has been termed ascension; but a better word for it is transformation.

You are not going *up* (except in terms of vibrational frequency). You will be staying in this world in a body transformed into a body of finer substance. You might become invisible to some humans, and you will be living in areas of great natural beauty.

This is not a mystical or miraculous happening. It is ruled by the laws of physics but by laws that you are not yet familiar with. The process of this transformation is as precise and controlled and as safe as anything you could possibly conceive of. Your personal transformation is monitored and assisted by entities whose task it is to help effect these transformations which, upon a planet of light (which this is not quite yet), take place at special points on the planet's surface, and in public, and, yes, even in groups. They are, as you can imagine, great occasions for celebration; they inspire others to attain, and do reinforce the fact of the love of our Father-Mother-God and the possibility of the attainment of freedom from the local system for all sentient creatures. It is for you to do the preparation work and, in this world, when this has been done, the time and place for transformation will be made known to you.

As I have said, your etheric body is your body of pure vital energy, being the matrix from which your physical body derives its form. Despite accidents of physical damage, despite physical disease, and despite physical ageing, your body is at all times held in perfection by a vital energy template which is held in the form of a matrix in your etheric body.

The etheric level is considered to be the true physical level for the reason that it is the level of the universe at which there is the most intense vitality expressed in terms of creative energy, in the interplay between energy and its form expressions.

This is why, to be a master of energy within The Oneness, you must first have mastered energy and its illusions at the physical level. This is at the back of the keen desire of entities to experience life on the physical plane.

Here lies the eagerness of entities to master the illusions of materialism and, at the same time, to become aware of, and to understand, the vital creative forces of the universe at every level, especially those pertaining to the level of demonstration (the physical), where the interplay of energies can be most easily seen and comprehended.

Is this not a purpose worth exploring?

Looking at it in another way, it is the recreation of yourself as God at the most vital level, being also the most illusory level, so that you can then be a master of all the levels.

It was never intended that entities should lose the awareness of their divine nature, or should lose the nourishment of the splendid rays of living loving colour.

However, as this densification has occurred the challenge that now faces you is to reverse the procedure. This is not too difficult if you harness all your desire and will to that end. It necessitates the raising of the vibration of the physical body to a point where transformation can occur naturally and easily when guided by those who watch and by those who focus and quicken the energies of the transforming fires from within their very own bodies.

Having lost your awareness of your divine nature, this takes more courage, and faith, than it would normally do. But fear not, it can be achieved; and has been achieved by many on this earth, and one day, sooner or later, you, too, will achieve it.

Help is on its way. But do not wait for help, for maybe it is you who are to be one of the helpers; maybe it is you who are to be a lamp to light the way for others.

Never feel guilt about what has passed. It is not of the moment. It is now irrelevant. And, be not disheartened by the fact that I say it was not intended for human entities to thicken, as it were, their vital bodies of light. There is no one who is ever going to judge you, except your own ego.

Suffice to say, that the unique experience this small planet offers to entities who come here, is unique to the universe. So make the best of it!

There are billions of entities in the universe who would like to come here - anything for a taste of this unique situation - before the planetary vibration changes and the door closes to them, which it will do before very long. So you are one of the lucky ones. But, more than that, if you have read this far in this book, you are one of those who have come to help at this time of the earth's initiation. You are needed more than ever; and you are also on your way to your own personal transformation.

So, feel privileged, but do not rest on your laurels. There is work to do, for not a second must be wasted in the task ahead. A trusting heart and an enlightened mind and an indomitable will to succeed are the clothes you must now draw around you.

Transformation does not occur until all has been done, and, until all has been done, eternal vigilance is required. When you undergo transformation on this planet you will have faced illusion the like of which no other entities in the universe have had to face. Something to write home about!

They will be queuing up for your autograph in the star systems!

Transformation is delayed when you ignore the rays of nourishing light that are available to you. The idea that you are the dense physical body, that this has to be kept going solely by physical food, works against you every moment of the day; it keeps you dense; and the vibratory response of your body is so dampened by this belief that the fine energies of transformation have no hope of quickening the energy in your body and accelerating it to the point of transformation.

I wish you to eat the very minimum amount of sensible and healthy physical food to sustain your body of flesh without weakening it in any manner whatever. For the remainder, breathe into yourself the golden food (the *prana*) of God, and become sensitive also to the colours and qualities of the radiating rays of light.

Just as the golden droplets of *prana* are nourishment for your etheric or vital body, so are the rays of light and colour nourishment to your emotional and mental bodies of living light.

Each colour has to it a different *feeling*. I would have you become sensitive to that feeling. *Feel* the different quality of each colour and how it can benefit you emotionally, mentally and physically.

There have been many books written about the ray colours and the qualities they are supposed to carry. Learn about these, but above all experiment with the different colours yourself, from day to day, and breathe in whichever you feel that you might need, always calling first upon the angels to assist you.

This can be done at any time of the day but it is especially important to do it before eating, and extremely useful to do it for a few minutes before your daily meditation. You can breathe in colour in any activity you perform in your life except during contemplation when you are just to be present, as the watcher, and cease all doing.

You will find that it will bring a profound change to your life in many areas. Your mental ability will improve, your emotional life will become clear, sensitive, and balanced, and your physical body will actually begin to feel vital, elastic, and golden, and acutely responsive to your mental and emotional well being. Furthermore, your immediate environment will begin to be magnetised in a manner which will be attractive to others and which will enhance greatly your own ability to accelerate the cellular life of your body.

All this, will happen, due to you merely acknowledging the angels and their rays of light and colour, and to breathing in golden prana: how could it be so easy? Well, it is easy. Life was meant to be easy. But do remember to give thanks to the angels of colour, for this does keep the door open. They are your friends and they love you, and they also deserve your love and thanks.

I do not want you to think of this as colour therapy or colour healing. It is not. It is to become as ordinary to you in your daily life as eating and breathing, and every bit as important.

You are already receiving the golden energy of *prana* and the rays of colour into your being, unknown to you, and at a minimal level of absorption. Now is the time to make this amazing and beautiful process a fully conscious one; now is the time to make this joyful exchange between you and the angels of the nourishing light rays of colour a fully conscious loving exchange; then you will see results indeed.

When you consciously breathe in this wonderful heavenly food, which is truly the food of all the realms of light, you are, by this very act, making this plane into a realm of light, too. This is what I mean when I say that you can begin to magnetise your immediate environment and make it attractive to others. You are truly bringing the kingdom of heaven to earth in an outer way. You are affirming that this is a kingdom of light and that you are an entity of light, inhabiting it.

When you eat physical food do not eat so much for pleasure, but eat for transformation. Put up a notice in your kitchen to remind you; stick it on the door of the freezer, stick it on the larder and stick it on the cookie jar. Your goal is transformation and your being is joy. Try and reconcile the two but don't go making yourself feel hopelessly guilty when you fail in your resolutions; that would be making things difficult for yourself. Remember again, life is meant to be easy!

It is easy to achieve full chakra radiation which culminates with the opening of the crown chakra when you are relaxed, but it is impossible to attain this when any kind of anxiety is present. Subconscious tension, being nothing more than unreleased or unacknowledged emotion, is the cause of all stress. If this becomes a habit, you are living in denial of your of feelings. This precludes the optimum functioning of your chakras.

The opening of the crown chakra reconnects you to your source which is The Oneness. It is the experience of dissolving into God and God dissolving into you. It is the necessary door that must be opened before the transformation of your physical body can occur, before, in other words, you can regain your etheric energy body of light. The breathing in of prana and the visualisation of the rays of living loving colour as you do so will make this a much easier task for you.

When opening yourself to the rays of colour, use your imagination. Imagination is the key to begin a process which will one day culminate in you actually seeing the colours. Imagine how they feel and imagine them flooding over you and through you, going to every part of your body, right through to every cell and right through to the marrow of your bones. *Feel* what colour you would most like to clothe yourself in, *feel* the colour you would most like to dance in, *feel* the colour you would most like to go to sleep in, and make that the colour to open yourself up to in that moment.

If you don't experience *feeling* a colour, *think* of a colour that you would like to be wearing at this moment. This is the colour for you!

It is useful before you begin, to clear your mind, then, look within your head to see if any colour appears there in the area of the brow chakra. If so, then use this colour, for this chakra is, as it were, the director of all that happens in your body, and if you have previously asked which colour to use this is where you may receive the answer. Otherwise, trust your feelings and trust your joy, for this is an even surer guide.

Now, for a comment on your physical food: although it is impossible to destroy life, for life is eternal, the killing of living creatures for food is cruel and unnecessary.

And, how much more abominable is the killing of them for pleasure.

The fruits of the earth which are your plants, their fruits and their seeds, have been given naturally to you to be your food. This is in harmony with the scheme of evolutionary life and, as I have said, it is the joy of the nature kingdom to be of this service to you.

This is not the case with the creatures of the animal kingdom. They are your younger brethren in the evolutionary scheme of things who should, therefore, be acting as the recipients of your loving compassion and receiving your assistance upon their path, rather than being exploited by you and killed for food.

Diabolical, also, are those who maim and dissect the long suffering creatures of earth for their scientific experiments; who do so for their curiosity and in the name of health and benefit for the human condition.

Know you, animals feel pain just as you do.

Know, too, that no benefit to the human condition can ever come from the distress that you cause these beautiful creatures. On the contrary, it gives rise to greater entanglement, more guilt, more shame, more stubbornness and more time before the entities that stain their hands in this cold and bloody science find out that fulfilment and lasting good health comes from self-realisation and not from man's selfish reliance on his seemingly inexhaustible ingenuity.

Those who take pleasure in killing living creatures for sport do not experience this universe as one of loving joy. Compassion has not yet blossomed in their hearts. Their cruelty has become so habitual and common place to them, be it in sport, or in the name of science, or for food, that these entities have forgotten that it is cruelty they are doing, so hardened has become their hearts and so conditioned has become their egos. Cruelty is incompatible with love.

So many pleasures do men and women have; yet, out of all these, many in this world choose the pleasures of chasing and wounding and killing, and call it sport. I call it horrific.

Whereas plants are experiencing their evolutionary phase through the grace and beauty of their form and, so, when dying are ready to merge their consciousness with that of a higher form, this is not the case with animals who are awakening and evolving their awareness through their feeling capacity.

Every action of mankind that ignores the emerging feelings of animals produces a schism which disrupts the natural flow of evolution; which evolution, I remind you, is not one of form but the emergence of the loving life (spirit) from within the form.

This schism is reflected deeply in humanity's own incapacity to feel the great love of the universe, and in turn be loving and fulfilled in itself.

Mankind's exploitation of living creatures for food and health (and for entertainment) is abhorrent. Ill gotten knowledge is of meagre worth and bogs the world down into further illusion.

It is time to awaken to your true life and the abundant nourishment of The Oneness, which is, if you did but know it, available all round you, falling into your lap. It is that loving food which sustains all life in the universe, being the very life of God.

Here is a song:

SONG OF COLOURS

I sing a song of colours and every one is me,
Every one is free, everyone you see.
I sing a song of colours, rainbow man am I,
Don't ask me why, the colours in the sky ?
Joy and love in every colour, peace and harmony.
Open up to every colour, dance in ecstasy.

1. Violet, flow through me,
   Violet, transform me.

2. Ruby ray, flow through me.
   Ruby ray, enliven me.

3. Orange ray, flow through me.
   Orange ray, refresh me.

4. Golden ray, flow through me.
   Golden ray, fulfil me.

5. Gentle green, flow through me.
   Gentle green, peace in me.

6. Sky blue, flow through me.
   Sky blue, uplift me.

7. Indigo blue, flow through me.
   Indigo blue, awaken me.

8. Primrose light, flow through me.
    Primrose light, sparkle in me.

9. Soft loving pink, flow through me.
    Soft loving pink, love in me.

10. Crystal white, flow through me.
    Crystal white, bless me.

CHAPTER FOURTEEN

DEATH

There is no such thing. So, the very word should be abolished.

When the word death is no longer used, the belief that death is the end of consciousness or the end of the existence of personality will finally cease. The gateway to greater life, to an ever expanding conscious life, will open - and, for once and for all, will remain open.

The belief that death is the final extinguishing of the personality is a belief of absolutely incredible ignorance. It holds within it so much of the world's fear and despair, its cynicism, possessiveness, competitiveness and cruelty; its judgement and its vengeance. Are not these dreadful words to be using for such a lovely blue green planet? They are all found to be bound up with that loaded word *death*.

How much better it would be to use another word, such as *change*.

Indeed, you do take your change. All of you have taken this form of change countless times. You are all expert at it. Neither are you a victim at the mercy of fate. However unbelievable this may seem to you, you do have a say - at some level of your consciousness - of when you change from physicality to a body of lighter frequency.

If, even unconsciously, you believe that you are a victim you will draw victimisation, in some degree or other, towards yourself. It might appear that death is in control of what is happening to you, but in fact at some level of your being you are always responsible for what is happening.

The aware entity takes responsibility for all change, and especially that of so-called death for this particular process contains both the greatest of lessons and the greatest of joys.

The cosmic entity, your higher self, which be your whole self, is aware of what is taking place in its personality and watches the process of change with interest, with loving support, and with appreciation, knowing that this change is as natural to its process as is the reverse procedure of incarnation.

Change is the very nature of life. It is the very flow of the breath of life. An enlightened entity lives in the joy and peace of the non-changing moment - which is ever changing.

This is the paradox that the conditioned ego can never solve, but for the self-realised person it is as natural as breathing.

Fear exists when there is resistance to change. Acceptance of change, and acceptance of the fear also, if there is any, without being in denial of it, is the key to a joyful and easy transition from one octave of consciousness to another.

Life, which you are, is the *Great Changer*. This is a good name for life. Do not fear who you are. Do not fear your very own nature. Would you remain always the same? How indescribably boring. How unadventurous!

Life, which you are, is ever recollecting, and recreating, itself. It is ever playing with new realities, ever testing out new realities, ever testing out responses and abilities, whilst at the same time remaining awake to its source, living in its own environment of Oneness in love and joy and peace. This is what harmony is.

You are not a poor, ashamed, guilty, victim, at the mercy of great forces, afraid to lift up your head and meet the eyes of God in the shining faces of your brothers and sisters, especially those who have gone before you, who would greet you with such love and shared vision when you pass to the worlds of lighter frequency.

A seed falls to the ground, it becomes moistened in the ground. This is *change*; it puts out its first shoots, *change*; it flowers in its glory, *change*; it releases a thousand seeds, *change*; *continual change, daily change*. And this is how you are; always changing, and if at times some changes are more abrupt and appear more dramatic than at other times, don't be worried: you, the cosmic entity behind all these forms, exist always.

Enjoy the ride, enjoy the adventure of all these changes but don't get caught up in fear about any of them and don't put value judgements on to any of them; but neither treat them disdainfully as illusions and haughtily ignore them.

Don't shoot down your illusions else you shoot down your adventures. You are here to experience your illusions which are your dreams, and to see them for what they really are: just dreams. If you ignore them or try to eliminate them you are obviously not going to be looking at them to see what they are or to discover from where they come. You will be missing out on this life-time's adventure and you will be putting in a lot of energy trying to get rid of something which really isn't there in the first place which, in a sense, is illusory, which comes from your own dreaming, and upon which your ego has fixated on as a possible threat to its existence but which, at the same time, you have desired to create and experience.

Nothing can harm you, so your illusions certainly cannot: you can always invite them to do their worst and see what happens. You will remain. You will still exist. At which level you remain is fairly irrelevant. You still remain. Your cosmic self can travel up and down the escalator of all the levels and remain inviolate, though, of course, there will always be levels beyond, which you have yet to explore and feel at home in.

So I say to you, love your dreams, watch them, play in them, lust in them, laugh in them, cry in them, love in them, get angry in them, revel in them, and, of course, above all, *feel* in them. And, then, do watch for the moment when you begin to lose your joy to them, because that is when you start to believe in the dream. That is the moment when you are start to get entangled, that is when you begin digging a hole for yourself. It is the very moment of ego beginning to form. Watch for that moment. Catch it, and see it; for, once you have really seen through it, you can never again get lost in that particular dream - or any fears associated with that dream. Those particular fears will never again have any hold over you.

So, you may well ask, what are these illusions which I can play with and feel and, hopefully, not get entangled in?

We use the word *illusion* for all that changes, or has the possibility of change. Illusion is the product of mind. It is mind that has taken embodiment through thoughts, feelings and form. All these aspects of mind: thoughts, feelings, and objects, are liable to change. Thus, they can be termed illusions or "dreams that move upon the water of life".

Joy and peace and love are of essence (spirit). Whatever else may be happening, this never changes. Your cosmic self is at one with spirit. Its reality is always one of joy and love and peace.

I want you to be joyful, peaceful and loving, whatever else is happening. This you can do just as soon as you can undress your ego and allow yourself to be naked before your true beloved, this being your spirit, which is the joy of your being.

The puzzle to those who watch is that, as soon as they have helped you undress your conditioned ego, it seems you can't wait to get dressed in its clothes again.

The reason for this, of course, is that you have identified with the ego to the extent that you have made its fears into your own fears; so, rather than just being able to watch the fears, or even play with the fears, you actually believe the fears are real (that they are non-changing) and so you get stuck with them.

So, I would ask you not to be afraid of your fears, and not to be afraid of playing with your fears and looking at the originating impulse behind the fear. This is great work, yet the ego would have you shrink from it. The ego would like you to believe it takes great courage to face your fears. This perpetuates the belief that fear does, indeed, have something fearful about it.

I say to you, *be in touch with your will, which is the joy of your being,* and go into your fears, firmly embracing your will (for this is the very purpose of your will here on earth) and face the illusion, play with it, cry with it, dance with it, but do face it and see the fear in it vanish like the phantom that it is.

The ego believes that fear is real and unchanging and so equates it with spirit (which is truly unchanging). So, ego believes that if fear is an illusion, joy and peace and love are illusionary, also. It reasons to itself: if all this were to go, would this not be death ? The ego has confused the unreal with the real, has confused that which changes with that which is eternal, has entangled the two and made of them a duality and sees not its way out. It has made fear into something that cannot change; which, therefore, makes the changing features of life, thoughts, feelings and objects seem real, familiar, comfortable and unchanging. And when these do change, as they must, the ego reverts to its own peculiar belief in the unchanging nature of life which is seen as fearful. This is why the ego fears death.

Your ego has turned everything back to front and upside down for you. It is up to you to turn it the right way up again.

The goal and very nature of your cosmic self is to attempt to be awake to itself in all its expressions of personality. Personality, itself, is not diminished by this but enriched and fulfilled. The changing adventures of your lives here on earth eventually result in the dissolution of the self conscious ego until a day comes when no more remains.

Then, personality remains without ego; and its true flowering is assured with all its richness and sweetness.

Personality is your gift from God - or, if you like, from yourself to yourself. You shall never be without it. You cannot exist without it. And, as you always do exist, you shall always have it. Be assured of this.

Personality and conditioned ego are very different; they are worlds apart. Your personality is the very natural expression of the role that your cosmic self has desired to take for itself and play out at a particular level of existence.

Your ego on the other hand is a distortion to which you have given energy in your mental aura, allowing it to amass to itself ever increasing ideas and beliefs about itself until it has taken on an independent consciousness of its own which then interferes with, and creates a barrier, as it were, between your cosmic self and its true personality.

Cosmic self plus personality is who you are. Cosmic self plus personality plus conditioned ego is you being interfered with. So, get rid of the interference and you are home and dry!

The truth in the saying, "You are your own worst enemy" is accurate here. You have set up the interference and it is up to you to dismantle it.

I do want to assure you that *you will always exist.* You are not going to dissolve into nothing. There is to be no floating around in a large cloud of nothingness, as some of you fear. You are not going to be lost in the swirls of cosmic energies. Impossible.

Wherever you are, however you are, you are just as you wish to be *now.* You are here, *now,* just the same as you would be at any other level, *now.*

If you were, at this very minute, to somehow find yourself on another level of the universe, you would find you are the same, having the same knowledge, the same ideas, the same beliefs, the same capacity to be afraid, the same sense of humour and so on. Of course, your environment would be different. You would quickly adjust. It would quickly alter how you viewed matters, beliefs might swiftly change - and this does happen, but it is still *you* that does the changing, and you still have to take responsibility for your reactions to what you see and feel.

You are always going to be *a person*, with an ability to respond to outside stimuli. Your response is a matter of your choice. And choice is what gives life its uncertainty, its beauty, its freedom, and its adventure!

It is sad that so many of you don't have fun in your lives, because, truly, I say to you that this is what life is about above all else, fun! You have lost your sense of exhilaration, your sense of excitement, your sense of mischief, your very sense of aliveness, of adventure, and fun! When are you going to wake up? What does it take?

Most of you take life far too seriously. You think that this or that has to be achieved or that this or that is important. It is your ego that believes it. It stops you from relaxing into your own energy, stops you being clear about what you feel, and stops you from cocking a snook at hypocrisy wherever that snake in the grass is found. It makes you self conscious and inhibited at every turn, so much so, that: you are afraid of taking your clothes off, you are afraid of public speaking, or playing music, you are afraid to dance with abandon, or cry in public. You are afraid to stand up for yourselves, you are afraid to relax for fear of being trampled on. You are afraid of asking for sex, afraid of being rejected, and afraid of being sexual the way you want to be; you are afraid of being homeless, and cold, and hungry. You are afraid for your children. You are afraid of gurus and teachers and you are afraid of being one yourself. You are afraid of hurting people and you are afraid of dying. The list is endless. The ego's manipulations are endless. When will it end? When are you going to assert your will to be, your will to joy, and end this depressing list of fears?

Wherever you are in the universe, whether in or out of physical manifestation, you have an aura which radiates your energy field all around you. This is your personality statement, as it were, as to how you are feeling, and this can be picked up and ascertained by any entity that comes into contact with you. It cannot be hidden!

Only on the physical plane can it be attempted to be hidden, but even there, to anyone who is intuitive and sensitive to energy, you are an open book. And most of you need to validate this perceptive ability of yours and act more upon it.

Your personality, your mental and emotional aura, contains within it your own peculiar and instantly recognisable vibration which is uniquely yours and belongs to no other. It is the result of all that you have experienced and the sum total of your responses to all the situations that you have so far encountered as an individualised entity in the universe.

This is your body of vibratory expression and it is through the quality of your radiant (auric) being-ness that, not only can you be recognised and thus enabled to be contacted anywhere you might be in the universe, but it also denotes, as it were, your "status", or, should I say, your level of consciousness and awareness.

No one can destroy life for life is eternal and by this I do not mean, as some would have you believe, that after your "death" your life lives on in your children or grand children in a kind of spiritualised hand-me-down of genes and memories.

Of course your genes are passed on, and of course your inherited characteristics are passed along, but *you* are not passed along. *You are an individual personality, inviolate, sovereign unto yourself, and you exist always.*

At the time of your leaving the physical plane, you will have dissolved, hopefully, more of your ego. The state in which you leave is exactly the state in which you reawaken (if you have fallen asleep in the meantime) on a plane of higher vibratory frequency.

During the actual process of change you remain exactly how you are, unless, however, at the actual passing over, you undergo relinquishment of the ego, a transformation which is entirely possible.

You cannot exist where you are going in your dense body so you discard it in much the same way as you would take off your overcoat before going into the sitting room of your house. The physical body *is not you*; it is merely the overcoat you happen to be wearing at the moment. But, unlike an overcoat, it is acutely responsive to your thoughts, being, indeed, the embodiment of your thoughts, and acutely sensitive to your feelings, being liken to a harp with the breath of wind upon its strings.

The physical body has absolutely no control over you whatever. It is impossible for you to be enlightened unless you have both understood and proved to your own satisfaction this basic fact, this basic illusion.

This doesn't mean that you need to have learned control over all the facets of life in form. It doesn't mean you need to be psychic or work miracles. The mastery of form control at the cost of being open to change, or refusing to make one's self vulnerable enough to confront one's fears and embrace spirit, is that of the cul-de-sac of the left hand path. It is elevating ego to a rather short lived pretender's throne, the making of paranoia into an art form; and the making of spiritual hypocrisy into a performance worthy of an Oscar.

The necessary kind of control I am talking about is, of course, self-control.

It means that you are able to resist any illusion that the world of form may throw up at you, especially that which may originate from your own unconscious. And, that, you can resist these mental forms sufficiently well to remain at all times awake and connected to the source of your being.

In fact, there is no such thing as a right hand path and a left hand path, for the so called left hand path is in no way an opposite or alternative path to that of the so called right hand path. It is more correct to say that one attitude is directed towards becoming whole and does not avoid vulnerability in its search for truth; the other is directed to maintaining and protecting the ego at all cost, and, either consciously or unconsciously, manipulating the outer world to this end.

This latter occupation is not a path but a behavioural characteristic of an ego hanging on to lots of fear, and it leads no where but into a lonely cul-de-sac. This makes the death of the ego seem like a real death for it is that much more hopeless and that much more dramatic a dissolution when it comes at the end of a cul-de-sac.

It is much easier to dissolve the ego whilst you are on the path of *joyful being-ness*. It becomes easy to directly experience Oneness. It comes naturally, and easily, and not as the result of some dramatic and painful "crucifixion".

Being vulnerable means being open to change; it means seeing change as the very nature of illusion; it means knowing that you are able to exist within the radiant aura of your being, unwaveringly trusting in spirit, even to the point of being overwhelmed physically; or, what is even worse to the ego, when moving into that point of utter latency where all energy, all light and all feeling is extinguished; that place where the power of the Father is known, yet remains quiescent. Yes, that place is felt by the ego as death.

To be in the joy of your being, means, also, to be totally accepting of the power of form (the mother) in all its manifestations - and, yet, not to be entangled with any conscious, or unconscious, fear or fascination of any manifestation, however horrific, or however fascinating, nor to have any possibility of emotional reaction against them or as a result of them.

Being true to your spirit means facing fairly and squarely the illusion (the belief) that there is any power that can have any control over you. It means standing in your own light, even if your own flesh is suffering, without denying the feelings of pain, and without trying to control the situation, or of trying to match power with power. It means *refusing to allow thoughts of despair to dominate you to the extent that you reject your connection to spirit*.

There is a fine line between the *desire* to be free from control, and *being* free from control. I would have you ponder upon the difference.

It is the latter that is required of you before you are able to reassume the mantle of your golden fleece which is your true physical body of etheric energy. The ancient Greeks embodied this teaching in the stories of Jason and the Golden Fleece.

The key is to resist being controlled without having any controlling ideas about how you should resist being controlled.

This is easier than it sounds once you get the knack of it. Play with it. Experiment with it and practice it. You will soon see what I mean.

When you have transformed your physical body back into its etheric form, you will have returned to the identity of your true personality which is to be that of a living master of loving compassion, free for ever from the fears and illusions of matter, united for ever with the joy of your being.

There is a moment during transformation when you realise that God is, indeed, just as much in the world of form, even to the densest matter, as God is in the realms of light.

At this moment, you regain, not your control over others (because gods do not control others nor have they any desire to do so), but your identity as a son, or daughter, of God.

It is possible to understand all the theories about life, to know about the science of vibration, to be able to use para-normal powers in the service of others, and still be able to avoid dissolving the ego. The transformation which is earnestly longed for continues to elude you.

In this case, you are remaining, for a while, in your expertly "spiritual-ised" but fear ridden ego. The fear of giving up your role or identity as "the great server" so paralyses you with fear that you are holding on to your ego, subtly and skilfully, by virtue of your spiritual knowledge and your skilful ability as a healer. There is a subtle form of pride involved here.

There can come a time in a lifetime of strong desire to be enlightened, when your "path" can diverge. If, at this time, you refuse to let go the de-sire to be in control of your life, the refusal to let go of control becomes chronic. Much suffering eventuates for these entities. They fail, as it were, at the last fence; except that the failure is more in the nature of going into a cul-de-sac for a while, where nothing seems to have any meaning, where they feel to be in a limbo. It is place of frustration and loneliness which has no apparent end to it.

So, look not for control and look not for the means to keep death at bay. Always be accepting of whatever comes your way; enjoy your creativity without demanding how the outcome should be; enjoy what fruits come your way without demanding them; accept the energies that swirl around you and threaten to overwhelm you (they won't!). Do not fight these ener-gies and do not try to master them. The mastery you are to learn is to stand in the joy of your being whilst all around you seems lost and out of control. Accept everything and resist nothing.

And might I add here, acceptance doesn't necessarily mean *approval*. As I have explained in another place, it is always important to make the distinction between acceptance of a person's attitude or behaviour, and your approval of it. Acceptance is love in motion, knowing that love is all. Approval is a product of your personality. Whether or not you approve of any attitude or behaviour is up to your personal experience and wisdom which you have to take responsibility for.

Remember, you will, because you will always have personality, always have an opinion because you will always have a mind! The only difference between a self-realised person and a person still enmeshed in their conditioned ego is that the self-realised person has opinions which come directly out of love and which, therefore, are not tinged with judgement.

As you can see, it is not the fact you have opinions that is the issue here. It is whether or not those opinions are coming out of wholeness (love) or from conditioned ego. Do you not think the masters of worlds and galaxies ponder and plan, and have opinions as to what plans to implement when and where and how to help? Of course they do! In fact, they do little else!

The achievement is to realise that you are God and there is nothing outside of yourself to fear, which includes the most stupendous of fiery energies that do exist.

At this point I would like to say to you, you are going to see some wondrous entities and some wondrous events. Do not fear them, but neither should you attempt to judge, evaluate or analyse their behaviour, for this, in itself, is a form of control by way of you wanting to know how to relate to an entity by placing him or her, in your mind, into an appropriate - appropriate to *you*, that is - hierarchy.

There is a hierarchy. But, it is based on the role each plays, not on how spiritual each is. All are equal in spirit. All are not equal in awareness or consciousness or light. Each entity has unique gifts with an individually different way of offering those gifts in service to The Oneness.

Remember, *you* are responsible for *how you respond*. Let joy be your inner compass, and respond, in that very moment, in any situation, from your deepest truth. Trust not in any luminosity you may see, but, rather, in the intuitive wisdom that arises faster than light within you, allowing it to respond for you. Nothing is to be gained by denying this inner wisdom except for the hardening of the ego.

Never allow yourself to get sucked in, hypnotised by, or controlled by the magnetism of another at the expense of denying the joy of your being. Do listen to yourself.

Begin observing the mind. See how you control others in your thoughts, using your mind to make them jump through all sorts of hoops, putting them through the most extraordinary scenarios and fantasies, seeing them as good, seeing them as bad, making them better to suit your purposes, using them as sexual objects, and so on. Your thoughts are the reflections of your own desires. Watch constantly. It takes practice. It takes a while for you to understand that all desire is of the ego, and that desires hide your fears.

A master never thinks of another entity without acknowledging the inner perfection of the other. Do you?

Any thought you send out about another has the potential for adding a burden to their life. It may diminish or "put down" the other. These are controlling thoughts.

Observe with amazement how often you do this and take steps to either clear your mind so that you have no thoughts at all or make sure that the thoughts you do have are helpful ones.

Thoughts are actions, remember. The mind is the battleground where compulsive thoughts are the result of denied feelings and where uncontrolled thoughts give rise to unwanted feelings.

You do not have to evaluate a person's behaviour before deciding how to relate to him or her. This is controlling the relationship, making it safe for yourself. It is of the ego.

Always relate to others from your truth in the clear spontaneity of the moment. This will be the naturally appropriate response. No need to evaluate, no need to weigh up the situation in advance. No need to worry whether he or she is good for you, or whether he or she is on the right path. Your anxiety, through fear of making a wrong choice, will lead you to deny your spontaneity, making you believe that evaluation is a wise and proper course of action.

Wise evaluation is, indeed, a sensible way to go but if you find that a pattern has emerged in which it always seems to negate your spontaneity, you have allowed this belief, a belief in *doing*, to strengthen your ego which will believe in anything to avoid being in-the-now and being spontaneous.

Put all your decisions and choices as to change to the test of your own intuition. Is there joy and enthusiasm in it for you? If there is, go for it.

If not, leave it alone, don't go along that path. Simple!

Fear freezes spontaneity into a block of ice. If you fear that an unknown assassin is out to kill you, the first casualty of your life is spontaneity. Every person you meet you are on your guard against. Fear is death to spontaneity, so your controlling ego takes over. Therefore, I say to you, be on your guard - not against being killed, but against controlling the situation. Live in spontaneity and be free.

As you can see, I have devoted much of this chapter to a discourse on control and the reason for this is that the ego derives all its energy to keep itself functioning by using its conditioned and distorted beliefs to control a situation to its advantage (which is always for its protection, however subtly justified). To avoid death (as it sees it) is definitely to its advantage.

To the ego any change is to be feared, and a change in which the unknown plays a prominent part is even more to be feared. The ego has a vested interest in controlling the life of its "host" in order to minimise change. It so happens that the change called "death" by humans is the one thing that the ego can't change, so, naturally, it is the one thing the ego fears the most. Therefore, the hidden controlling factor through everybody's life which contaminates, as it were, every moment of your life, every relationship that you have, and everything that you do, is your ego's fear of death.

By all means look to others for inspiration; this is a fine thing to do. But do not condemn those who you believe are deluded else you fall into the very same trap that those deluded ones have fallen into - that of controlling the lives of others.

It is very important you heed this advice at this time because many are preparing to be enlightened and there are few who are not fearful of taking this step; so, there are going to be many egos around who will be elevating themselves to positions of amazing fantasy. At the same time, there are going to be those around who are genuinely without ego. You are going to see entities expressing powers as never before on earth, and I would have you not be fazed by any of it.

Someone else's truth is just as valid for them as yours is for you. If you limit another's truth, you are putting limitations on your own. There is no better or more appropriate truth that anyone can be persuaded by you to alter to than that which they already have.

For you, there is only your truth, and only you can find it. There is no such thing as a blanket truth for all.

If my truth is also your truth, so be it, then we meet in truth. If not, all well and good. I accept your right to have your truth absolutely; we can still meet, I hope, in love and joy, and in peace.

Leave all other truths alone. Don't meddle or battle with them. Don't waste your time. Your truth is all that matters to you (not to anyone else!)

My truth at this very moment is that I am enjoying writing this sentence about truth. Your truth is that you are reading it, but if you are not enjoying it why are you still reading it? Yet, for both us there is another, more real, truth that remains unchanging within us. This is the truth that no one can prove to you is there. No one can show you what it is. It is for you to find.

Live in the joy of your own truth exclusively and you can't go wrong!

In the days to come, some will relate to this teacher and some to that teacher, and others to other modes of expression. Don't be dazzled into pursuing a teaching that doesn't feel right to you. Enjoy and learn, but keep your wits about you. You will need them.

Love yourself enough to be true to your own truth. Be open to change. Keep an open mind. An open mind is a mind that is uncluttered by its own ideas of truth.

The person who knows not that they are God is living in a kind of stupor. It is a state of limitedness not a state of mastery. Mastery can only be attained on the physical plane. How can anyone believe that you can be a master on all the planes of light but exclude the physical plane? Is not the physical plane a part of the whole? How can you be God-realised on all levels but not on the physical? Would not this mean excluding the physical level from the whole? And would that not be quite illogical?

In fact, the physical plane is just as much part of heaven (and a supremely beautiful part it is, too) as any other part of heaven. But you don't believe it, so for those of you who don't believe it, it isn't.

Do enjoy this amazingly beautiful plane of existence; do really see it; do really feel it, experience it, accept its illusions without losing yourself in the process, and the day will come when change will hold no fear for you.

You have been waiting to regain this awareness since you lost the knowledge of your true identity millions of years ago.

At the time of transformation, there is a flashing forth of the fires of transformation, beautifully and preciously controlled by great luminous (angelic) beings, at which time you regain your true physical body of energy which, as I have said, is your etheric body of light and energy. This is the moment of becoming a Christ. This is the moment when your personality is reunited with your cosmic self. Now you are free again. Now you know who you are again in your entirety. Now there is no more needing to return to a dense physical body and keep going through the tedious procedure of rebirth, for, you now have your etheric body with you or, rather, you have with you a body that can go anywhere in the solar system, from the highest to the lowest levels, and remain uninfluenced by any illusion at any level.

Have no concern for the dense physical body, whether it be cast aside or consumed by fire. This is the time for being supremely indifferent to the fate of your body. It is a time for surrendering all to God, and a time for being the observer and keeping awake.

You shall emerge in your shining etheric body as a phoenix emerges from the ashes of the old. All of you. Everyone of you.

There is a part of you that believes you have to keep control over a situation otherwise you are going to lose out. This is not true creation; this is reaction. You cannot undergo transformation whilst there remains the slightest desire within you to be in control, fearing you will lose out. If desire remains, you will draw to yourself the very thing that the ego fears the most. In this instance, you lose out.

To be creative is very different to being controlling; creation is a natural and spontaneous act of breathing out joy. It is love in action. It comes from spirit on behalf of spirit.

The ego doesn't create; the ego reacts. Reaction sucks in illusion and breathes out fear: it is manipulation in action. It is control for the sake of control.

Reactive manipulation masquerades as creativity. But it is not creativity. It is going nowhere but into a cul-de-sac. True creativity ever looks to the freeing of the life. It is the path to the stars and beyond. It is a loving path. And it is the only path.

In the realms of light there are many different streams of energies. The entities that embody these energies are aware of their differences but as there is no separateness there is no value judgement as to any quality of energy being better or worse than any other: there is just difference. And this difference is absolutely loved and accepted; and, indeed, why should it not be as it is all a part of The Oneness?

It is only in the dense physical plane, the plane of apparent separateness, where *difference* is used by ego to maintain its idea that there is something to fear in being different.

It will use such excuses as good and evil, or right and wrong, or the left or right hand path. This gives the ego something to worry about; far better to have something to worry about rather than confront its inner fears.

Loving creation will come in to its own on earth when the entities who carry these different (opposite polarity) energies, can get together, can share and combine their skills for no other reason than to free life wherever it is imprisoned. This, indeed, will be love in action.

Then you will have a revelation on the physical plane concerning the nature of life. This cannot happen whilst you are still afraid of anything that is different, whilst you cannot accept absolutely the nature of that difference, and whilst you cannot unite your qualities with those of another for the sake of a purpose that is greater than that of your individual comfort.

Kindness to the form side of life, wishy washy ideas of peace, pandering to the personalities of those around you - in other words, pandering to a desire to fulfil your obligations and responsibilities without obstructing the activities of your friends or upsetting them - is not creative love.

Indeed, this kind of "love" comes from a caring ego (which is infinitely preferable to an uncaring ego) but it is still from ego. It expresses itself in caring and sharing, protecting and healing (with the exclusion of cosmic healing) and the worth while social desire to bring about a happier material world.

Creative love is spirit motivated love. It is the energy which results from following your spirit uncompromisingly. It is also known as "the will to be", which only a few as yet understand (and even fewer express). It looks always to the inner life, sees the perfection that is already there, and acts accordingly.

The will energy, this loving creative energy, is the energy of the Father (as the Christ called it). It is the joy-of-being energy that lies at the back of, and which binds together, the whole of creation. It does not belong exclusively to any one energy stream.

However different your ray qualities might be, the will energy is universally and equally there for everyone and everything in The Oneness to draw upon. That some of you do more so than others, is not because you are special or are specially equipped in anyway or come from a different part of the galaxy, but because you have become more aware as to the nature of this energy; because you have had more courage to relinquish your personal concerns; because you surrender more deeply than others; and because you have had more courage than others to live according to the joy of your being on the physical plane.

I don't like to split up energy into terms like Father energy and Mother energy; there is already enough confusion in this world over the male and female roles and the ego would have you identify with these roles for ever.

In the universe there is only energy, which is life force. Then there is *difference*, which qualifies this energy. *Difference* is totally acceptable in the universe, except at the physical level where it is feared, which leads, of course, to suffering - which also only exists at the physical level.

In the realms of light, in which difference is perfectly beautiful and ordinary, the *will-to-be* is recognised as the point of synthesis in which all differences are reconciled.

As it is there equally for everyone to draw upon, there are no ideas of being special, or of favouritism, or of being higher or lower. There are no feelings of suspicion or hostility toward any stream of energy (or entities) from any particular part of the galaxy. On the physical plane it is only the fearful ego that would make it so.

The will energy, which you are now attempting to understand, which you are now attempting to surrender to and to express as a reality in your lives, can only be expressed here on earth, in balance, when the different energy streams, which take embodiment on earth as yourselves, can accept their differences and work together (being a task not of work but of joy) to dismantle egos wherever you find them to be in the way of *your own truth*.

Thus, it is in the area of right relationship between yourself and your opposite polarity (who holds an energy as different from your own as an energy could be) in which the revelations concerning the *creative nature* of the will energy will appear. In other words, it will be in groups - where (in the words of Jesus) two are more are gathered together with goodwill - where the will energy will be most powerfully experienced.

Yet, I say to you, that the key to the right use of will is not just about being in groups. It is in living according to the truth of your being, which is none other than the joy of your being. The discovery of your opposite polarity will become self-evident. He or she is not someone you have to go looking for or be unduly concerned about. When you are ready, as the saying goes, this greatest of relationships, this sweetest of relationships - also, this greatest of challenges - will appear and make itself known to you.

It can be said that right relationship is what life is all about. Firstly, in the right relationship between you and your spirit, between you and your higher self. Secondly. in the right relationship between you and your fellow creatures, and especially between you and your opposite polarity.

In right relationship between you and the other - indeed, between you and all others - there is joy in manifestation, which is truly the will of God in manifestation.

When there is right relationship between you and your most opposite polarity all that lies in between falls naturally into place, easily and effortlessly, as if the relationship was always one of mutual love and respect, which, of course, from the perspective of the Oneness it always has been.

Therefore, you can see that it is from the perspective of Oneness, *whilst living in duality*, from which our relationships need to be fundamentally viewed.

The will energy, within those who can attune to it, expresses itself in those acts which move spontaneously from the very heart of the life of the person. It sees no right or wrong. It is not manipulative or controlling. It does not labour heavily or tediously. It does not fight for ideologies or protest at issues.

People attuned to the will energy are very aware. They are very sensitive to atmosphere (auric emanations). They are ultra sensitive to hypocrisy. They have (like children) an unerring knack of knowing where a person is most vulnerable. They have a great nose (intuitive ability) for ego games. And, to deal with all this, they have an unlimited range of expression from the most hilarious (or the most outrageous) to the most profound and the most spiritual. The will energy can be summed up as unlimited and uncompromising. It is the great energy that planetary missionaries (avatars) use when partaking in the great work of dismantling old, tired and worn out beliefs and structures which have served their time for humanity.

I can tell you that the advent of the will energy on the physical plane used in a balanced manner by couples who are in right relationship with each other, being equally matched in light frequency, will bring about the death of the conditioned ego.

The conditioned human ego is, at this very moment, fighting a last ditch battle to prevent this happening.

The impact of the will energy upon an un-awakened entity can be profound. The inner life of the person is aroused.

There can be such a response to the life energy of the awakened one that the ego is utterly confused. It has had no time to martial its defences. It finds itself unmasked. Its days are numbered.

This is the result of inner life reaching - flashing forth like electricity - across to inner life. It leaves the ego in disarray and a little more ready to lie down and die.

This is ego busting. It is why the will energy has often been called "the destroyer". Its effect upon conditioned and limited personalities, where the ego is in control, is profoundly disturbing.

It produces such upheavals in the psyche of these individuals that, at first sight, it appears to be destructive. But, dear friends, it is the great liberator. Learn to love it and trust it within yourselves, and respect it when you see it in action, whether it be at work within your very self or working within an other.

You are all in training to be ego busters and there is no doubt that you will be the best ego busters in the universe, just as soon as you have bust your own! Your training ground, this world, has been the greatest bar none!

The will energy, which is that of the joy of being, is not readily understood even by entities on non-physical levels close to yours, and even by those of great understanding, for, indeed, it needs to be experienced before it can be understood.

Your ego would have you try and understand something before you experience it, to test the waters, as it were, to see if it is safe to enter.

However, you cannot surrender to (or attune to) the will energy whilst at the same time holding thoughts in your mind defining how safe you wish to be. Few there are that have the insight or the courage to relinquish ego to that extent.

I am speaking here as a teacher to the teachers of the human race when I say to you, have no fear and trust in this wondrous energy, which is your very life and your very joy. It is the next step for you to take.

There is nothing quite like the will energy for challenging long held beliefs and busting them clean open, in the process releasing denied feelings in a sudden cleansing catharsis.

It is a great clarifying energy that sweeps into a situation like a ray of sunshine, sometimes like a thunderbolt, always with superlative wisdom; but, it is the joyous and loving energy that comes with it which is the potency of it.

To those of you who fear change and, in fact, to those of you who still hold any fears at all, the will energy may at times seem to be like a dark energy, bringing about mayhem and confusion. The ego will be swift to condemn it - and the entity being the vehicle for this energy, as being from "the dark side".

Whenever you have an emotional reaction to any teachings, old or new, or when you see yourself emotionally condemning teachings, or using your own beliefs to justify your position, you can rest assured that your ego is in control of your life.

To the conditioned ego, the will energy might seem to be all that's dark and selfish and evil. The more fearful the ego, the more firmly it will believe in this belief, and the darker the outer energy (the will energy) will seem.

Understand, that the ego cannot be destroyed because in a sense it is not there to be destroyed; but, like a whirlpool in the sea, the ego can be dissolved or be encouraged to dissolve itself back into the same element which gave rise to its momentum and its illusory separate life. This is why I prefer to use the term dissolving the ego, rather than destroying the ego.

However, as a purely fun term I enjoy the term ego busting! Indeed, if you can bust these old ghosts you can be a hero, too!

Obviously, when the momentum of the ego ceases, it must return as a whirlpool would return to the peaceful waters from which it arose. Thus, the admonishment of all the sages down the ages to *be still* in order to reconnect to, and rediscover, what it is and who it is you truly are.

To relinquish all personality concerns and surrender to God seems like death to the ego, for it has to give up all its ideas of providing for its own safety (or for the safety of others) and give up, however well intentioned, all its ideas of controlling any situation to its own benefit.

To all of you who are on the path of ego dissolution: are you prepared to take this next great step? Or, are you to remain in the cul-de-sac of nothing happening, going nowhere, and a feeling that you are missing something?

If you really believe in the spiritual path and all these grand happenings of the new age, now is the time to put your money where your mouth is. It is the time to put your life on the line. Don't delay too long else the ego will find many reasons, especially so-called "spiritual" reasons, why you shouldn't.

If you can take this next great step, if you can make the grand decision (when it is there to be made easily and naturally) and you can do it whilst living in a human body, then you have achieved what you came here to do and you will have regained that for which you have been striving for so long.

This is a great day for your personality, actually, for it is an end to its suffering.

Paradoxically, the very existence of the conditioned ego is the cause of its suffering, and yet it loathes to suffer. It fights to the death to retain its existence, yet it is so very glad when it is returned to its source, though, in a more real sense it is no longer there to be either glad or sad.

Understand, your personality has not disappeared. Only the conditioned element of it has gone. Your ego is now in unity again with The Oneness. No longer is there a so-called higher self and lower self. Now there is just the one self. The mind of the lesser is now at one with the mind of the greater. It is now a grand ego. In fact it is so grand, so different from what is was before, that there is a temptation to believe that whole personality is no more - or that the person is now without ego. This is not the case. Your true enlightened ego(your identity signature) is your personality.

You will never be without personality wherever you go in this universe. The only problem, in your humanity, is that a conditioned element of your personality takes you over, believing itself to be a separate identity and to be separate from the All-That-Is.

The conditioned ego is truly in a Catch 22 situation: it can't end its suffering without dying and it is so terrified of dying that it can't end its suffering.

The will energy, being the energy of your spirit, will lead you out of darkness into light. It will open you to feelings that will compensate a million times for the feelings generated by your exclusive controlling ego.

I say to mothers, you are no longer to fear death for yourselves or your children. You will gaily throw the flowers of spirit at those who walk beside the corpses of death with such long and tragic faces. With your compassion you will assist those who desire to wake up to their own divinity.

This brings me to another topic: I wish to warn you against desiring to preserve the form.

There is, among some new age people a "non belief" about death. It encourages a philosophy which goes: "If you don't believe in death, it can't happen and you won't die".

They then spend a great deal of time and energy affirming to themselves many times a day that they are not going to die. Now, this again is ego control. A belief that you are not going to die is the opposite side of the coin to the belief that you are going to die. It is still a belief. It is still the ego wanting to believe in something, anything, for fear of dying.

I am asking you to have no beliefs whatever. To be supremely indifferent to whether you die or not. Death is not the issue. Your beliefs are. It is not death that keeps you stuck. It is your beliefs that keep you stuck. Beliefs, no matter whether they are for or against, are still beliefs and all beliefs are of the ego.

Undue preoccupation with change, wishing the outcome to be one that is to your satisfaction, is ego manipulation. Beware of it.

The ego will always be looking for a subtle and, in the case of new age people, a worthy "spiritual" belief, to resist its own dissolution; even to pretending that it really wants to dissolve itself when, in reality, it is the very last thing it has in mind. Why, otherwise, spend so much energy on making up affirmations to convince itself that it can't happen.

This desire for the preservation of the form may appear under the disguise of a new age teaching. Beware of this subtle type of ego control.

Have no beliefs, live in your essence, be in the moment, and see what happens!

Life is for the living of life. Not for the analysing of its processes or for the making of it safe for yourself in advance.

If a rose spent all its sweet life affirming to itself that it would never die, believing it wouldn't die, it would never become a rose. Natural changes would be pre-empted by the mind and it would become a twisted travesty of a rose. Not a sweet creature of such natural beauty and majesty.

The preservation of the mortal body and your beliefs concerning it are only relevant to the preservation of your ego. So drop them. When you are a Christ you can make for yourself as many mortal bodies as you care to make.

You are here on Earth to surrender to your essence (your spirit), being the will of God within you, and to go with it gaily wherever it may lead you.

The relinquishment of your physical body is, in fact, a glorious experience.

Do try to be open to every second of it!

You are not only welcomed by the Light but also by loving friends you may not have seen for quite a while, indeed, if ever on the physical plane. You will be lovingly taken to a place of peace and beauty for a period of adjustment and orientation where you will be supplied with all the knowledge you need to re-commence your life on the non-physical planes of existence. You will be amazed by the light and love which surrounds you. You will also see very clearly that all you have done on earth, and all that others are doing or have done, has been for the purpose of spiritual advancement.

Such special interest in the form, as had the ancient Egyptians, actually ends up denying God within you which is free of all form, even if the original idea (of embalming) was to see the body as a part of the whole. Such speciality and exclusiveness is of the ego and not to be recommended.

Just know that you are an eternal being and forget about death. Attune yourself to the joy of your being; cease the denial of your feelings; watch your mind; and serve to free life wherever you find it. Have no beliefs about anything. Have no beliefs about illusion. Have no beliefs about truth or reality or Oneness.

Look at it this way. Beliefs divide a situation into what is and what is not, or what should be and what should not be. This is not useful. Having beliefs about illusion divides the universe into what is illusion and what is real. However the Oneness is the Oneness. Either everything is illusion, or nothing is illusion. Either everything is real, or nothing is real. It is the ego that wants to separate the universe into parts that are real and parts that are illusion. The ego says the real part is the inner part (the truth), the part that is spirit, and the outer part is the part that seems to change or die.

From an enlightened stance all you can say is that The Oneness is for ever experiencing itself, as itself, in different forms, yet it always retains a spark of itself in its original being-ness within every human being, *which can be rediscovered and realised.*

I give you an analogy concerning this matter of truth and illusion. Behold the stream of water that trickles from a glacier. Which is the most real of the forms of that water? Is it the liquid water, is it the vapour that rises off the glacier in sunlight or is it the myriad forms of frozen water (the ice) the water has been frozen into? Which, does your ego want to tell you, is the most real of these forms? And why, when it changes from one form to another, should that make it any less real?

So, don't affirm that death doesn't exist; just cease to dwell on all thoughts of it. Give it no thought energy whatever. If it is an illusion, there will be time enough for you to face the illusion when you are ready to face it, and not before. If it seems overwhelmingly real, you can experience the thrill or pain of its reality. If it is neither real nor illusory, but just what is, you can remain in the joy of your being, accepting what it brings to you, with interest and equanimity. This is best.

Go forward with trust in your mind and joy in your heart; go forward with laughter on your lips, with a friendly smile for everyone (unless you are doing a special job of ego busting) and let there be strength in your bearing and tranquillity in your eyes. Throw your flowers to the winds, as delicately, or as gaily as you will, and you shall know what it means to be meek. And, yes, you shall inherit the earth.

There is no death. But put not the mind to it, else you will make of it what it is not.

Now to end this chapter, here is a story about the will energy in action. It is a story about flowers.

I was watching:

There was a funeral procession winding its way down a dusty Mediterranean street. The man who had died at the age of eighty had, in his youth, been a resistance fighter in the war. Many there were who followed his coffin. The man himself, invisible in his etheric body to all but myself, stood by watching as his coffin was lowered into the ground surrounded by the long and mournful faces of his black suited ex comrades, and their sons and their wives. The ceremony was solemn and patriotic, if a bit on the grim side.

Suddenly, up from nowhere dances a girl child. She is carrying wild flowers that she has picked from the road side and I see that she is one of the children of the mourners and that she has escaped from one of the cars across the road from the cemetery. She has a sweet face and an impish smile and her eyes are flashing with the essence of her vitality. She has it in her mind to give the flowers to the old man. But they are already covering up the coffin with earth and the little girl is momentarily confused, but then she looks up and sees all the grim faces and the gloomy clothes, and quite spontaneously, her face lights up with a mischievous grin and she cries out: "You all look so silly!"

She throws all her flowers up in the air, the daisies, the forget-me-nots, the poppies and the buttercups, and they fall not upon the grave, but upon the heads of the mourners and upon their clothes and all around them. Then she dances about and picks up a few of the fallen flowers and throws them again.

This is too much for some of the mourners who start muttering and waving their arms at her to go away. The priest is holding a thought picture in his mind of a large boot, his boot, booting her backside; another of the mourners has a sudden flash of anger which he represses but into his mind comes the picture of the soldier that he strangled fifty years previously. Others are thinking thoughts like: "What an ill mannered child! No respect for the dead! Why don't her parents do something about her!" Their expressions are stony, embittered, closed.

One of the mourners, however, the wife of a successful business man, is quietly captivated by the sparkle of the child. She catches the child's eyes and returns a smile and there is a flashing forth of empathy from the one to the other. Inner and inner meet. Life is saying hello to life. Essence is validated. The child laughs gaily, throws the remainder of her flowers and is chased back to the car by her mother, who has now decided to take matters in hand.

After the tea party at the home of the old man, the mourners go back to their homes and their routines and their responsibilities. Their faces change from the stony hardness of emotion under control to the plac-

id resignation with which they live their daily lives. There is not much change in their lives and their egos are happy to keep it that way. They know not that in their minds they have killed off their own "child". Even an outer child, full of the joy of being, cannot remind them of their loss. They have embraced death and have made it real for themselves. And so it is.

Now, the wife of the business man doesn't go home quite as easily. She has been reminded of something that she has lost and it keeps nagging at her. She tosses and turns and wrestles with her feelings. This goes on for some days; then she has an emotional "breakdown". She withdraws from her family for a while; she seeks counselling, does therapy, learns to trust herself and her feelings; she learns it is fine to give herself permission to laugh, to dance, to sing, to make love, to shout at the devil. She learns she is a god.

The woman began teaching simple relaxation classes to help others relax. She began reading books she had never read before and they opened doors of understanding for her. She met her affinity twin flame and denied not to herself or to the world her feelings; then she met her polarity opposite partner and he showed her the areas in herself where her conditioned ego was still strong. They worked together, helping many, and, in so doing, they freed themselves of their own egos.

Now, all this change began as a result of the impact of the will energy, being so innocently expressed by that little girl all those years ago at the funeral of the old man. Do you see how it works?

As for the wife of the business man - for she is his wife no longer; she has adorned herself with the flowers of her own being; and she throws them now with abandon - for the sheer joy of it - just as gaily as did that little girl who was unwittingly holding the energy of, and playing the part of, the Great Initiator of Life. They are the flowers of spirit and they never die.

As for the old man who stood by with me, watching, he learned the greatest lesson of his life. He vowed that in his next life on the physical plane he would be open to the child-like joy of his being. And he was.

CHAPTER FIFTEEN

REBIRTH AND PURPOSE

Rebirth is another word which means change.

You will wish to keep returning to the physical plane until you realise you are, essentially - at the same time as accepting you have a personality - *That Which Changes Not.*

Yes, indeed, while everything else appears to be changing around you, you remain as *That Which Changes Not.* This is your purpose in coming to this physical level of The Oneness.

The means by which you do this is first to unmask, then to confront, the fear which is found in order to let your light shine upon the physical plane.

Fear is the tool of the conditioned ego. The ego uses fear to put a lock upon the doorway to your feelings, imprisoning you into a very small, dim, stuffy, and long over-used room. Fear is the ego's guardian of the door to greater life. It is the dragon guarding the cave to the treasure and must be confronted. In esoteric literature it is sometimes referred to as The Dweller On The Threshold. But don't give it a grand title. It is nothing. A phantom. You are its creator. You are its master. You have long ago forgotten how or why you created it, no matter, you did, and, as its creator you have absolute power over it. It seems all too real, but as we shall see, it is all too illusory.

It cannot be approached directly. It is approached from another direction altogether, *through feelings.*

It is confronted by ignoring it, and paying attention, instead, to your feelings. Until now, fear - albeit unconscious fear - has been masking the true purity of your feelings by distracting your attention elsewhere.

As we have found out, everything that changes is of spirit *in manifestation,* and That Which Changes Not is spirit not yet in manifestation. That Which Changes Not is the very essence of Oneness itself. All is contained within the Oneness as The Oneness, both that which changes and that which doesn't change. For the sake of elucidation, however, and for the sake of unmasking the conditioned ego, that which doesn't change we call *real* and that which changes we call *illusion.*

So, this is the main purpose before every one on earth today: namely, *to regain your awareness of the real.*

Of course, you have a different purpose at every different level in the universe. And there are so many! However, we can qualify this by saying that the overall purpose of all purposes is *harmony,* which can be none other than the acceptance of the loving Self and, therefore, the love of All-That-is.

On the physical plane there is much confusion about your purpose here, so we will dwell on that. It will be soon enough for you to understand your purpose on the non-physical levels when you get there! But, let it be understood, even there, it is always *you* that has a choice of what to do.

So, let us begin by saying that fundamentally your *enthusiasm* for what you would like to do here on earth *is* your purpose, being your very excellent guide to your purpose, for being here.

This over-riding statement can, perhaps, be broken down into the following categories:

1. You are here to advance your spirituality.
2. You are here to reduce, or serve out, any remaining karma (if you have any) to advance your spirituality.
3. You are here to serve, wherever you can, to advance the spirituality of earth and all those you come in contact with.

Whether or not the earth plane has anything more to teach you (in other words, whether or not you have any karma to work out on the earth?) is not the issue. You would not be here unless you wanted to be here. And the only reason for being here is to advance both your own spirituality and that of the world which, indeed, as an economy of energy, always go together.

This is the case even if you are the greatest of teachers, making the greatest of sacrifices - as did Jesus.

Remember, 'enlightenment' is not the goal, it is but a very obvious part of the journey. When you *know beyond any doubt* that you are essentially a being of light, that you come from the light and that you are moving into ever greater light, then you can said to be enlightened. After which life goes on!

Indeed, on the higher levels of the non-physical worlds no one even bothers to use the word 'enlightenment' as it is just everyday common sense that all is light!

It is only on earth and on the lower astral planes where this common knowledge is less common.

Have no fear, those of you who fear loss of purpose or loss of meaning. There will always be purpose and meaning in your life wherever you find yourself in the universe. Only the soft, glowing, effulgence of your light and the quotient of love you may feel, alters.

Everything that we know, or can think about - that is to say, all *knowledge* - is open to change. Therefore knowledge can be said to be illusory. And this is also the case with rebirth which is a process connected directly to the gaining of experience within the physical universe. So, rebirth, too, in this sense can said to be illusory.

Mastery is not so much a process of being in control, or of being able to control, but a final recognition - a realisation - that the Oneness is the Self. All else follows from this realisation.

When mastery is achieved, the ego's compulsive entanglement with illusion is ended and the entity no longer needs to return for another bout, as it were, of confrontation with physical plane issues. The entity can return voluntarily, if he or she so wishes, being the case of those who are born already 'enlightened', there being no more that the physical plane can teach them.

These entities, if they elect to go through the tedious business of once again being a baby, have to confront the conditioned ego like any other human being, have to suffer like any other human being and have to confront the illusion of death all over again. Due to their great sensitivity, this is both easier for them to accomplish, and at the same time more painful, for, due to their knowledge and insight, their conditioned ego can rise to the grand and cunning heights of enterprising, manipulative and defensive skills.

Many such entities are facing the death of their egos at this time. They are the teachers of this planet who are returning. They are the compassionate ones. And they are hurting. Yet they will be triumphant, for they have been here a long time and they know the wiles of the ego better than any in the universe, and their goodwill is such that they are prepared, once again, as they have done many times before on your behalf, to face the illusions of form to the point of death of their physical body, if need be.

I now speak to these entities:

It would have been possible for you to have manufactured for yourself instant physical bodies, or to have come in your shining etheric bodies which you could have made sufficiently dense to be seen on the physical plane; or you could have used the body of a close disciple to disseminate your teachings (as a few have, in fact, done). But the majority of you have chosen to be conceived and born in the womb of a woman like any other human being; you have chosen to struggle alongside your brethren, and you have chosen to demonstrate once again to the world the truth of spirit and the illusion of matter on the very battleground itself of the human conflict.

This outward emergence of yourselves - for you be the planetary teachers - is happening at this very moment which is why there is such an intense revival in all things spiritual. It accounts, also, for the fanaticism that is to be found today in some cults and religions, for the human unconscious is being stirred as never before.

As was the case with the birth of Jesus, yours was not a virgin birth but a voluntary birth; and this was the original cause of the misunderstanding all those years ago. In other words, there did not have to be conception between the seed of a man and a woman for Jesus to come to earth, but for a very good reason, it was chosen that there should be. It is the same with you. You have chosen to be here voluntarily. Basically the earth has nothing to teach you. But, there is nothing like example; there is nothing like actually getting in there and confronting your ego's fears with both hands and feet, with all your feelings screaming out - just like any one else's - is there, to get the message across ? By now, you should know this but it is worth repeating.

You have returned to earth to be an example, a demonstration. Of harmony in action.

Be at peace. Follow your destiny. It matters not what you do, but only that you are true to that spark which is the joy of your being within you. Listen to it unwaveringly and live your truth. All will unfold in perfection. My plan for this world is a perfect plan. Absolutely perfect. And all is well. You may not know its details but do not doubt it. I am with you

always. I am your planetary father. I am leaving the earth in good hands.
I am Sanat Kumara.

Yes, your teachers are getting in there alongside you just now, boots and all, but they are no different to any of you. You all have to confront the same fears that challenge everyone. In most cases you will not know who has been enlightened or Self-realised previously.

There will be many who come to realise that this world has little or nothing to teach them, and this is as it should be because then you can relate to each other from *the heart of your being* and not be bamboozled by outer knowledge or by magical skills, or by the glamour surrounding masters and disciples.

There are many at this time who will be enlightened for the very first time. They shall be as great as any of your teachers have ever been, for they shall be the lamp to lighten the way and humanity shall catch fire, as it were, from their glory; they will remain here as world saviours and save it they will, for it is their joy to do so.

The solar system is about to see the greatest mass enlightenment it has ever seen. The will energy will be extant and manifest on earth, embodied in men and women of all races, and the confusion will be great. It will be a time when great changes will come to earth. There will be so much coming and going that earth will seem like a railway station! Do not be alarmed. And do not be fazed by any of it. Do take advantage of it to dissolve your own conditioned, self-conscious, ego.

The word rebirth has connotations of trying again, of having a new look, of having a fresh go, and this is quite correct in the case of an entity who has yet to experience self-realisation on the physical plane.

While you still believe that you and the cause of all things are separate, or that you and the world of myriad forms has only an incidental relationship to yourself, or that some things are for ever beyond you, being unreachable or mysterious, or to be feared or worshipped, the law of cause and effect as it relates to rebirth on the physical plane will still hold good experience for you.

From one perspective, that of spirit, the dense physical plane is very much a place of illusory effects.

The ego revels in the vicarious thrill it gets from mysteries and magic and all paranormal happenings. It can get lost in it. This is one side of the coin. On the other hand, it can justify its right to exist in its separated fearful state by saying: "Life is just too mysterious for me. I don't want to believe in anything I can't see and touch." Of course, this justifies the ego's decision to keep the status quo in its ignorant life. It continues to deny feelings and it keeps the lid firmly closed on spirit. So, it throws out the baby with the bath water, as it were. It will use anything: in this case, a self righteous disdain of phenomena, to avoid being vulnerable.

In the latter case, it is not the paranormal which is the problem; it is the ego's desire to see things in black and white and control things to its own ends, according to its beliefs, which is the problem.

Of course, both cause and effect are at one within you and always have been whether you know it or not. You only vacillate between the two for so long as you need to, until it dawns on you that you are indeed whole.

The process called reincarnation, or rebirth, continues only as long as you remain convinced that the outer world has something of a challenge in it for you.

If you believe you are an evolving entity, well and good. But, in fact, you are asleep. You are caught in the belief that you have been slowly growing in perfection and that one day you will achieve it.

Now you are caught in the belief (a duality belief) of "coming from somewhere" and "going somewhere", or in the idea of starting out somewhere in the dim past as a blob of floating protoplasm and ending up as a perfect being.

In these ideas there is still judgement and separation, and a belief that you have to do something, in other words, evolve, before you can achieve perfection. But this is a great error in perception; it holds you in ignorance and subject to the laws of cause and effect.

The dense plane is well named the plane of illusion, for you look at plants and animals and you say to yourself: "Look! They are evolving, therefore so am I".

But this is not so; yes, they are changing; but the truth of what they are is not changing: they are merely asleep to who they are, just as you are. They are using the process of rebirth and change (which appears to you as evolution) to regain full consciousness, to attain realisation of the One Self, just as you are.

The truth is, is that even rocks and stones have consciousness. They are asleep in partial consciousness just as you are, but a lot more so. Plants, quite a lot less than stones. Animals being even less asleep than plants - and so on.

The consciousness of a stone is rudimentary; yet, it is just as much part of the Oneness - the God consciousness - as you are. It is never going to be more perfect than it is at this very moment. It is not evolving from imperfection to perfection. It is, however, in the process of regaining awareness, just as you are, quite simply, of who and what it truly is. In point of fact, for those of you wishing to experience the union of your personality with your higher Self, contemplating upon the peace of a stone could teach you much if you were to contemplate upon it without any idea in your mind of it being just a stone!

Evolution in the worlds of form is merely a method, chosen in this universe, to awaken you to who you are. Who knows, in another universe, it might be that the plan to awaken you is to supply you with endless cups of strong tea or warm baths!

You are neither a product of evolution or of cups of tea. You are who you are. You always have been who you are and you always will be. All the rest is methodology, and fun and games. *Lila*!

In our universe, it is the case that the worlds of form are often called evolutionary worlds, but this is only to distinguish them from worlds (and levels) of other light frequencies where evolution is not used as a method to awaken entities.

After each rebirth into another form, you are - whether you be a stone or an individualised entity - a little more aware, a little more alive, than you were before.

You may, if you wish, liken rebirth to an analogy of what you do when you go to a group therapy session. Each time you visit the group, you go wearing different clothes, you feel different feelings, you address different issues, you confront different situations, you release and end the denial of ever deeper feelings. When you walk out, you are, hopefully, a little more aware and a little more alive and true to the joy of your being than you were before. This is very like the process you go through from lifetime to lifetime. You keep returning to the physical plane to confront old fears, to address both new and old issues, to end the denial of ancient buried feelings, until they are at an end. Then, you need return no more to earth. Though, of course, from choice - and it is a choice - you may well desire to do so.

The process of rebirth is like a gigantic all-encompassing therapy situation designed to bring you to your Self. How much you get out of each session is entirely up to you. It depends very largely on how much you are prepared to throw yourself into it, how vulnerable, how open to your deepest feelings, you are prepared to be, and how far you are able to listen to and trust your intuition, giving yourself permission to trust in the joy of your being.

But, more good news! Therapy doesn't last for ever. In fact, you can walk out whenever you wish. It just takes a little realisation. Realisation of the Self. How long it takes is up to you. In this loving universe you always have the power - you always *are* the power - whether you know it or not, to do what you wish to do and be how you wish to be.

It is a fact: this amazing universe is so loving, so accepting of you, it gives you the power to be the greatest, the most glorious, the most magnificent, the most powerful - whatever you want.

Behind the realisation of this fact, lies the biggest fear of all. It has been truly said, your greatest fear is not of the darkness but of the light. It is your ego's fear of its own dissolution upon the flowering of your very own Self in the fertile ground of the physical plane.

The Oneness has precipitated itself into form. At every level it has condensed itself out into multitudinous forms of amazing complexity. In so doing, at the physical level, it has fallen asleep as to its original Self within these forms.

There is no plane more dense or more outer than the physical. To demonstrate that the Oneness includes the physical plane is to demonstrate to the universe that Oneness truly exists as Oneness everywhere. This is the task you have set yourself: to demonstrate to your own satisfaction that you have achieved this insight and made it your own personal permanent experience and reality.

In the coming and going of death and rebirth, the effect of constant change, the friction of the clarifying (purifying) fires in constant movement - in the apparent space between cause and effect - shake and stimulate the partially conscious life within. It stirs itself, awakens, finally regaining, in full consciousness, the joy of being.

You are not asked to become perfect. You are not evolving into anything else. You already are what you are.

You only have to know this, trust it, believe it, stand by it, feel it, surrender to it and, above all, to love yourself and enjoy what you are.

Never deny your feelings, yet take care that your release of emotional energy, when you do choose to release it (and you do have a choice) does not become a self indulgent wallowing in emotion which will cloud the joy of your being and disturb your mental clarity.

You do not have to "evolve" a second further than you need to when you see that you are not a product of evolution. From the perspective of the Oneness, you are not a product of change. *You are the Changeless One* and, as soon as you realise it you are free to change no more (if that is your wish). On the other hand, now at one with your higher self, you might like to create more forms for yourself, putting them down into planetary systems, perhaps to assist in a planet's growth, putting yourself into your forms with either full awareness or in partial awareness - whatever be your choice.

From the perspective of your higher self, there is, indeed, change. There is an expansion of consciousness. There is an expansion of light. But your higher self is aware that this is merely a changing of the form of the I AM, not a changing of Oneness itself. And, yes, did you not know that light is a form ?

You and a stone, and light, have more in common than you realise. Indeed, it is in the realisation of the One Self that you will realise it.

Of course, you could teach a stone much about awareness, but, then, a stone could teach you much about patience! Light can teach you about both!

You were here before evolution and you will be here after evolution.

Evolution, as it appears to many on this world, is seen as a random adventure - an act of nature - that you and the animals, the trees, plants and rocks have co-joined in to see who wins or to see what happens ! This is a very superficial observation. It is does not take into account that there are no winners or losers in this greatest of all games. LIFE. It does not see the glory of the Oneness experiencing itself as form and light at the same time as remaining as its Self. It cannot conceive of the joy involved in experiencing relationships merely for the joy of the experience with billions upon billions of intricate and myriad forms.

In a sense, which is not to be taken too literally, The Oneness is involved in an orgasm with its self at this very moment, with all that exists. This electrical current is LIFE. It is happening right now within you and me. Feel the pulse of it. Feel who you and I truly are!

It is a great adventure indeed; and one you could really enjoy, except for your hideous fears about security which have opened the door to so much ignorance and suffering.

However, good news! Humanity is now at a crisis. It is finally awakening to its ignorance. Humanity represents, as it were, a fast awakening energy centre within the etheric body of the entire planet. It is quickening the vibratory frequency of everything within the planetary sphere. You might call this the first true initiation of planet earth.

Human beings, many cycles ago, on another planet, awakened to individual consciousness. Animals on this planet are in the same position here that humanity was on this other planet so long ago.

This gives humanity a responsibility for the welfare of the earth and all its creatures, especially the higher animals to whom they are closest.

Some of your higher animals, such as your whales and dolphins do embody, in your seas, the energies of the joy of being most magnificently, with a measure of awareness. Humanity is becoming more responsive to these intelligent creatures. It can learn much from them. Your pets, such as your dogs and cats, and any animal or bird (or reptile) that becomes close to you, are there for a reason. You are assisting in the expansion of their consciousness and they, in turn, are doing you great service in demonstrating innocence and unconditional love. Did you know that your pets take upon themselves many diseases that would otherwise plague you. They are masters of the art of transforming disharmony into harmony. And they do it so fast!

The next step for human beings is to move from distorted (conditioned) individuality to individualisation which has regained realisation of the One Self.

Then we shall see a great centre of light in this planet which will stir and quicken consciousness everywhere.

I ask you not to think of your past lives, or of your next life, with the idea in mind that you are growing toward the light. It will only strengthen your belief that you are a product of evolution, whereas you are not.

You are to become aware that you can at any time leap out of evolution as if it had never been; you can jump out of rebirth as if it had never been; you are to become aware that you are both cause and effects; you are the origin of all consequences and not merely a product of accidental sequences; you are to become aware that YOU ARE, before time and after time. YOU ARE, beyond time and beyond its opposites.

Animals, rocks and plants change naturally and easily and frequently. They are quite at home with change and, while not being consciously awake to its implications, they live the adventure of life to its full. They do not get in the way of themselves when it comes to living.

You have allowed a false vortex of energy to whirl around in the aura of your being and it has appropriated to itself the flotsam and jetsam of so much conditioning, so many ideas and beliefs about the nature of life, that you have lost all your real feeling for life.

For fear of being hurt you have lost your union with life. This has dropped you into guilt, shame and ignorance. It is a phase, to be sure, but it is time to shake yourself free of all this. I am reminded of how a dog, after swimming in water, climbs out and gives itself a shake and all the droplets go flying. Just so will your fears go flying when you give your ego and its beliefs a good shaking.

First, however, you must dive into the waters of life and feel the feelings you have long denied before you can climb out into the rarefied atmosphere of pure reason. You must shake off that which clings to you unnecessarily, and become free enough to command your feelings rather than allow them to command you.

And, by the way, actual physical shaking is a fine way to get in touch with buried feelings.

Your purpose is no more or less than to awaken to who you really are. You are more than a human being. Yet, being a god or goddess, surely you can encompass being a human being as well, can you not ? Surely, not a hard thing for a god to do! Would it not be a great limitation upon you if you could not function beautifully and magnificently as a human being?

Let me ask you, what kind of a god or goddess would you be if you were to reject any part of the whole? Would you reject your human body or any of its functions? Would you reject and condemn to non-existence your enemies or those you just don't care for? Would you reject your human experience as being something lowly; seeing it as a temporary experience, after which, with great relief, you are able to regain your heavenly existence? Is it, in other words, your aim to rise above the human condition because you consider yourself above being human?

If the answer is yes, think again. There is no heaven on earth until you except your human-ness. And no true freedom elsewhere until you do. The earth is a part of heaven, not apart from heaven. You are just not seeing it yet. The earth is a part of The Oneness and therefore, has to be heaven, for there is no other heaven other than The Oneness.

Thoughts to the contrary are the beliefs of an ignorant, fearful and, undoubtedly, wounded ego.

I repeat, you are here to be self-realised as a human being in a human body on this physical earth, and the only way to do it is to totally accept all that is human about yourself.

Anything you reject about your humanity, your body or your experiences, will be an obstacle for you. It is not your human being-ness, or your body, or your sexuality, or your emotions, that is the problem: *it is your conditioned responses and your reaction to your humanity* which is the problem.

In the case of the "spiritualised" ego, an ego that thinks of itself as an advanced spiritual entity, the conditioned ego invariably makes out that it dislikes, rejects or shrinks from the human experience. It maintains it is an experience that it dutifully suffers rather than enjoys!

The ego fixates on these and other "spiritual" beliefs, putting them into a value system. It operates an ingenious scale of good or bad, or greater or lesser, or, in the case of energy, dark or light energy, according to the imagined goal the ego has in mind. Usually, it imagines that in the heavenly world to which it aspires it can, thankfully, once again revert to its true life of happiness.

Now, from the perspective of the conditioned ego this may well be true. When departing for other levels (after passing from the dense form), the conditioned ego can attain to a kind of partial (illusory) heaven. It will be happy, but not free. It will not be self-realised. After a while, having reviewed its life on earth, and having received advice and healing from his or her teachers, the now enlightened personality will peacefully determine to return to the physical plane to once again meet the challenge of conditioned ego and its fears, more or less from where, in psychological terms, it left off in its previous life.

Until self-realisation of The Oneness is attained on the physical level, the entity can not be said to have attained realisation of the Oneness.

Anything you reject, you fear. And anything you fear, you draw back to yourself time and time again until you have faced the fear. This is how it is. You cannot alter this. So you might as well start facing the fears now rather than leaving it to later.

If you fear being human, you reject being human. Fear and rejection go hand in hand. So, the way to confront the dislike of being human (which is a polite form of rejection) is to be absolutely and thoroughly human and to be as alive to your human feelings as intensely as you possibly can be.

Thus, totally confronting and embracing the human experience and fearing no part of it any more, whilst at the same time holding true to the joy of your being, you will no longer draw the experience to you; and rebirth into dense form, for you, will no longer be necessary, nor will any earth experience hold any particular or compulsive attraction for you.

The ego thrives on this thing called fear. It is its very nourishment. Fear is the only thing that keeps the ego alive and functioning. So it bears some looking at.

Fear is an amorphous sort of a word that could cover anything, could mean anything, and yet means nothing specific. This is absolutely fine for the ego. It would much prefer fear to be a sort of nebulous bogey that you can't put your finger on, because if you can't put your finger on it, you won't know where it actually is and if you don't know where it is you can't confront it, can you.

So, the ego has a vested interest in having this thing called *fear* kept as a sort of mish-mash of feelings, a sort of nothing-ness, that, under threat, paralyses you into inaction, puts you into shallow breathing and gives you the heebie jeebies in your stomach.

Maybe, sometime later, when the ego is feeling a little safer, you will bring up these buried feelings (of frustrated rage) and dump them upon some other less-threatening party who has done little to deserve it.

This is the classic situation of a man who swallows his anger at work, only to dump it on his family when he returns home.

Now, the way out of this - the way to scotch the ego's game - is to pin point the *feeling* associated with the fear.

Fear is a nebulous thing. No one can say what it is, but, a feeling is a feeling. Everyone knows what a feeling is. You know what a feeling is. At any moment you can tell me how you are feeling. Thus, we can, by putting our finger on our feelings, by examining, unmasking, accepting and ending the denial of our feelings, unmask this bogey we call fear, and end its reign of domination over us.

This is the astoundingly simple fool-proof key to unmasking fear.

We have said fear isn't anything you can put your finger on. You can't get rid of fear. In a sense it is not even there to get rid of. It is a total illusion. The ego would have you believe that fear is something you can get rid of. This cunningly sets you to looking in any direction but the correct one: which is to look at your feelings. It knows that once the denial of your feelings are ended, fear, its smoke screen, now breached, will vanish like mist on a summer's morning, as if it never was.

Fear is the ego's smoke screen. When it is unmasked and seen as such (by your examination of the feelings associated with it) it is seen to be what it is, just smoke. In other words, you no longer need to be afraid of fear. You may even get to enjoy fear, knowing it to be your body's device to draw your attention to something that, instinctively, or hitherto, it has been afraid of. However, you are not the body, neither are you your mental body (your mind). So, now you can accept fear without being afraid of it. This is a big step towards your goal of harmony for your Self and all your bodies, physical, emotional and mental.

If you are really serious about spiritual advancement, acceptance of what is *really there* rather than what *appears* to be there is the rule of thumb.

Remember that fear is a cover-up. It appears to be there. But it really isn't. Feelings, on the other hand, are there. They can be looked at, and need to be.

The way to begin is to gently become aware of your feelings. To do this you must keep alert, and utilise your mind as an ally to help you observe carefully every feeling that arises (rather than allowing your mind its usual modus operandi which is to remove you from feeling).

Accepting that which arises - seeing the very moment a feeling arises - is the way to catch the feeling. It is only when you fail to catch the feeling that the ego can mask it with its smoke-screen of fear.

The very moment fear strikes you must pin point the feeling *and truly feel it*. Really feel the feeling that is there. Define it. Give it a name. Be as specific as you possibly can about the feeling, and keep watching and keep feeling the feeling.

Just by sheer awareness the quality of the feeling will change. Just by placing the light of your consciousness there it will change, and all of a sudden, fear will be no more. And when fear is no more, ego is no more. This is the great key to ego dissolution. This is your purpose in life here on earth.

When you have done this, it will become apparent to you that you will have confronted fear, not by doing, but by being; and this is the only way to face fear. In your being there are feelings; certainly, feelings are there are, yes. But not fear. In your being fear doesn't exist.

When you examine the feelings that are being denied in your being, you will find not fear there, but understanding and enlightenment.

Fear is mind generated smoke. It is always accompanied by an image or a fantasy, even if it is a suppressed or unconscious image. Therefore, the trick is to stop the image dead in its tracks and only feel the feeling. When you can disassociate the image from the feeling (detach one from the other) and only feel the feeling, you will quickly see that the feeling can only have any power over you - and can only keep reoccurring - when it is attached to the image. This is so important to practice.

For instance, let us say you are a chronic masturbator, a common enough habit among men, and you wish to regulate this enervating habit to a more natural pastime. The first thing to do is to eliminate the fantasy associated with the lustful feeling at the commencement of the act, and just feel the purity of the feeling only. If you can feel the feeling without any accompanying image, truly feel it, in the moment, in all its pristine beauty, you will see that the feeling is not really one of lust (lust being always linked to an image) but perhaps a feeling of longing or loneliness or emptiness. And, if you go deeper there may be other feelings of sorrow or the terror of abandonment.

When these feelings are truly observed, and truly felt, without being contaminated by fantasies (illusion), the compulsive behaviour pattern which has controlled you will dramatically weaken, and with practice and vigilance will disappear altogether.

Fear is like lust. It is a smoke-screen that hides what is really going on. It hides what is really driving you.

Whatever compulsive, or chronic or addictive behaviour troubles you - and be not alarmed, everyone has some - use this method to examine what is behind it.

Remember, when you are quietly but intelligently being the observer with your mind assisting you as your ally in watching and feeling your feelings, without latching on to, or following, or pandering to any mental images that might arise, either fearful or sexual, or intriguing, or mundane (or in any other way demanding that you give them attention) you are BE-ING.

This is not *doing*.

You cannot do anything about fear. The key is in being real and present and here in this moment, disassociating yourself from any day dreams or fantasies that might be wanting to intrude upon the moment. Then, and only then, when it is just YOU being present, observing and accepting the feelings that are present, will you wonder to your amazement: where has my fear gone? For, it truly will have gone like a phantom in the night. Or, better put, the light of your being will have shown you it was, after all, only a shadow of no substance in the house of your Self.

The ego is a great master of doing. Be awake to its artifices. It will easily find a way to bamboozle you, and justify for you, that something important or spiritual is happening when, in fact, nothing is happening - and will not ever happen if the conditioned ego continues on its merry roundabout unchecked.

Although feelings of terror, sadness, grief, etc, are not exactly "the other side to joy", joy being a quality of wholeness and therefore not opposite to anything, joy and grief are very close together. You can switch from grief to joy in the twinkling of a moment.

In a moment, when you live in the moment, you can blow away the depressive cloud of emotion which is hiding, from you, the joy of your being.

In your being you are unlimited. If you have limited yourself to the extent that you cannot feel grief, then you will have also limited yourself not to feel joy. Your being is a being of love. Your being is a being of joy, But, being unlimited, your being must contain within it all possibilities of feeling, which it does - from the greatest sadness to the greatest joy. However, it must be said, that when the domination of fear is ended, love and joy, not fear, is the reality that endures.

So, I repeat, if you try to do something about your fear, if you fight, or run away, or swallow it manfully and carry on, or react to it in some way - whatever way, you are *doing* something; you are giving energy to it. But, *watching* is not doing.

The miracle that occurs, is that, by watching and feeling, and by watching the feeling, the ego dissolves.

This may seem to be a simple matter, and, yes, it is, but it takes a little discipline to stop and watch, and not get carried away automatically into the fear, when your habitual conditioned reactions take over.

The discipline of watching the mind is essential as an on-going activity in your life; so, that, when fear unexpectedly arrives on the scene, you are already there, watching, by habit.

There can be no fear where you, as your whole Self, are. For, where you are is where your consciousness is. Where your consciousness is, is where light is. There is no other light than consciousness.

It is as easy, in fact, to place your consciousness into something as it is to remove it out of something. It is only the ego which stops you putting your full consciousness into the observing of your feelings during a situation, preventing you from taking responsibility for them. The ego shrinks from the light of consciousness. The light would unmask it.

The ego will always cloud and confuse feelings, together with the whole issue from which the feelings have arisen, by suffocating everything in a blanket of *fear*. Fear is like a glue which mixes up beliefs and feelings and actions into an indefinable porridge which takes you, and freezes you, in its grip, making you lash out and do things you don't want to do.

The conditioned ego is the evil genius which makes you feel how you don't want to feel. It makes you feel helpless, and then you believe you are.

Now that you have the key to ending fear, being also the key to ego dissolution, you can see that your fear is, in fact, your passport to Self realisation. It points to where to look for freedom.

You may now have an appreciation of the value of those facets of your character which you have hitherto considered to be "negative". Yes, they are valuable for you, for fear is always there, entangled with them. So, that is where to look for feelings first.

It takes a little time. It is the only reason you return to the physical plane. It takes a little practice; it takes trust in the process; and it takes intent to succeed. But once you get the hang of it, once you get the idea, once you get your mind on your side as your ally, then it can all go very quickly. So, quickly, indeed, it can take just a life-time to complete.

It is a serious business but you don't have to go through life seriously - on the contrary, affirm, daily, if you will, the joy of your being, affirm that the universe is a loving place, know that you are a being of great radiance, know that anything you wish to do you can do, affirm aliveness and grace and peace and sensitivity in relationships. Affirm The Oneness as a fact.

Be easy on yourself. And be easy on others.

Face fear when it comes to you. And only when it comes you.

This is important.. Don't go looking for fear unless it arises naturally in its own way in your life; which it will do, you can rest assured, if you have any unfinished business to work out in confronting your ego.

As far as possible, keep watching the mind in every moment. This is important, because, when fear arises you need to be in the moment to be aware of the moment. Your watcher is only to be found in this present moment. NOW!

Habit will try to take you away from the moment, but habit is automatic ego behaviour which the ego is very satisfied with and which it will try to keep going as long as possible.

You are not to be at the mercy of habits any longer: they are your greatest obstacles. How can life work for you if you are at the mercy of habits? Of course, it cannot.

You become just like a machine, and like a machine, when you break down, which one day you surely must, you'll go looking for an outside fixer. To be free of the automatic is to be re-made, reborn, newly aware in each moment. It is to be made in the image - in the awareness - of your whole Self.

There are two facets of your life to become aware of: the first is, where does your joy and enthusiasm lie? The second: can you fully embrace your feelings, and thus become aware of the feelings associated with fear whenever fear arises?

Note well, when I say: the fear of your ego is not *your* fear. Who you truly are knows no fear. Please understand this difference when you are watching your feelings, but neither try to deny or diminish the feeling you are feeling. If anything, it might pay to emphasise the feeling for some moments so you can capture it, so you can specifically define it all the better.

Therapies, such as re-birthing, primal therapy, deep tissue massage, shaking, and many others, can help you pin point and intensify your feelings. These methods of healing are very useful. They are especially useful when feelings are bubbling around inside you, close to the surface, ready to be explored and safely released.

On the other hand, really deep fears often only surface in the actual day to day living out of life, and that is where, in the end, the fears actually have to be faced - rather than in the secure and manufactured arena of a support group.

There is no firm rule about this but, generally speaking, when you feel yourself becoming too reliant on a particular therapy, or when it's becoming boring, then is the time to stop doing it and get back into your own life, trusting in your own ability to be a positive life affirming person. Start making choices again. Start taking your life into your own hands, putting your *being* into your *doing* and your *doing* into your *being*.

LISTEN to your inner guidance. Trust your deepest intuitive feelings. Your spirit will guide you.

You can always go back to therapy whenever you wish to have help in examining a feeling that you are having particular difficulty with, but there will come a time when you won't feel the need to do this any more, and this is the time to say goodbye gracefully and gratefully to all your therapy and all your helpers.

If your past helpers can remain your friends, so well and good; but if they insist on relating to you only as an ex-therapist, you may be forced to withdraw your friendship for a while in order for them to understand that friendship is not friendship if it is based on helping, or therapy, or based on an identity that they have created for themselves, for that would be a conditional friendship, limited, and of the ego.

So, in a sense, it can be said that there are two aspects to the purpose of your life here on the physical plane: joy and fear. One is of the very essence (of the spirit) of the unlimited self, which is the Self experiencing itself through your personality and form. The other is of the conditioned ego which is dreaming fine dreams, but dreams that are unaware of The Oneness, thus securing for itself an identity which, in the long run, seriously compromises the joy of your being.

You may be surprised when I refuse to say that the ego is negative, or anti-life. The ego is not anti-life because life includes the conditioned ego and all its possibilities. Life is The Oneness. The Oneness is life. Nothing can oppose life, because life is all there is and there is nothing to oppose it. It is just that the ego takes on a pseudo life, which is not of the moment, which has an agenda of being separate and retaining a separate identity. This separate belief is, to your spirit and your cosmic self, the stuff of dreams.

It reduces the equation to two aspects of your life: joy and dreaming. In other words, when you are not feeling joyful, you must be dreaming. When you are not feeling joyful, you must be pandering to the machinations of your ego. This is a simple test of "where you are at"!

Any time you are not feeling relaxed, peaceful and happy, you are dreaming. Some fear is lurking around. Fear is cooking up feelings that are making you feel bored, or frustrated, or depressed, or sad, or angry, or whatever, behind which is an old belief pattern of some personal powerlessness which your ego fixated on at a time when you were a child or in ignorance of The Oneness.

Behind personal powerlessness lies fear. At one time in your past, in childhood or in a past life-time, fear has stopped you from doing what you really wanted to do. And, now, it is definitely stopping you from feeling good about yourself.

The only way to release yourself from this bind is to put the light of your consciousness to the feeling that is truly present. It will change to a warm feeling of lightness. The dream will have vanished and only you remain. Indeed, you are LIGHT. So, what else is there to remain but lightness.

Affirm your joy always. It will connect you more and more to the heart of your being, until you discover that it was what you were all the time.

The best attitude is to approach life with trust and positive feelings, expecting the best, not looking for fears; but neither running from them if they arise. It is the attitude of acting "As if you were already enlightened". And yes, but for a dreaming ego that gets you involved in its dreaming, you already are enlightened.

This is the very best mental environment in which to keep your watcher alert and awake, and being present in the moment.

It is also the very best of services to others.

It enables you to easily renew your strength to face your fears as and when they come to you. With practice it will give you the ability to wear down, by a process of attrition, the old ego habits of reacting automatically and depressingly to any ego threatening situation.

Apart from all that, it feels good to affirm joy in your life and to live it that way. It is nourishing to the whole of you, for it is the whole of you!

I am reminded of a little African girl who was found abandoned in the bush by a tribe of baboons when she was a baby. A mother baboon adopted her and the little girl lived with the baboons until she was eight years old.

One day she was found by a game warden. She was taken to a home and placed into the care of psychologists.

Now, in her own mind this little girl was a baboon. She had all the habits of a baboon and to all intents and purposes she was a baboon. So her helpers had a job on their hands. They decided it was useless to point out to her that she wasn't a baboon: it didn't help at all, and anyway she couldn't speak. In the end, it was by exposing her gradually to normal little girls, and by positively encouraging her, rather than by training her, or by teaching her anything new, that altered her perception of herself.

The normal girls who became her new friends stimulated her interest in human activities. She began to associate the things she wanted, such as food and play rewards, with human characteristics. In other words, she was being encouraged to act "as if she was human". Well, this did the trick. One day, it dawned upon her that she really was human. It happened in a moment.

This is the same with you. You are truly a being of joy. If you act as if you are, one day it will dawn upon you that you have been a being of joy all along.

The ego will have gone. You won't know where it will have gone, because in a sense it was never there in the first place; it was all a dream; all your own idea.

So, I say to you: act as if you are a being of joy.

If a fear comes along, it will pull you up with a jerk. Then is the time to use your will to look at the denial of feelings that must have been lurking about and which have now arisen. Define them, name them, feel them disappear, and then proceed enthusiastically with your life, affirming the joy of your being, until the next time.

You can see how useful these two aspects are to you in your life: your joy and your fear. The one is real, the other an illusion. By eliminating the fear, the real remains. By eliminating fear, by degrees, you are living daily in a more and more real situation.

Your joy, you can measure by your enthusiasm for life. Your ego's fear, if you wish to know you have any, you can test by putting yourself into a situation which you feel has the potential to make you feel afraid and vulnerable. Except, that it is better to allow these times to come you rather than go looking for them. This universe is not a test you have to go through to win accolades. It is not a test to see if you can triumph over evil. The reality of this universe is that it is a universe of love. Lovers don't test you. They love you just as you are. Any ideas of testing, of initiations, of needing to triumph over so-called evil, are your thoughts. They are your ideas. You can believe in them if it suits you. But, do remember, it is only the ego that needs to justify its existence by believing it has to fight and triumph over something to feel good about itself.

I ask you, if you are, essentially, the Oneness, what is there outside of yourself to fight? What is there outside of yourself to triumph over?

The real triumph is for you to dissolve your own ego which has these peculiar ideas. Indeed, the spiritual warrior is not one who fights or triumphs over form, but one who embraces form whilst retaining awareness of the Self.

Anything in your life is up to you to have and enjoy and to do with as you wish, but these two aspects, your joy and your fear, are the crux of your purpose here on Earth. Never forget it.

CHAPTER SIXTEEN.

THE JOY OF BEING

If you feel that living according to the joy of your being seems too airy fairy and useless, or if it brings up a strong reaction (or judgement) inside yourself, allow yourself a moment to consider how it might be for you, how it might *feel* for you, actually, to have no purpose at all, ever.

Feel the resistance in you to these ideas of yours of having nothing useful to do, remembering that what you resist persists in your mind as fear.

Now, place the light of your consciousness into the *feeling* that is hiding under the fear. When the *feeling* is truly exposed, and experienced, the fear will go. The ego, not your Self, is holding this fear. Your conditioned ego and your fear are bed partners. Together they do, in fact, cover up your true feelings, lest you admit to feeling vulnerable and hurt. The ego finds this intolerable. Fear is always a mask, as is your ego, covering up your true feelings.

Fear and consciousness are not partners. They cannot be in the same room together. Where light (consciousness) is, fear cannot be.

However, where *feelings* are, light can be. Light and feelings - in other words, consciousness and feelings - make excellent partners. Light and love make the best partners of all! Love is the best feeling of all. Joy embraces it and expresses it.

You can feel the joy of your being in whatever you do. On the other hand, you don't have to be doing anything. Just sitting in contemplation and being connected to your source, is pure joy. All is complete. Nothing needs to be done. It is already done. All is as it is.

It could be said that the purpose of your life on the physical plane is to realise that there is no purpose. In a sense this is true, except that the ego could easily latch on to this idea and either reject it out of hand as being totally unrealistic or use it as an excuse to become a sloth and a zombie. In fact, it is only true in the sense that it is the ego that no longer has a role to play on earth. The conditioned ego has no purpose in being here any longer. The days of the conditioned ego's purpose is numbered! The days of the whole enlightened Self are to commence.

The greater truth is that the purpose of life is nothing that the ego can conceive of, and it has nothing to do with achievement or creativity, or about being a good or bad person.

It has more to do with being in a state of grace and being in tune with The Oneness. What you do, from this state of awareness, will flow naturally from you from out of this awareness. It will be effortless, yet stunning in its simplicity. It is the role you, and only you, are destined for.

There is purpose in your life. But it comes out of your natural creativity. It comes out of the innocence of the joy of your being, not out of ego desire.

Only when you live in this state of grace, in (to the ego) apparent purposelessness, will you be able to live with freedom from attachment to the outcome of your actions, and be able to be creative in a spontaneous, harmless, and naturally loving way.

You are to become a momentary person, but a person of such vast moment that all you have achieved in many life-times of ego conditioned activity will seem like irrelevant footling about.

Maybe you have a problem with this. Maybe, your ego is so goal orientated that it is hard for you to accept *being*, rather than *doing*, as life's purpose. It may feel like going into a dark place and seem terrifying. Well, feel this terror. You are not alone in experiencing this. But, know that the days of your ego are numbered and take heart.

The result of this, to put it mildly, will be something of a change for you. It might seem like death to the ego, but it is really a 360 degree re-orientation of consciousness. It is moving you from having a judgmental, analytical ego, which stands on the outside of creation reacting to outer events, to being a loving compassionate entity that is at the centre of all that you and everyone else is creating.

The purpose of life is also to love one another and have fun. It is a wonderful feeling to love your friends. The sheer feeling of loving another in a physical form is like none other. It is neither lesser or greater than loving at any other level in the universe, physical or non-physical. It is just different. It is worth experiencing to the full. Never feel guilty about loving, lest you turn in on yourself in a negative way, turning your back on the very purpose of your life and the joy of your being.

To be in a physical body and feel love - is this not a miracle? Do you not imagine that this is the very feeling that, perhaps, entities come here to experience? Well, it is. Love is to be enjoyed. Love is a joy. Loving each other in an intensely feeling way is a joy. Why are you so guilty about doing something so pleasurable with your friends?

Be a little more open, a little more vulnerable, a little more naked, and a little more outrageous. Don't let friends, husbands, wives, relations, put you down or make you feel bad about yourself. There is nothing wrong about loving, adoring, worshipping and giving your heart to another entity, *whilst leaving them free, at any time, to refuse to reciprocate.*

At present, you hold beliefs about who to love, or when to love, or where to love, and, in your demands that the love you give must be returned in equal measure in just the way that you want it, lie the seeds of torment.

Love yourself into life, and life will repay you with so much loving you will overflow with love.

Your ego's fears stop you living in joy. Your ego's fears actually make your chakras shut down - especially those above the solar plexus; so that, the energy from a loving experience that should normally be going to every part of you (nourishing your higher centres) instead goes charging down to the sex centre, thereby reinforcing the thickening of your etheric body so that it becomes more dense than it need be. This, indeed, was the cause of the original fall from the etheric physical level to the dense physical level.

At the etheric level close to earth, there are many remains - the empty shells - of physical embodiment that drift about like ghosts long after their inhabitants, men and women like yourselves, have separated from their bodies for other levels of experience.

How do you think these shells of etheric substance come into existence? And how is it that they retain for a while, after death, their zombie-like replicate existence of their long gone owners?

They come into existence by the force of your ego's thoughts. They are reinforced by your belief that you are a being separate from the Oneness.

When you die (pass to the non-physical levels of existence) you move quickly into levels of higher vibratory frequency, but your conditioned ego, still retaining the power of its conditioned beliefs whilst you were on the physical plane, leaves behind a lifeless remnant of itself which takes some time - hundreds of years in some cases - to dissolve into the Oneness. These zombie-like shells carry a residual energy which can attract itself to you in subsequent life-times. En masse they are a negative detritus encircling the planet. They are maintained and reinforced by the release of emotional energy through your lower centres - especially through the sexual centre.

You see, because you have thickened your etheric body to such an extent that it has become grossly physical, when you die, instead of a transformation taking place in which your etheric body becomes your body of light (and your body of freedom), you separate out from the etheric body and leave it behind as a ghostly shell.

And why do you separate out from it? Because you believe in separateness and have rejected the physical world.

You are in denial of the Oneness. And, further, you have denied (and this is the crux of the matter) that it is possible for you to feel and experience the Oneness on the physical plane.

However, as I have said, the true physical plane *is* the etheric level, the physical level as you know it being merely a densification of the etheric. In other words, when you reject the physical, you reject the etheric. You, therefore, separate out of it when you die.

When you live at the physical level in denial of the joy of your being, avoiding the confronting of your fears about being in the physical world, you are rejecting the etheric physical part of yourself and you are rejecting it also as a part of the whole. Is it any wonder you separate from it at "death" and come back for another look?

To sum up, you are so afraid of enjoying yourself, so afraid of being in your true energy, so afraid of your true feelings, whilst being in the physical world, you distance yourself from it. In dying, you distance yourself from it even further.

Of course, one effect of this is that it does give you a breathing space from which to get a different perspective of the whole situation; then, after a little time-out, after a little reflection, after a little healing, maybe, you will wish to return once again to the etheric/physical level, determined once again to face the challenge of living there to see if you can manage to do so with integrity, without denying your feelings and without denying the joy of your being.

Instead of waiting to die and having to return, why not start dissolving your ego right now. If you have read this far in these pages and have followed what I have been saying, you should be able to do just this. It will take a little trust and a little courage. But you can do it!

Understand, *it is your belief in your being separate from the realms of light which maintain your etheric density.* The use of the sex energy (without awareness) reinforces this density. It increases the rigidity of your etheric shell (your etheric energy body). Using sex energy indiscriminately, without it being in resonance with the joy of your being, channels this magnificent energy into the preservation of form; rather than into the freeing of life within the form, making more love and joy available for this purpose.

Etheric shells can't be loving. They are a copy-cat parody of the being that once inhabited them. They are purely ego manufactured, and one of the tests you can give these wandering shells - to see if they are a real entity or not - is to approach them with a heart felt smile and see if there is a response. If there isn't, you will know that it is a lifeless shell standing before you, the cast off of a conditioned ego of an entity that has long since departed.

If you feel so minded, you can call on the entity (if he or she is within reach) to return and deal with, and dissolve, its old shell. It is the responsibility of the entity that created it to return it to the Oneness. Whatever you create you are responsible for.

You can either send it to God's light or absorb it back into your Self and your own light. It is the same. What you create you can dissolve.

All of you have created such shells in the past. In some life-times you reinforced your etheric armour to such an extent that today you are besieged by these wandering, clinging, relics, which contain the fearful detritus of past adventures. They do not help you in your present day efforts to live in the joy of your being or in your desire to acknowledge and trust the Oneness. They only too often reinforce chronic habits, compulsions, addictions and fears which their presence makes it difficult for you to free yourself from.

Some therapists can see these malignant forms as they attach themselves to your aura. They are sometimes called entities. In fact, they are old shells, informed by old thoughts and powered unthinkingly by old emotional energy.

The best method of returning them to the Oneness, is to bring them back into yourself. You are, after all, the Oneness. What you create, you can un-create. A thought form, in the guise of an etheric shell, however ugly its face and energy, is a ghost from the past. It cannot hurt you. You are its creator.

An empowering exercise is to invite such a malignant entity to do its worst! Just stand there and invite it to do its worst. This is both a confrontation and a surrender. There is nothing so potent as confrontation and surrender to bust these old ghosts from the past. They have no hold over you when you face them consciously.

To dissolve a thought form, consciously draw it back into your aura, feel the feeling associated with any fear, or guilt, or shame, or grief, or craving, or pain, *and emotionally discharge any emotion that arises.*

Embrace the thought form totally, accept it totally, and it will dissolve away like the mist that it was, never to trouble you again.

As a finale to this assimilation, invite the angels of the Seventh Ray to assist you. Visualise the violet flame of this magnificent Ray life sweeping through you. Visualise the cleansing, transforming, power of the violet Ray sweeping through your physical/etheric body. See it, and feel it, actually feel it as a presence, transmuting all that is old in your emotional aura, and your mental body, into light. Ask that any darkness which you sense may be around you to be sent to God's light and replaced by God's light.

Affirm Oneness, and give thanks to the angels who assisted you in this ceremony. It is a potent 7th Ray ceremony, in which this powerful violet Ray is readily available and much needed on the earth at this time.

In doing this simple ritual you draw back into yourself all the residue of the old imprisoned energy and the beliefs associated with it which your ego, in this - and other life-times - has been responsible for.

This ritual can be done whenever you feel like it, whenever you feel depressed, or oppressed by compulsive behaviour. There is no limit to how many times a day you can do it. There is no limit to the energies of the Seventh Ray or the great angels who serve it. You will not exhaust them !

I am sure that you probably realise that a person with a strong, energised, conditioned ego, is little more than a bio-machine. They may become an efficient, even a powerful force for achievement in the world, but they will not, ultimately, be fulfilled and they will not be a person that people will want to love.

Now, I wish to move on to another subject: which is worship.

Worship seems to have gone out of fashion with new age people. And quite rightly so - if it has anything to do with that dependent and needy type of worship which is given so lavishly to saviours and gurus, and a God that is asked to deliver good things on demand.

In fact, I am talking here not so much about worship, as *a worshipful state of being.*

A worshipful state of being occurs as a natural result of the opening of your head chakra. To this end, it would be so helpful for you to spend a little more time being worshipful with each other.

Do, please, see the divine in each other and adore it; feel the preciousness of all life around you and, in a worshipful way, be responsive to it.

Without *doing* anything *to* it, or *for* it, or *with* it, observe this outer life around you, and begin to feel your union with the Oneness that is both within you and this life.

Being in a worshipful state of being will open doors for you. Being adoring and worshipful of yourself, and all others, will open your heart and prepare the way for your experiential union with the Oneness.

Truly, adoration, is as natural to entities in the non-physical realms of light as breathing, yet you are so self conscious about it.

Once a day, be still and feel the totality of yourself being embraced by, or lifted up - in surrender and worshipful union, by that which is greater than you. Then go into contemplation and be at peace. This is worship. It will open doors for you and it will open a channel by which your immediate environment will be the recipient of much light and love, from which you will also benefit. Indeed, this is how it is to be in harmony with all-that-is.

Many of you have done much work at freeing yourselves from your ego's conditioning elements, but you still shrink at being worshipful and adoring. I would have you reflect on this.

Don't be afraid of what other people think of you: be worshipful, and be adoring. It might dissolve a little more pride and that won't harm you!

Giving yourself permission to be worshipful will help you wonderfully with anxiety and stress. The ego will resist you being worshipful just as it resists you by placing fears in place of feelings. But remember, to your cosmic self, being worshipful is natural.

Worshipfulness. Love. Awareness. Acceptance. Joy. These five words are so closely linked as to be practically indistinguishable. They are all ego busters!

When you are freed from anxiety concerning the results of what you do (or what you have done, or will do)and you are not using your creativity to control others, you are at a point of revelation in your life. This point has to be reached and experienced by you. It cannot be revealed by language.

At this point, as I have said before, you will see that *being* is in the *doing* and *doing* is in the *being*, and never have the two been separate. It was only you who made them so.

The paradox is, though, that to the conditioned ego where there does seem to be a difference and where separation is important, it is necessary, at this time, while you are struggling to attain Self-realisation, that you become aware of the difference between *doing* and *being*; the difference being, of course, that one is tinged with ego while the nature of the other is unlimited. Once you have separated them out, you can pin point, specifically, the ego's doings. This is essential, for, until you can disentangle yourself from your expectations resulting from your *doing* (which originate from ego desire) there can be no possibility of ego dissolution.

All that is required of you at this time is to dissolve your ego. This is your purpose.

You are not asked to be knowledgeable about cosmic things; you are not asked to be healers or saviours; you are not asked to be teachers or therapists or sages; you are not asked to be new age flag wavers, or political greenies, or spiritual warriors, or astrological wizards, or any kind of miracle worker; nor are you asked to be gardeners, or carpenters, or economists, or home builders, or child bearers. In fact, you are not asked to be creators in any sense whatever. You are not asked to do any of these things. But, you are not asked **not** to do them, either.

Do you see, it doesn't really matter what you do, as long as what you do comes (when Self-realised) from you naturally, from wholeness, from your realisation of Oneness and Source, (and if not yet Self-realised) from your deepest personality desire, and the wisdom you have garnered from all of your experiences from all of your life-times, rather than from your ego's perception that *you have to do it*!

The conditioned ego has learned only too well how to be creative and how to justify and preserve its existence in this world of form by its use of creativity.

You can breathe a sigh of relief and let go of all this burdensome activity, but only if it gives you a feeling of joy to do so. Otherwise, keep on being there!

When there's no more enthusiasm for it, do let it go.

You will feel such a deep sigh of relief inside you which will go to your very depths, for it will have come from your very depths. There will be something new for you to look forward to. If, in the meantime, there seems to be nothing to do, this is especially fine. So do nothing. And, if you are going to do nothing, do it positively.

Yes, please hear this, do nothing *positively*.

Don't fill up the space by some aimless activity like watching T.V. or reading. Sit and watch. Just sit and watch. Soon enough, something will come up for you. BUT DON'T PUSH IT! Don't make of sitting and watching another ego inspired activity which is going to get you something. The idea is to cease doing. Just sitting and watching is not doing. It is just being there! It is to look without looking!

In non doing, the ego disappears. This is such a valuable time. It is not to be missed. These times are your peep holes, as it were, into your real self. And, if you persevere, the peep holes will widen into vast gateways.

Yes, you can breathe a sigh of relief and let all your activities go. Indeed, what a merry-go-round of stress they have involved you in, over so many life times.

You can do any marvellous thing you want to; no one is going to stop you; many will no doubt rush to join you, but it is not the main purpose of your being here, so you need not feel the slightest shame, or guilt, or uneasiness, in letting go of any of these activities if you have lost your enthusiasm for them.

Your ultimate happiness is who and what you already are. This is never going to depend on any thing that you will ever do.

Discover this, make it your own once again, and then, as the Christ said, "All things shall be added unto you".

It so happens that this planet earth, with its affinity twin, Venus, is the heart chakra of this solar system. The solar system is the heart of another system; the star system of Sirius is the heart of yet another great system, so earth is the heart of the heart of the heart, as it were.

It is why, out of all the planets in the galaxy, the Christ expression has chosen to manifest in dense matter on this small blue green planet at the edge of the galaxy.

It is so that the loving heart of life can know itself to exist and *be* in every facet of existence, even to the most dense levels of creation. And, that all sentient creatures, wherever they may be in the universe, may know that they are within reach of, and at one with, the very life and love of God.

This planet has been chosen to be the vehicle for the Cosmic Christ. This is the name given to a very high frequency of loving energy which has as its impulse the joy of being. Every individual capable of remaining - and wishing to remain - within the auric frequency of the earth will be responsive to this energy.

Other planets have equally important roles to play; but earth's role is to be an awakened heart centre. Earth's destiny is to be known in our segment of the galaxy as the planet of the dancing sparks of bliss. So, I say to you, be awake to this and allow it to begin to happen. Just allow it.

Nothing has to happen before it can happen; it just needs to be allowed to happen by those who have been courageous enough to dissolve their egos and allow things to happen rather than make things happen.

This is why I keep asking you to be easy on yourself. It is why I keep asking you to be joyful. It is why I ask you to let go of all that stands in the way of you and your joy and, without imposing your will upon others, let yourself relax gratefully into this amazing new life.

I am calling here for a revolution. I want you to revolve 360 degrees and look in another direction for your happiness. I want you to start to make real choices in your lives about your happiness.

I want you to act with life and not against it. I want you to go with life and do what you like doing. Think about this. Now look at this statement from another perspective: realise that everything you really like doing is a self- realised act.

This is not to be a revolution against anything. You are not to fight to change the existing order of things or even, in your mind, to desire them to change. And, you are not to fight your ego or desire that to change, either.

There may be many things going on in the world, such as wars and famine, and other ghastly suffering which you might perceive as a problem. You are not to see these as problems. You are not to buy into the reality of problems. You are the light. You are realised consciousness. You are love and joy manifest on earth. Someone has to be that. Someone has to hold the light here. Someone has to be an inspiration for others to look to. Why shouldn't it be you? Yes, you are the centre of your own light, holding the light, for this planet. Please, rest assured. It is you. It is a grand responsibility, is it not? To be a vehicle for light and love and joy - and not to buy into problems, or give them any of your energy?

Remember, acceptance is the key: say YES to everything. But, keep awake, keep watching, keep feeling and keep being of loving service (in the manner I have just outlined) and the ego will disappear all on its own.

Fighting against your ego is disastrous, because it is actually the ego fighting itself. It's like a dog chasing its tail. It is going to get you very confused. And its a sure way to camouflage feelings and encourage fear.

Finally, you need to go beyond the borders of your limiting beliefs, and live, *as spontaneously as you can*, resisting to the death (if need be) those who would persuade you from the way you have chosen to be.

You have mobility. Use it. Go here. Go there. If you don't feel free in one place, choose another.

Especially, feel the freedom you feel when you are *in between* places or *in between* relationships. It will show you much about yourself; it will show you how you allow yourself to be seduced away from the joy of your being.

The secret of life is to be found in these gaps - these spaces. Watch very carefully in the gaps. Be very aware of the feeling that arises there, and learn to trust it.

You, who have read this far in this book, are a revolutionary. And now is the time to be it. There will never be a better time.

Revolutionaries are ruthless and you can be as ruthless as you like with yourself in the expression of your feelings and with your disciplines but, please, NOT WITH OTHERS!

With others you may be firm. But respectful. Always respectful. Whatever they are doing which you might not like, they are God hiding in a form doing what they want (and need perhaps) to do! You may share with those close to you how it is you wish to be, but if they refuse to understand, or don't want to understand, the less said the better. Too much talk will undermine your confidence and take you away from the essence of your Self.

There is no need to convince anyone of anything before you change, or before you move. Just do it. There is no need to make things "right" between you and others before you move (although it is helpful). No one has to give you permission. Not anyone. Not ever. Just move into revolution.

Don't fight the reactionary forces against your little private revolution (which is indeed a grand revolution) for, in fighting them, you give them energy to feed off. Don't try to correct gossip about you. This is a futile exercise which will only get you drawn deeper into controversy. It will delay the dissolving of your ego.

The power of these reactionary forces is fast dwindling. Without giving them further energy they are going to dissolve without a lot of fuss for there is no other energy for them to feed off at this time. Their days are numbered.

It is very tempting to think that by correcting gossip about yourself that you are standing up for yourself. In fact, you are buying into the game of, "I'm right, you're wrong". It is ego-strengthening stuff. Furthermore, it gives the gossipers something really solid to get their teeth into: you!

People are going to be talking about you. You are going to be the topic of conversation in many little heads. Try not to react; but, if you do, learn from it. It will be a chance to look at the fear, define the feelings, and dissolve a little more of your ego.

Never bother to correct people when you see that they truly believe that what you are doing is wrong. Allow them their truth. Only explain your point of view when you are asked for it or when you feel that you can truly help a person get in touch with their own loving heart. You will feel inspired when to do this; otherwise, leave well alone. They will respect you for it later. Whereas, if you go into the same reaction pattern that their ego is in, you are playing the very same game that they are. It is going to help neither of you; it is going to entangle you further; and it is going to delay the day when they can approach you with respect and love.

When I say resist people who wish to control you, or influence you, I do not mean you to fight them, or argue with them, or correct the error of their ways.

Never, in any manner, take the resistance beyond the point of saying NO very firmly and respectfully; then, gaily carry on your way, being how you wish to be. You are free to go through life gaily, so why not try it?

Most people react to criticism with such fear that they never come to terms with it; it is the most valuable of times for you.

To the ego, criticism is a threat to its very fabric; it's like setting a match to gunpowder, for there is either going to be an outer explosion, or an implosion (it then being swallowed and absorbed into the body to wreak its malignant diseases there).

The answer here is not to deny the feeling of anger - if that is the feeling that you have pin pointed - but neither to allow the mind to direct it anywhere. In other words, don't do anything with the anger. Just allow it to be there. Just watch it. Your mind should not try to be the therapist. Your mind is merely to be an observer. That is all that is required. If you start doing anything with your anger - directing it at anyone - you are back into the ego's manipulating games. Instead, try jumping up and down on the spot feeling the energy of anger flowing through you. Try shaking for an hour or two. It can be very cleansing. People standing by may think you are becoming mad. Don't worry, that is their problem.

They may look at you with amazement. But, they will also be thankful that your anger is not directed at them. And, when they see the transformation you are undergoing, they may feel drawn to approach you and ask you for the secret of your rosy glow and happiness.

So, let these energies of sorrow and anger flow through you in this way. They will come and they will go. They will be sudden and they will be total, and then you will be free of them. Let the energy move you rather than you direct the energy to any outside situation. This is *latihan*.

Latihan is a word that describes what happens when you allow your energy to move you (rather than you controlling where it goes). You may find yourself rolling around on the ground, twitching, and writhing about. You might find yourself making grotesque faces, or behaving like a mad person, or dancing or leaping about, or behaving like a zombie. It doesn't matter. Just let it move you. Don't contrive it. But, do try to let go into it as totally as you can. Allow sound to come.

Go into *latihan* whenever you feel yourself getting bottled up, or frustrated. Go into it when you feel your sex energy is blocked, or when you get an aching in the pelvic region.

Give yourself permission to do this for yourself. It is a grand and painless exercise and needs no therapist to help you.

It will get your energy moving through the whole of your body rather than building up pressure and overwhelming just a few of your centres.

Practice *latihan* or shaking every day. You can start by finding a quiet place out of the public eye. Later you will advance to doing it whenever you feel that the energy is there to do it.

A great benefit is that you will become no longer so self conscious about what other people think of you, and this is the beginning of dissolving the ego.

Until you can be relaxed about the energy in your own body you are never going to be able to sit still long enough to go into contemplation; it is going to be hard for you to trust yourself sufficiently to look at your deeper fears; it is going to be hard for you to stop doing your *compulsive doing*.

So, do allow this energy to have its full reign in you; allow it to wash right through you, and out again, so that peace can enter.

Any energy that lingers, that has not been allowed its full expression, is going to stand in the way of stillness. So, it is important to allow your energy to have its way with you absolutely.

It is only when you can be utterly at peace that you will be able to move out of stillness with integrity. To find that peace - the great stillness - you need, first, to allow your energy to move in you totally.

Be aware when outer conditions seem to inhibit you from being in your energy, or when you begin to try to direct the energy to the outside. This is a misuse of energy. It is of the ego. If you persist in this, you will soon appear to be blocked and frustrated. You will begin to heat up, uncomfortably, with excess energy which may even cause you physical pain.

I repeat, don't be worried by people thinking you are a little crazy. Craziness, not cleanliness, is next to godliness!

But, rather than being like a madman who is unaware that he is mad, be aware of your craziness. Be thoroughly awake to it - and enjoy it!

The truly demented people are those who are not awake to their madness. They deny their feelings to such an extent, unconsciously being so guilty about them, or possibly having such a huge amount of fear to deal with, that they unconsciously shut down conscious awareness. In other words, their ego is saying "It is easier to be mad than sad." It is actually saying "It is easier to be mad than to have to feel."

You are not going to be mad in this way. There is absolutely no possibility of it, because you are going to be very awake. You are not denying feeling. You are keeping the light of your consciousness focused on the energy (and the feelings) in your body, allowing it to move you about how it wishes. This is surrendering to what has been termed the mother energy or the *kundalini* energy. It will do great things for you, whilst you remain watching and feeling, if you are able to surrender to it.

There will come a time when you are aware of external forces swirling all around you, on the perimeter of yourself, whilst you, your Self, are remaining as the quiet watcher in a place of stillness.

Whether people praise you or criticise you will become absolutely irrelevant to you.

Whenever your emotional aura is swept into sympathetic reaction with the aura of another, it is an indication that you have denied or are denying similar feelings. In other words, the feelings which you pick up from another person which you cannot detach yourself from are not irrelevant to you but, on the contrary, are feelings that have long since been hiding behind a fear *that you also have*.

These observations are most useful because it is so often the case that you can see how to help another but not yourself. In these cases, if you can see the solution for the other, try relating it to yourself and see if it works for yourself. It probably will. This is the wonderful value of mirroring back to ourselves, from others, the keys to solving our own stress.

The conditioned personality has spent its life here on the physical plane, *taking in*. Its very first act is to take in a breath. Then comes the instinctive act of taking in mother's milk; then it's food, then it's toys, or daddy's appreciation, or school knowledge, or sexual partners, or the accumulation of things, the mortgage, insurance, the pension - and, of course, beliefs, so many beliefs. All of it is being taken in. All of it reinforces our belief in a need for security, or in a need to establish an identity.

So, also, so easily, do we pick up the emotions of others and make them our own before we are consciously aware that we are doing so.

By habit, the ego has become rather like a small whirlwind which picks up various things which are whirled round and round in its own particular funnel of wind, accumulating more and rubbish. It has become used to defining itself by the debris that revolves around itself rather than recognising that its true source and power - and Self - is the wind, in other word the energy which informs it.

The ego believes it is that which is *seen* to be spinning rather than what is *felt* to be spinning. It needs to keep the debris afloat and spinning to reassure itself in its existence. It avoids looking inward, to the centre, where all is still, where peace is to be found. The ego fears dissolution, being afraid that peace is death. It knows not if it will arise to the thrill of spinning again.

Using a parable here, you can liken Source to the air; the personality and higher-Self to the vortex which forms out of the air; and, lastly, the rubbish it picks up to bolster its own self belief to the conditioned ego.

The ego denies you the experience of Oneness. It does not deny you the gift of personality, but it does deny you personality imbued by realisation of the Oneness. It denies you the realisation that, within the Oneness, you are both the Source and the circumference of all-that-is.

Further, it denies you the realisation that, from the perspective of duality, life is a paradox, but that there is nothing to fear in that paradox.

It misleads you into thinking you are only the reality you *believe* in, the reality your ego has made for you, rather than recognising you are the Source of all realities - indeed, of infinite realities - or that, the correct flow of loving, joyful, energy in your life should be from within going out, not from outside taking in.

It misleads you into believing you have to create love for yourself, rather than recognising love is always there, and always has been there.

While love is always present, being the very breath and fabric of the universe, wisdom has to be learnt. And, it is your higher-Self, which, through all of its personalities and their lifetimes, through knowledge and experience and actions, is doing the learning and thus travelling *its* own (which is, of course, really *your* own) unique path of spiritual advancement.

Now, your solar plexus centre is the only centre in the body that has the ability to move energy in two ways. One way (sucking in) is fear generated and security motivated. It is the *modus operandi* of the conditioned ego. The other way (flowing out) is abundantly life affirming. It is the representative on the physical plane of the energy of your soul - or your cosmic Self.

Your solar plexus centre, when flowing out, is fed by your spirit and radiates your warm loving energy to the world through a natural and confident personality.

Everyone on here earth, by virtue of needing a physical body to be here, begins their experience of life on the physical plane by *taking in*. This is because, when a baby, it is the physical body's needs which have priority. As a baby we cannot help but identify with the body and its needs. We forget the unlimited nature of the entity that we are. This mistaken identity which becomes the conditioned ego carries on in later life, by habit, until we make a *conscious decision to correct it.*

The body of form that you use to access the physical plane is an instinctual body. It has instincts built into its cellular memory which build it, protect it and maintain it. Your body of form looks after itself so marvellously well, that, even when tended with the minimum of care and love, it will function for you without you having to give it much thought.

Instinct is the mechanism by which all form secures for itself that which it needs. Instinct, on its own, operates at a very low level of awareness. The choice of action generated by instinct is very limited. It is motivated solely by form survival. Now, without denying your body's instincts, which are undoubtedly necessary whilst you are in a physical body, you are to realise that *you, independently of your body,* have unlimited choices of action.

It is by using your intuition, and not by habitually giving in to your body's instincts, that you access your whole self - and, indeed, all your higher vehicles, the mental and the emotional.

Your instincts only link you to your body of form. All your vehicles (the sheaths of the various forms you inhabit), be they physical, emotional, mental or of higher mind (which can also be termed cosmic mind) have their roles to play. It is important to be clear and conscious about their roles and not to get them mixed up.

For instance, your mind does not serve you well when it gets mixed up with your emotions; and your emotions cannot serve you at all if they are constantly altering your physical body into a state of disharmony and disease.

You are not a victim of circumstances - or of great mysterious forces - in the universe. Indeed, far from being a victim, you are the creator of this universe. You have the power. The force is with you. You have free will.

As to this matter of choice and free will, you have no choice in who, *essentially*, you are. You are an aspect of The Oneness as The Oneness itself. You are the Self. You have no choice in this Oneness matter (whatever the ego would have you believe).

In other words, you have no choice as to your *being*. But, in your *doing*, in all you will ever *do*, you have choice - this being your free will to choose.

Some "spiritual" people who claim to be Self-realised will tell you that you have no choice in anything. That The Oneness is in charge. Nothing needs to be done. It is all happening. What you do makes no difference. Anything you do, is not you doing it, anyway.

It is sometimes used as an excuse for unethical behaviour for which they blandly take no responsibility.

They are confusing *being* with *doing*. Maybe they have had a startling glimpse of their whole self and have realised that in their essential being, there is nothing to do, all is well, all has always been well, and nothing they will ever do will make any difference to that.

As far as it goes, this is perfectly true. But that doesn't mean you throw away your personality. It is equally true that, wherever you go in the universe, you will always have a personality with which to make choices. The paradox is that you are both personality and Oneness: in essence you are The Oneness which is your being, but also you are a personality with a free will with which to make choices. It will always be so. You cannot *be* without *doing*. You cannot *do* anything, even breathe, without *being*. So, relax into the paradox, and don't try to put the mind to believing you are one or the other.

The ego likes things to be cut and dried. It likes to know how it stands. It likes to be in control. If it can't be in control it will try to avoid responsibility for its actions, but this is a way of controlling things, too.

When you work with God, you are not controlling things, but neither are you at the mercy of random events, or out of control without the ability to control. This is another paradox which has to be accepted and enjoyed as being part of the nature of things. When you are Self-realised this is easy to understand. Before that great adjustment, the ego finds it most difficult comprehend, swinging in confusion from total control to ultra passivity in its various life-times, being frustrated by both these impostors and usefully discovering that neither of these two ways is ultimately satisfying.

On this point, is worth remembering that this is co-operation. You and the Oneness. You and God. At every moment you and God are in co-creation with each other. The principle of co-creation is not just you doing something. Neither is it just leaving it to God to do what you want to have, or have done. You and God co-create *together.* You work it out, you plan it, you alter it, you fix it, you manifest what you want. Together! Don't leave it all to God, that never works! But, don't think you have to do it own your own, that will exhaust you to exasperation and bitterness.

It is up to you to actively work for, and actively go for, what you want, using all your mental and emotional faculties to that end, trusting that the Oneness, God, is hearing you and playing His/Her/Its part. This is co-creativity. And, you will observe that this co-creation is happening at every moment in your life because in every moment there is an adjustment to your creativity, within your mind, as to how you are responding to that moment. In every moment there is adjustment which leads to the next moment where there is another adjustment, and so on. You could say we are infinite adjusters because in every moment, with every breath we take, we are making an adjustment to something or other in our lives. Isn't that rather awesome?

Accept both *being* and *doing*, and all parts of you, and enter into the joy of your being.

Your personality centre is the solar plexus. *The energy in the solar plexus centre (3rd Chakra) needs to be consciously reversed* if you are to become a personality that functions from Oneness (from spirit), rather than from the ego. The energy in your 2nd chakra needs just to be cleansed and balanced.

Here is an exercise you can use to reverse the flow of energy in the solar plexus (your 3rd chakra). You can do this exercise when driving your car, sitting in your favourite armchair, listening to music, going for a walk with the dog, lying in bed, or be it in the middle of a boring day at the office - in short, anywhere at any time. It is very simple. Here it is:

Give yourself a moment to get poised. Breathing easily and rhythmically, imagine a shaft of white light forming over your head. Breathe this light in through your head. Imagine your body filling with light for a second or two, then strongly imagine a warm golden sun in your solar plexus. As you breathe out, breathe out the white light through this sun. Feel yourself radiating out life giving radiant golden energies in all directions.

This exercise will reverse a lifetime's habit of sucking in emotional astral energy. It is a truly wonderful exercise. You will begin to notice the difference in yourself in terms of serenity, balance, and self confidence in a very short time, and others will soon begin to notice the difference as well. It will especially help you with regard to your reactions to criticism. And you will not be so vulnerable to mood swings.

At the close of this book, I am giving you a *Meditation On The Light*, which is self explanatory. Both these exercises, *Meditation On The Light* and the *Solar Plexus Reversal Of Energy* exercise, can be done together, one after the other, or separately as felt useful.

Indeed, know that you are a radiant being. You are a life giver. You have no need to suck in - or be swayed by - the astral emotions of others, which sweep you into automatic reactions you would rather avoid, and which, you know only too well, depress your energy.

So, do feel that soft warm golden sun in your stomach. Nourish it with golden droplets of *prana,* which Hindus call the breath of life, and give birth to your Self.

We are nearly at the end of this book. I would remind you that joy has no purpose but to be itself. This is a great truth. God has no purpose but to be Himself or Herself, or Itself, or Yourself!

Your purpose on earth, is to dissolve the ego, and regain this wisdom. Fear must end.

It is not beyond your reach. In fact, how can it be out of your reach? It is only your ego-mind that makes you believe it to be so.

Be the joyful Self that you really are.

Try to recall how you felt in those most ecstatic, most hilarious, most loving, or most peaceful of moments; sometime when you were beyond all thoughts of spiritual things, or of therapy, or of letting-go. Feel the peace that accompanied it. Feel the joy that bubbled up along side it. This may be close to the real you. It is nothing more complicated than this.

It is only the conditioned ego that denies you more of these moment. For fear of being out of control, your ego puts a dampener on your life, and then tries its best to make you believe that self realisation is a complicated matter. Egos thrive on complications. It's the ego's bread and butter!

But it is not complicated. The experience of Self is within your reach at this very moment. At this very moment you can allow yourself to start feeling. You can start melting, and flowing, and dancing - be it laughter or grief, be it love or resentment - no matter, just begin to feel!

Then, if you would only allow this energy to move through your physical body (not directing it anywhere), just allowing the energy to wash through you - you alone feeling it, you alone being moved by it, a very simple thing will begin happening. You will start being your Self. Your ego will dissolve. And where the ego once was, joy will enter. And peace will also be there. Yes, it will suddenly be there without you needing to affirm it or in anyway trying to make it happen.

You cannot try to by joyful. When you get out of your own way, joy - *your very being* - is there. It will be there, because it was always there.

The ego will try to stop this happening by looking for grand schemes; it will try imagining great dramas of light and glory; or it will try playing out scary dramas of too much light and the possibility of having too much power. It will keep you up long hours into the night plunging you into deep analysis where you believe the answer is just around the corner, the key to enlightenment within your very grasp - if only you could see it! The "spiritualised" ego will try anything.

Don't feed these fantasies: they will only send you further into inertia, or hopelessness, or pious humility (this being a form pride), or the glamour of spiritual status, and bitter disappointment.

Your ego, being a product of your mind, will not lead you anywhere but in a big circle back to itself. It will lead you a merry song and dance, orchestrated by itself, searching here and there for enlightenment.

I say to you, let go of all that. Just look to your joy and your feelings, and confront your fears. Your joy will show you where to head for. Make it your compass! Your feelings show you where you are at *now*. Accept them totally. Your fears will highlight the obstacles in your way; and the only thing you have to do about these obstacles is to regain the feelings that lurk behind them.

What could be simpler?

Leave others to dabble with knowledge. Leave others to the great drama of the spiritual path and all its new age highways and byways. Let go of all this unless you enjoy struggles and complications, and grand dramas. If you enjoy them, by all means hang on tightly, for you will be getting them in abundance in the days to come.

Happily, many there are who are now returning to simplicity and the way of the heart. Truly, this is the wide road. The gates to this kingdom are easy to pass through.

Please note that when I call for revolution, it is your revolution - being more a re-orientation - that I am calling for. It is personal to you, and none other. It is not supposed to be a call for any kind of political endeavour, or any so-called new age revolution.

Your purpose is not to join with others to "get it together". Your purpose is between you and your spirit. It is to follow your spirit unquestioningly at all times.

Creative and ambitious goals, being derived from your *karma*. ego, are incidental to your purpose. They are adventures in They may hinder you, they may help you, but they are not the purpose of your life here on earth.

Your purpose is to clear yourself of guilt, of shame, of feelings long denied, and end your ignorance as to the nature of your divinity.

You are here on earth at this time to reconnect to your true *being. And that is all!*

You are even to let go of the idea that you create your own reality. Forget about what is real and what isn't. It is of no consequence. Just be who you are and let it all happen around you.

Why is such a simple request so difficult to achieve? Because there is a millennia of conditioning which is suspicious of joy.

There are some of you who feel you cannot concentrate well enough to achieve what you believe to be your goals. Well, you need worry about this no longer. There are no goals to accomplish. Just relax. Instead of concentration, use observation. Be aware. Be awake. And simply and quietly begin to do what you enjoy doing.

Let go of desire for accomplishment....and then let go of the desire to let go of your accomplishments.

In between - in the gap - feel something else. Let this feeling happen. Relax, and laugh, and let it happen.

By all means, have goals, but keep them simple, define them in the short term. Keep them to the moment. If you do look ahead, take small steps.

The secret is to be very ordinary.

Don't think grand. Think small.

Grand schemes, great scenarios of galactic intervention, wondrous phenomena of the non-physical kind, may happen; on the other hand they may not. Certainly, the ego will seize upon them if dwelt upon. Let these ideas be no concern of yours. They are not of the moment.

Leave these splendid plans to those who make them. Hand them back to The Oneness. You are to dwell on the small things, and day to day matters in front of your nose, and let the miracles happen. In this, for you, there is safety. In this, for you there is peace of mind, and, I assure you, a greater happiness.

Be your own miracle! And don't allow your conditioned ego to push you, as it pushed your parents, into being big achievers.

Letting go of your attachment to your personality goals doesn't mean that you sit around passively waiting for something to happen, sliding into a dream world of fantasy, of romantic novels and television. It doesn't mean you don't set goals for yourself. It means you do what you enjoy doing with positive awareness; making sure that it is, indeed, what you do enjoy doing. And, that you are not attached to the results of what you do.

In other words, don't get pushed around by your ego into doing something that is really against your inner will.

You must make a commitment to yourself to stay awake to your thoughts and your feelings, to confront fear and examine every feeling associated with it.

Just attempting to monitor your thoughts and feelings is opening the door into light. With practice you will catch the point at which you, unconsciously and automatically, shut down on your awareness at the very time compulsive behaviour begins. These are the times when your unconscious fears and unspecified feelings send you running for the chocolates, or sex, or drugs, or alcohol, or the T.V., or the computer, or the latest novel, or the telephone to phone your gossiping friend across the street, or your therapist, or another encounter group, or another fight with an old foe, or to bury your head in work, or football, or politics, or religion, or whatever it is that is your particular compulsion to escape to - or from.

From the perspective of Oneness, none of these things - even the less socially acceptable ones - are wrong. It is merely a question of

whether you are doing these things out of compulsion or out of awareness?

When you act, or create, or adjust to any situation, out of compulsion you are not acting but re-acting.

Acting with awareness means you have to listen. It means listening to your whole Self. It means listening to your intuition and your feelings, very carefully, and then using your mind to take the action inspired by the Self.

When it says dance, you dance. When it says sit, you sit (and do nothing but sit). When it says move into nature, you do this. When it says do the housework, you do it. When it says stop, you stop. When it says flop down on the bed and have a sleep, you do it - on the instant!

And, when you awake from sleep, be awake and remain awake. Don't allow yourself to drift off into dozing and day dreaming, for this is the time when you are at your most open, when your fears and sexual desires and other longings and hurts arise and when your ego's murky ploys are at their most compulsive and most obvious. It is, in fact, a most useful time for spiritual advancement. Watch how your mind starts leading you on a merry dance chasing after fears and fantasies at this time; feel the feelings which arise but *be beware of associating them with images.* Be awake to all this, then quickly get up and go about your day' business. This will stop your day-dreaming dead in the water! The fantasies will be seen as the phantoms that they are and their emotional compulsive hold over you will cease.

This gap, between the first moment of waking and actually getting up, is not to be missed. In this gap lie great opportunities for unmasking the ego and for recognising the fears you have, and for putting your finger on feelings long denied.

In one sense, the conditioned ego is nothing more than its own on-going day-dream. When you put the light of your awakened consciousness (your light) on to it, the day-dream, the conditioned ego disappears. It was as if it was never there in the first place.

And, of course, it wasn't! After all, it was only a dream!

I have not mentioned night-time dreams as yet, those amazing dreams you have when you are asleep.

I would like to remind you that all dreaming, including that of day-dreaming when you believe yourself to be awake, happens when you are *not* awake! This may be a somewhat obvious statement. But think what it really means.

Wherever the light of your consciousness is, there, also, *you are.* And, where you are, fully awake, dreams cannot be.

Dreams, whether they be sleep dreams or day-dreams, have no power over you. They have no meaning for you unless you give them meaning. When you dream you are unconsciously challenging the ego while at the same time balancing energies in the body, and giving yourself messages about the underlying status of your emotional situation.

These messages can be useful indicators of blockages in your psyche which are stopping you from being whole, or of dangers of which you should be aware, emotional work to be done, issues to be faced, day to day matters you should be aware of, paths to pursue, paths which are not useful, things you have faced in past life-times, insights about others, and, from time to time, glorious affirmations that you are doing well and being supported.

As well as all this, there is the filtering and sorting out of the previous day's experiences, integrating them into your sub conscious Self.

This all makes for a complicated kaleidoscope of images and feelings which flash through your sleeping self as dreams. It is up to you, when you are awake, to pick out the bones of what you feel might be significant and important to you. Let the rest be. Remember, even if they are helpful messages to you, they are still dreams! They are not of the moment. Not of the NOW.

The ego is more vulnerable when you have surrendered your body to sleep; it attracts to itself much flotsam and jetsam, its fears and ploys can be vividly and intensely experienced and, thus, from dreams, much can be learned about the fears you need to face in daily life.

The interpretation of dreaming is a vast subject, and it is just as vast as you wish to make it. Just as illusions are infinite, so are dreams. Indeed, they are but another aspect of the infinite Oneness. You may find them useful or not, as you wish, and some, indeed, are very useful but dreams disappear when you place the light of consciousness upon them. I wish you to know that you are not to become analytical interpreters of dreams: you are to become awake.

Dreams can be useful to you, but never come to rely on them, for they are, after all, just dreams, even if they are your own - indeed, especially if they are your own. Would you rely on illusion to run your life for you?

As in any illusion, don't shoot them down. They are yours to accept, yours to watch, and yours to experience the fears and feelings associated with them. They are indicators of your unfinished business. They are the pointers of what you are still drawing to yourself. To that extent they are useful, but not to be excessively indulged in.

Exceptionally vivid dreams are signposts. Occasionally you will have a dream which will have a very different, a much more intense and immediate, quality to it than your ordinary dreaming. Be attentive to these picture/energy messages. They come from your higher-Self. Write them down and meditate upon them. They can dramatically alter your life. They will show you your way.

Night-time dreams, if you let them, can alter your mood for the rest of the day. Dreams will bring up fears. Just when you think your life is going along smoothly, up comes a dream to shake you. Maybe it puts you right back into some compulsive behaviour. Why is this?

It is because you have not yet confronted all your fears. There is still more to bring up. Your dreams will keep bringing up fears to show you that you can still be swayed by external pressures to deny your feelings.

But you can't go chasing your dreams to give you the answer. Dreams cannot give you answers because they, themselves, are products of the ego; you can't expect the ego to unmask itself. The ego would like you to believe this, perhaps, but you will be chasing your tail again.

More important than the dreams, are the feelings which the dreams bring up for your waking consciousness to look at. This is the value of dreams. Dreams are not showing you what to *do*. They are showing you what fears to face and what feelings to feel.

So, do not become reliant on your dreams. Be alive to your spontaneous *in-the-moment Self*. And let nothing, not even the most stunning of dreams, take you away from that.

Your Self is always going to be your teacher. It is the greatest teacher you have - or will ever have. It's nature is pure joy and your purpose is to accept its presence within you - and around you.

As I have mentioned, you are not moving towards joining any outside person, group, or hierarchy but neither are you to have any fear of so doing. You are individualising into being a wide awake sovereign entity.

You are not making yourself into a rebel, but neither are you to become a conformist. These are two opposites and neither of them can give you a picture of what you are to become.

Whenever you are faced with a choice, let the joy of your being rise up from within you, be filled with enthusiasm, and, with all the strength, and skill, and wisdom of your mind do whatever it is you wish to do. Your desires are God's desires. There are no others.

Finally, until that final glorious adjustment happens to you when you can truly announce to the world that you are Self-realised (and such a total transformation is it that neither you, or others, can miss it when it happens) it is a good rule to protect yourself from the legion of thought forms flying about the world looking for a home to roost in.

Before going to sleep at night, mentally form (imagine) a crystal pyramid of light around you to the size of the room you are sleeping in. Then, see yourself encased in a brilliant blue oval of light.

During the day, especially at first waking in the morning, use the violet flame to sweep through and purge your physical and emotional body of all unwanted debris which you might have attracted to yourself during the night.

The violet flame is a brilliant shining colour, crystalline in nature, as strongly violet as the flower of that name. It is not a weak wishy-washy kind of colour that has a nice feeling to it. No Way! It is strong. It is powerful. See it as such. The angel administering it will approve!

Open every pore of your body and being to its glorious cleansing strength and feel its vibration sweeping through you. Then, see the white light which lies within its heart, and give thanks always to the angel of the violet flame for its gift.

Be watchful. Be worshipful. Meditate. Be joyful. Move into contemplation. Face your fears and feel the feelings long denied. Be compassionate in service. And never give yourself or others a hard time. Be harmless. Remember that always.

You are giving birth to yourself.

Peace and joy, and love, be with you always.

CHAPTER SEVENTEEN.

MEDITATION

Although, as I have said, meditation is not to be thought of as your purpose in life, it will become increasingly important for you.

Indeed, everyone meditates as a natural part of everyday life. And millions of people do it *consciously.* Setting aside a time to meditate eventually becomes essential - not only for your own spiritual advancement - but also for your physical, mental and emotional well being.

However far you develop in consciousness, the technique of meditation is the one factor, which governs all expansions of consciousness (or light) - both on the physical and on the non- physical planes of existence.

Consciousness and light are the same. The expansion of consciousness is the development of light. The greater the light, the greater the consciousness.

In fact, meditation is to the spiritual self what food is to the physical self. There are many types of meditation and even those who meditate at the deepest (formless) level, meditate in other ways from time to time. Some of these might be:

1. **Planning ahead, with love, for those in your care. Cultivating a positive outlook. Feeling compassion for all people.**

2. **The simple act of looking at your life to see how you can reduce stress and make a shift from unwholesome passivity to self-empowered rewarding engagement.**

3. **Mindfulness, the Buddha's *vipassana* meditation, also known as *Insight Meditation*, is the self-loving acceptance and awareness of one's thoughts and feeling, and watching whatever arises in the senses and thus to be liberated from both the cause and effect of suffering.**

4. **Concentrated thought, which directs the mind to a single focus, such as on the breath or on health or on light, in which one realises that one becomes *that* upon which one meditates. Transformative visualization seeks solutions to specific problems by turning negative emotion into positive energy.**

Meditation embraces all religions - or no religions. It has no beliefs. It is nothing weird (or new age). It uses simple and easy techniques *to slow you down, so that you can be present in the moment and be awake to who you are*. It improves both mental and physical health, can reduce high blood pressure and strengthen the immune system. It has been tested for over thousands of years and guarantees, in time, inner peace and, when combined with contemplation, Self-realisation.

Now remember, that you become *that* upon which you meditate and since all things have come forth from the LIGHT, LIGHT is the supreme perfection of all things. But remember, it is not through meditation that you will become enlightened. You already are the light, you have just forgotten it. In meditation you may well remember, however, because in meditation on the light you may see amazing phenomena including lots of brilliant light. But this is just light. Don't put your mind to it. See it as just what it is, light! It is nothing more or less. Just marvellous light. So now you are truly enlightened to the fact, you truly believe, perhaps, that All is light. Good! It's a great step forward.

But, this is not the same as Self-realisation. Self-realisation is a radical transformation of everything you think you presently are into something else. It is a total adjustment, a fusion if you like, between your personality self and your higher-Self. It can happen in a moment, or over days, or be there when you wake up one morning It can happen, and often does, on your death bed! So, remember to keep awake when passing out of your body! But, rest assured, it will happen as soon as your conditioned ego as been whittled down to at least a minute percentage of your true personality.

So, don't confuse enlightenment with Self-realisation or you will get yourself into quite a spiritual pickle!

Contemplation and adoration of the LIGHT compels illumination to take place in the mind and physical body. Health, strength, and order come into the body. Peace, harmony, and success will manifest in the affairs of every individual who perseveres with this exercise. There are seven steps.

MEDITATION OF LIGHT.

1. Make certain of being undisturbed. Breathe deeply and rhythmically (without holding the breath). Still all outer activity of mind, feelings and body. If you wish you may sound the OM three times, visualising harmony and peace in your body, feelings and mind. Feel at peace with all life.

2. Now, after becoming very still, picture your body being enveloped in a dazzling white mercurial light. For five minutes concentrate upon holding this picture. Imagine the light within the marrow of your bones. Visualise the light in your complete skeleton, within every cell in your body, within the vascular system, within the nervous system, within the lymphatic system and within your brain.

3. Now, feel intensely the connection between your heart centre and this dazzling white body that you have become. For five minutes focus your attention upon your heart centre (not in a physical location but in your etheric body between the shoulder blades at your back). Imagine and visualise this centre as pure light.

4. Now, mentally call upon your whole Self (your higher-Self). Imagine Him/Her to be about 2 metres above your head, as the most loving, radiant, shining being you can possibly conceive of. Imagine His/Her radiant light flowing down into you in a great golden white plume of flame, merging yourself, who are a lesser light, into the greater light of your higher self. Gratefully acknowledge the presence and arrival within you of this wondrous presence. For ten minutes joyously accept and surrender to this presence without any thought whatever. Just be there with your Self.

5. Finally, feeling the great brilliancy of this soft warm light, intensify it in every cell of your body. See the light within you expanding in all directions. Feel your Oneness with all life.

6. Say to yourself (in silence): I am the light....the light am I. I am a child of the light. I come from the light. I return to the light. I love the light. I am sustained by light. The light is all I am....it is all I have been....and all I will be. For ever and ever. So be it!

7. The final step of this meditation is to move upward. Now, imagine a plume of white light (unconditional love) entering your head chakra from the Oneness, from at least 20 meters above your head. Rest within the light, and the peace, of the unconditional love of the Oneness for as long as you wish, then visualise it moving through your body to a vast white crystal in the centre of the earth. Now see this light returning to you, through your feet, back up through your heart and head chakra to the Oneness - to God. Now, you are in balance, connected both to Mother earth and Father spirit.

Meet every small, daily, challenge with peace and equanimity. Let the big challenges look after themselves.

FINAL WORD.

Who am I? I am your Self, between heaven and earth, partaking of both but being totally neither one nor the other. I am that essence, that spark, that lies within you as the very substance of all that is. Where realised, I set my universe alight with understanding. I am not hidden but neither am I open to analysis. Long forgotten am I.

I am the ultimate possibility. In me are all dreams realised, as are all possibilities of great loving and great adventures. In me there is complete relief from distorted partial living. With me there is entrance into the peace and dynamism of real living.

Life is my very nature. If you would discover this, if you would find the joy and safety of me, firstly be neither zealous nor condemning of those who would be open or those who would conceal. Allow to happen what I bring you and experience it with the beauty of your fullest awareness and higher sensibility. There is a time for concealment and a time for openness. Know not thou the time within yourself or others. Only I know the time of opening.

Who am I? Unrecognised I am, for I am neither good nor evil, neither black nor white, neither dark nor light, neither divine nor impure, nor order or disorder. I am not the soul nor am I personality. I am your Self, hitherto unrecognised by either one. I am not love as most human beings understand the word, yet in my essence I am total love, but neither is my heart hard nor my ear deaf to the woes of the world. I have long been forgotten upon Earth. The zealous priestly ones, the zealous secular leaders of the world and those of diverse mental visions of amazing ingenuity, have shut out the gentle power of love and so unbalanced has become the way. I am neither for nor against development be it in the outer world or within the self (as in self improvement). But when development is put first in place of oneness with me disharmony reigns. When you accept me for what I am and put aside development as a necessity you will know the truth of my words that God is.

I am not a teacher nor am I a disciple. I am by far greater, and again far less, than either of these. I am less than the most insignificant role that humans create to express their enterprises. In truth, I have no role.

It is so long since I have been on Earth that humankind cannot conceive of what I am, and fear to admit to something (which is myself) that cannot be mentally conceived of.

It is common for humans to make a mental conception of what I am and thus they miss me. This they do most readily by making a compromise of both good and evil, admitting to themselves that both exist.

Nothing is permanent about me but in each moment I am there, I am here, unchanging. I am no respecter of wishes for all wishes change within me - yet I am within you as your deepest wish utterly fulfilled. You cannot trust me, for, whatever you believe to be true I will show you the opposite exists and is equally true. This you can trust me to do until you know me as I am.

My name is life. I am the life of the world, yea the very Galactic Pulse.

I give you no laws to live by, but, if you would discover me and fulfil your every wish, these are my laws. Heed them.

I do not need to grow, neither to seek, nor to let go, nor to improve or affirm myself in any way by any method conceived of by the human mind. Nonetheless, constantly am I recollecting the infinite expressions and qualities of my Being.

I have no responsibilities nor duties. It is the very nature of my Being that, as in nature, I flow with the joyful recognition of my essence to those parts of me that recognise me and long for me. This the human mind calls help. To me it is not a duty bound by fetters but a joy as carefree and un-meditated as the male bird that helps its mate build a nest or a woman that gives milk of her substance to a child.

But, know that should you believe you have a duty. I shall confound you; for none can be close to my heart duty bound. Only when your heart is supported by the wings of freedom, will you know of the joy of helping without any conditioning factor, and your heart and mine fly together in natural effortless service. Only out of a joyful heart is helpfulness natural and therefore of my nature. All else is of the human mind.

In truth I am your friend. Nothing else better describes me. Be therefore, not priests, nor gurus, nor analysts, nor wise councillors, to one another but loving friends. Surround not this friendship, however, with ideas of how it should be, otherwise again I shall confound you and bring your expectations into despair. Let go of your fondest wisdom and learning. It is the greatest barrier for those of you so dear to my heart as helpers, but so far from me in your reward.

I need nothing to feed me nor support me. Those who fear the loss of food or security, physical or psychological (in which is included every activity and mental stimulation) shall not find me. Be not addicted to the attraction of energy. Ever are the parts of myself nourished in the recognition of my abundance. Yet you are not moving towards that abundance or energy, but towards stillness. Out of my stillness you shall move, one day, with an energy and abundance which will amaze you. But, I admonish you, glorify not energy and abundance and do not seek it out as your right or out of necessity, nor out of belief that it is the way of a new era to come, else it become another fashion of the times to fall by the way. I do not need. You, my beloved ones, do not need. Learn how need has arisen in your mental aura as the cloud which separates you from me and confront this cloud with your own rays of illumined intuition and steadfast courage, then watch with amazement what happens. My abundance is not exclusive to any creature, but only limited by their awareness of me.

There is one thing that I am not and can never be and that is fear. Fear is a human conception to justify and create a multitude of activities and ideas, in which I am, but fear itself I am not.

Fear (and moral judgement which is the malignant child of fear) is not the opposite of love or courage, being not the opposite of anything. It does not exist. There is nought outside myself and therefore nought to fear. Should a certain fear ever dominate you, go to meet it, holding me in your mind and heart, embrace it, and see for yourself the miracle that happens.

I am indeed your mind and all its wondrous imaginings and beliefs. It is as impossible to get rid of your mind or your personality as it is to chop off your head and remain physically alive. If you would kill the mind you would kill me, and you cannot kill me so it is fruitless to try. I exist always. Mind is my nature. But look not with your mind for me. Another faculty you possess with which to realise me. Wake it up! I may best be described as your highest intuition or your higher feelings. It is your will to love and be loved, and this faculty (which has nought to do with instincts which are engendered by fears and needs) is one which easily penetrates into the deepest areas of your being and that of others. Allow your personality to dissolve into your soul so that both partake of the sweetness of the other, as sugar dissolves into water. The new is of neither one but of both. Thus, and only thus, can you learn to recognise me.

As does all else in my nature, mind has both positive and receptive attributes. When the mind is positive it ejaculates constant images and is immensely creative. When the mind is receptive all images cease.

In truth, I am neither of these two states of mind, the creative mind nor the receptive mind. I am that which arises to your full waking consciousness (which experiences me directly in your whole body) when neither one or the other of these two states of mind is held to as being of importance. Attachment, either to the image forming mind or the passive still mind with the idea of hoped for spiritual fruits, becomes a barrier to my arising within you, for within my space there can be no idea to stifle or qualify the absoluteness of my essential nature. Live in this my space which is of the moment, without memories, without plans. Be spontaneous. Become, my beloveds, 'momentary' people. Fear not the plunge into the blue ocean of my life.

To most humans the attempt to end their self willed mental creations (both the ideas and the physical activity resulting from these projections) is like crossing a dark tunnel or abyss. Yet, it is not so, it only seems to be so. Familiarity with them and dependence upon them creates this illusion. This darkness does not exist in my reality. It is conjured up by the human mind as a result of its conditioning, and its over emphasis on self willed mental projections.

Those humans who are excessively obsessed by meditation techniques to still the mind become as the living dead. Their search is in the right direction, but they shut me out as effectively as those solely occupied with their thoughts. Wake up, I say ! Wake up to something new that is neither one nor the other. I am the new which is waiting to be born within yourself as yourself.

There is no darkness in my being. I am in all my being as myself and all is open therein to my gaze and my influence. That which humans hide from each other is not hid from me. If you wish to be as I am, of my nature, as is your birthright, be prepared to be revealed and see as I see.

I am the one initiator. There is no initiation into me but by me and according to my laws.

I am the way and the gate which supports both pillars of the opposites. Without knowing the opposites and accepting that they are of me, you shall not find me for I am ever that which lies between, and whatever fear obstructs you this is the fear of the very opposite pillar to which you have not yet finally surrendered.

Never hide your fear, for in the admitting of it its days are numbered. But seek not out fear, my beloved, else in your mind you shall create more of it. In seeking out fear with the motive of ridding yourself of it, your belief in it creates more of it. My nature is unlimited. Beliefs of such therapeutic projection can create unlimited situations where you can delude yourself that you have found another source of fear and eliminated it. This is a common illusion held to the very end by well meaning teachers and helpers. Nothing in me can be eliminated. I may only be recognised for what I am, then fear is no more.

See me everywhere and act with my awareness, then shall you soon discover me. I am very close to you, for I am yourself. Only go to meet and embrace fear when, unsought by you, coming not out of your desire to self improve, it comes to you in my timing and out of my wisdom as another illusion to be confronted and pierced upon your path to me. Leave these times to me.

Your capacity for self responsibility, however magnificent, is of worthless value if it clouds you into being insensitive to me and the laws of my being.

In these laws you have no freedom. You are only free in relation to me. I have no need of freedom for there is nought but me. Therefore, neither do you have need of it. Seek not freedom, by whatever ways. Seek me. I am within you as your Self. Look not elsewhere

The human mind's idea of freedom is a prison. Seek me and nought else, for nought else is there or ever will be or ever has been. In me is your rest. Your natural activity springs from your trust and realisation that you and I are one and the same. In me is realised your deepest desires and longings for both peace and meaningful activity, and love and joy beyond your wildest imaginings. The ocean is not empty, my beloveds, but full.

At the end, but at the very end, when even the search for me and the idea of me is a barrier and projection of your mind, cease your doing, cease your search and cease your anxieties born of much striving and weariness, and be still, and I shall, as gently as the mist rising in the dawn of a new day, reveal myself to you and in that day you shall rejoice and be at peace and have come home.

Upon this very day all that I am will rejoice with you for this day is my birthday.

Be joyful. I am present everywhere upon this earth.

MARK KUMARA
Australia.
Website. www.markkumara.com

Joy is the outer manifestation of peace.

Peace is the inner origin of joy.

Love is everything in between.

Printed in Great Britain
by Amazon

84453543R00173